SWEET TIMES

SWEET TIMES

SWEET TIMES

Simple Desserts for Every Occasion

Dorie Greenspan

William Morrow and Company, Inc.
New York

Library of Congress Cataloging-in-Publication Data

Greenspan, Dorie.
    Sweet times : simple desserts for every occasion
  Dorie Greenspan.
      p.   cm.
  Includes index.
  ISBN 0-688-08300-5
  1. Desserts. I. Title.
TX773.G6986 1991
641.8'6—dc20   90-47277
                            CIP

Printed in the United States of America

First Edition

1 2 3 4 5 6 7 8 9 10

BOOK DESIGN BY STEPHANIE TEVONIAN

For Michael and Joshua, for all the sweet times

And in memory of Artie Rudick,
for my first lesson in chocolate and the
years of friendship that followed

S · W · E · E · T

Acknowledgments

While I was working on Sweet Times, a fortune-teller told me, "Expect help from no one." For sure she was reading someone else's life. Books don't get written without help, and from the start I was blessed with ace helpers.

In the beginning—and for every minute thereafter—there was my editor, Maria Guarnaschelli. I'm sure she had a desk filled with other projects while she was working with me on mine, but I certainly couldn't tell. Maria's concern, energy, enthusiasm, and attention to details were never less than total.

For a first-timer, publishing can be a puzzlement, but I was lucky to get encouragement and wise counsel from my agent, Susan Lescher—a woman with whom I've never had a conversation that didn't include a good laugh.

When whatever I was testing came out of the oven picture-perfect, I was delighted and it showed; but when cakes fell and cookies cracked, my spirits did the same. Grumpy as I was, good friends hung in. Mary Bralove, who years ago made the rule "You can talk about anything on a run," ran with me regularly and cheerfully listened to me go on about cakes and catastrophes, never once even hinting that I was anything other than fascinating. Ditto Kathie Laundy, my buddy and running mate in Connecticut; Bonnie Lee Black, whose help and encouragement were boundless; Karen Rosetti, "from the old neighborhood"; Maggie Simmons, who knew there would be a Sweet Times before I did; Virginia Slifka, a terrific hostess who tested my recipes on guests; the lunch bunch—Anne de Ravel and Jeanne Wilensky—great friends and smart women; and the dinner crew, my friends at The James Beard Foundation, most especially Len Pickell and Peter Kump, The Foundation's irrepressible president and the man who promises that one day I'll learn not to worry.

I worried a lot, but never about the final tests on my recipes. Everything was carefully retested by Anna Brandenburger, Amanda Cushman, and Denise Landis, whose testing notes were worthy of framing. Nor did I have to give a second thought to anything under the aegis of the swell team at William Morrow, particularly Deborah Weiss Geline, Liz Portland, Karen Lumley, Michelle Corallo, Lisa Queen, and Linda Kosarin.

When Sweet Times was just a stack of typed sheets, I got advice I needed and support I appreciated from Barbara Kafka, Pierre Franey, Suzanne Hamlin, Nick Malgieri, Jean Hewitt, and Jim Fobel, pros who read the manuscript. I know they'll find Sweet Times a more pleasurable read now that Stephanie Tevonian has put her considerable talents to the book's design.

Once the inside of the book was in good hands, the jacket became the challenge. Maria Guarnaschelli had the perfect idea, a bake shop window, and Louis Wallach had the genius to make it real. Lou created the set with the help of Judy Singer, prop stylist, and Carol Gelles, food stylist, then photographed it brilliantly, giving Sweet Times the jacket I dreamed it would have.

Finally, as always, and for always, I am grateful for the love and support of my family—my parents, Helen and Abe Burg; my mother-in-law, Esther Greenspan; and the two dearest men in the world, my husband, Michael, and our son, Joshua.

Contents

Ice Cream for Adults *137*

Café Society Sweets *155*
Little Luxuries to Keep Coffee and Conversation Company

Dinner Party Dazzlers *181*
Desserts to Show Off

Holiday Wrap-ups *211*
Finishes for the Feasts

Index *241*

Introduction

When I gave up my doctoral dissertation and a job in corporate America to bake cookies in the basement of a Greenwich Village restaurant, neither my parents, who were looking forward to introducing me as "our daughter, the doctor," nor my thesis committee, who'd worked with me on my study, nor my boss, for whom I wrote reports and speeches, was amused. I, on the other hand, was elated. I was finally doing just what I wanted to do.

No one would have predicted I'd become a baker. I didn't crack an egg before I turned twenty and probably would have remained a culinary innocent for many more years had I not gotten married. Michael and I were married while I was still in college, and we became the first of our friends to have a real apartment. "Real" meant we had some furniture, dishes that matched one another, and pots and pans that weren't our parents' castoffs. Our new apartment was tiny: It was called a three-room but it was actually a Lilliputian-size studio that the landlord had divided, carving a kitchen out of what had been a closet in a previous tenancy. There was barely enough space for the two of us (we had to stand on the bed and lean against the bureau to get into our clothing closet), yet four or five times a week—even on school nights—the place was packed with friends. It was for Michael and them that I learned my way around the kitchen and from them that I learned the joy of making food for people I care about.

I learned to cook from necessity—we had to eat and couldn't afford to go out—but I learned to bake for love. Serving meal after meal, it didn't take me long to realize that no matter how delicious dinner was, everyone was waiting for dessert. Dessert was—and still is—the most special course, the food that feels like a gift for both the giver and the getter.

As we all graduated from school, moved here and there around the country, and, in general, got busier, Michael and I entertained only slightly less, but I baked even more; I began to bake daily. I would come home from work, later from graduate school, and still later from work and school, and start mixing, rolling, and frosting my way through the recipes in Maida Heatter's and Gaston LeNotre's cookbooks. I took baking classes with Francis Lorenzini, who was the pastry chef at New York's Le Cygne restaurant, studied intensively with John Clancy, who was then the premier baking teacher in the city, and signed on for sessions with the patissiers at La Varenne in Paris. There were nights when I was certain there were more pastries in my kitchen than on the dessert trolley of any grand restaurant.

It took years for me to have what I now think of as my epiphany. One morning I walked into the kitchen (by this time we were living in a roomy apartment on Manhattan's Upper West Side, and the kitchen was actually large enough to walk into) and saw the pots of lemon marmalade I'd made the night before. They were lined up on the counter, sunny yellow, topped with calico and tied with ribbons. Just the sight of them warmed me. By the time I reached the office I'd asked myself the hard questions: Why doesn't the work I do all day satisfy me as much as those little pots of marmalade? And why, if there's something in this world that can please me so much, am I not doing it constantly? I quit my job that morning, deserted my dissertation just a few days after that, and started baking professionally.

I baked at the now-defunct Soho Charcuterie and the then-new Sarabeth's Kitchen, where our then-new son, Joshua, spent some part of every afternoon playing inside an industrial-size mixing bowl. I also worked solo, turning our *kitchen into a storeroom stocked with bins of flour, sugar, chocolate, and stacks of doilies, boxes, and odd-shaped pans. I baked birthday and wedding cakes for big parties, and pies and cakes for local restaurants. My father noted that, given the time I was putting in, I was barely pulling down a minimum wage, but that didn't stop me. I'd found my calling—almost.*

It wasn't until 1984 that it all came together. That's when my friend Maggie Simmons, who'd helped me get my first baking job, asked me why I didn't write about baking. After all, as she pointed out, I was a baker who had earned a living as a writer. Sometimes the obvious needs pointing out. That same month Food & Wine *magazine accepted my first piece, "Fireside Sweets"; I've been writing for them and other magazines ever since. (Years later the managing editor, Warren Picower, told me that they accepted the article in record time because they were won over by the Prune-Armagnac Truffles I sent along as samples.)*

In many ways, my career has come full circle. I started by baking for my family and friends; now I create new desserts so that others can bake them for their families and friends. Perhaps it's not so much coming full circle as making the circle fuller. In any case, what remains the same is the sharing, the most delicious part of any dessert.

I have written Sweet Times *with sharing in mind. These are the recipes I want to share with you, written in a way that will make the sweets easy for you to bake and share with others. I've created desserts that are simple, inviting, and do-able (even if you've never baked before); and I've given you the same information I always want to have when I'm baking, whether for my small family, a casual get-together with friends, or a dressy dinner party. I've included four special sections after each recipe: Serving (advice on cooling, cutting, and presenting each sweet); Storing (do's, don'ts, and directions for freezing the desserts); Best Match (top choices for go-alongs); and Playing Around (variations, ideas for revamping leftovers, and new recipes for the right add-ons). These sections, as well as the book's organization—the chapters are arranged by time of day and mood—take the guesswork out of party planning and make sharing a sweet a simple pleasure.*

I know how happy each of the sweets in this book makes the baker and the taster because I've had the delight of sharing every dessert in Sweet Times. I've had the thrill of seeing first-time bakers follow one of these recipes, pull a perfect cake from the oven, and beam with pride and astonishment; the excitement of seeing a class of eleven-year-old boys revel in their newly learned ability to produce a batch of chocolate truffles that looks storebought and tastes even better; the satisfaction of serving these desserts to hundreds of people and hearing them sigh with contentment; and the fun of giving a cookie to a grown-up and seeing a smile become a childish grin, as youthful memories bubble up at the almost forgotten taste of peanut butter.

It is my hope that now that I have passed these recipes along to you, you too will share these desserts, and with them hours of joy and endless sweet times.

DORIE GREENSPAN

New York City, 1991

Quick-Fix Matrix

When I've got a craving for a sweet, it never seems to be just an amorphous "something" I want; I've usually got an idea of what will quell the hankering. Sometimes the yen is for chocolate, sometimes for a creamy concoction, and sometimes it's crunch I'm after. When I'm in the midst of a "gotta-have," I don't think in terms of cakes, or cookies, or pies, but rather in terms of the craving itself, the need, for instance, for crunch, tang, or spice. Most cookbooks, as I'm sure you've noticed, are no help in this department; they're usually organized by type of dessert. Unless you know the recipes in the book very well, it will be a while before you find something that will do the trick.

That's why I came up with the Quick-Fix Matrix on the pages that follow. It's a craver's lifesaver. Look up your longing under creamy, light, hearty, fruity, spicy, crunchy, tangy, or, of course, chocolaty, and you're guaranteed to find the sweet to meet the need. The Matrix is also the perfect party planner. Look across the top of the chart to find the chapter that suits the occasion and balance your dessert menu by choosing sweets from several of the taste and texture categories. With this at hand, you can make the right choice in a snap.

Breakfast, Brunch, and Lunch Mates	Snackables	Teatime Treats	Comfort on a Spoon
CREAMY Almost-Like-Grandma's Sweet-Filled Blintzes Puffed Pancake Buttermilk Pie	Chocolate Cream Dream Pie		Triple Chocolate Old-Fashioned Pudding Chocolate-Laced Cinnamon Pudding Rich Bread Pudding with Buttery Apples Prune Bread Pudding Cups Slippery Slidey Lemon-Clove Cup Custard Honey-Yogurt Mousse Outrageous Rice Pudding
LIGHT Buttermilk Pie	Pecan Flats Mace-Lemon Softies Jelly Bellies for Grown-ups	Coconut Tea Cake Gently Spiced Carrot-Pecan Torte Shortbreads	Raspberry Peach en Papillote Slippery Slidey Lemon-Clove Cup Custard Honey-Yogurt Mousse
HEARTY French-Fried Toast Chockablock Bran Muffins Buttermilk Banana Waffles	Olivia's Oatmeal Fruit Bars Applesauce Spice Bars	Round Pound Cake with Blueberry Jam Burnt Butter Baby Cakes Cream Scones Chocolate Swirl Sour Cream Bundt Cake Buttermilk–Brown Sugar Pound Cake	Rich Bread Pudding with Buttery Apples Prune Bread Pudding Cups Pear-Cranberry Crisp Outrageous Rice Pudding Thoroughly Modern Betty
FRUITY Soft and Spicy Fresh Plum Cake Crumb-Topped Raspberry Coffeecake Cranberry Upside-Downer Blueberry-Corn Mini Muffins Apple-Nut Mini Muffins Chockablock Bran Muffins Gingered Peach Tart	Olivia's Oatmeal Fruit Bars Applesauce Spice Bars	Round Pound Cake with Blueberry Jam Orange Custard Bars Lemon-Drenched Zucchini Loaves	Rich Bread Pudding with Buttery Apples Prune Bread Pudding Cups Summer Pandowdy Raspberry Peach en Papillote Sweet Plums with Tart Cream Pear-Cranberry Crisp Thoroughly Modern Betty

Ice Cream for Adults	Café Society Sweets	Dinner Party Dazzlers	Holiday Wrap-ups
Tangy Pear Mascarpone Sherbet Eggnog-Pumpkin Ice Cream Cinnamon Ice Cream with Old-Time Creamery Hot Fudge Deepest Darkest Double Chocolate Sorbet Cardamom-Orange Ice Cream Raspberry Chocolate Truffle Ice Cream Cake Coffee–Almond Crunch Tart	Espresso Cheesecake Brownies Orange Caramel Mousse Chocolate Truffles	Frozen Chocolate–Peanut Butter Mousse Torte Minted White Chocolate Velvets Chilled Hazelnut-Chocolate Tartlets Frosty Double Chocolate Tart Mango-Berry Mousse Golden Cloud Cake	Banana-Pumpkin Pie Honeyed Ricotta-Almond Easter Cake Mulled Wine Tart
Tangy Pear Mascarpone Sherbet Ginger-Lemonade Sorbet	Orange Caramel Mousse Jean-Marc's Honeycomb Tuiles	Frozen Chocolate–Peanut Butter Mousse Torte Kir Coupes with Peaches Frozen Winter Sunshine Mango-Berry Mousse Golden Cloud Cake	Pomander Cake Christmas Clementines Valentine's Day Sweet Hearts Gene Ford's Fourth of July Sparkler
Eggnog-Pumpkin Ice Cream Coffee–Almond Crunch Tart Peanut Butter Fudge Ice Cream Sandwiches		Chilled Hazelnut-Chocolate Tartlets	Banana-Pumpkin Pie Holiday Gingerbread Cake Date and Nut Toasting Loaf
Tangy Pear Mascarpone Sherbet Cardamom-Orange Ice Cream Raspberry Chocolate Truffle Ice Cream Cake Tropical Freeze	Mixed Fruit with Bubbling Almond Cream Quick Prune Pithiviers Apple Paper Thins Thick-Cut Candied Peels	Apple Tatinettes Posh Pommes Frozen Winter Sunshine Mango-Berry Mousse Golden Cloud Cake	Giant Cranberry Turnover Christmas Clementines Fruit Fritters for Chanukah Gene Ford's Fourth of July Sparkler

Breakfast, Brunch, and Lunch Mates	Snackables	Teatime Treats	Comfort on a Spoon
SPICY Soft and Spicy Fresh Plum Cake Apple-Nut Mini Muffins Gingered Peach Tart Apple Butter Bundt Cake	Peanut Patty Cakes Mace-Lemon Softies Applesauce Spice Bars Cinnamon Fudge Brownies	Round Pound Cake with Blueberry Jam Flaky Cinnamon Twists Gently Spiced Carrot-Pecan Torte Lemon Drenched Zucchini Loves	Chocolate-Laced Cinnamon Pudding Prune Bread Pudding Cups Sweet Plums with Tart Cream Thoroughly Modern Betty
CRUNCHY Crumb-Topped Raspberry Coffeecake	PB & O Snackers Mocha-Almond Bars Nutty Granola Cookies Cocoa Snaps Jelly Bellies for Kids	Flaky Cinnamon Twists	Pear-Cranberry Crisp
TANGY Cranberry Upside-Downer	Olivia's Oatmeal Fruit Bars	Flaky Cinnamon Twists Orange Custard Bars Lemon-Drenched Zucchini Loaves	Sweet Plums with Tart Cream Slippery Slidey Lemon-Clove Cup Custard Honey-Yogurt Mousse
CHOCOLATY	PB & O Snackers Mocha-Almond Bars Cocoa Snaps Cinnamon Fudge Brownies Chocolate Cream Dream Pie	Chocolate-Dipped Walnut Wafers Shortbreads Lucky Devil's Cake	Triple Chocolate Old-Fashioned Pudding Chocolate-Laced Cinnamon Pudding

Ice Cream for Adults	Café Society Sweets	Dinner Party Dazzlers	Holiday Wrap-ups
Eggnog–Pumpkin Ice Cream Ginger-Lemonade Sorbet Cinnamon Ice Cream Cardamom-Orange Ice Cream	Thick-Cut Candied Peels Linzer Doubles		Banana–Pumpkin Pie Pomander Cake Holiday Gingerbread Cake Giant Cranberry Turnover Peppermill Squares Christmas Clementines Mulled Wine Tart
Coffee–Almond Crunch Tart Peanut Butter Fudge Ice Cream Sandwiches Tropical Freeze	Jean-Marc's Honeycomb Tuiles Raspberry Rugelach	Chilled Hazelnut-Chocolate Tartlets	Chocolate Pecan Tart Honeyed Ricotta-Almond Easter Cake
Tangy Pear Mascarpone Sherbet Ginger-Lemonade Sorbet	Orange Caramel Mousse Thick-Cut Candied Peels Raspberry Rugelach	Kir Coupes with Peaches Frozen Winter Sunshine Mango-Berry Mousse Golden Cloud Cake	Giant Cranberry Turnover Mulled Wine Tart
Cinnamon Ice Cream with Old-Time Creamery Hot Fudge Deepest Darkest Double Chocolate Sorbet Raspberry Chocolate Truffle Ice Cream Cake Peanut Butter Fudge Ice Cream Sandwiches	Fudge Buttons Espresso Cheesecake Brownies Chocolate Truffles Glossy-Topped Black Cherry Chocolate Bars	Frozen Chocolate-Peanut Butter Mousse Torte Minted White Chocolate Velvets Frosty Double Chocolate Tart 15 Minute Magic Chocolate Midnight Classic French Chocolate Gâteau	Chocolate-Pecan Tart Pomander Cake Holiday Gingerbread Cake Peppermill Squares

S • W • E • E • T

A Short Course in Dessertmaking

The first time an editor asked for my slug, I was stumped. I'd been writing for years without having learned that a slug is the shorthand name for an article. When I finally wised up, it wasn't because I asked my editor—I was too embarrassed—it was because my journalist friend, Mary Bralove, explained it to me. Mary, who's infinitely supportive, called the editor impolite for assuming I'd know the term and sloughed it off, saying, "It's just newspaper talk. Bet you say things in baking that wouldn't make sense to me."

This was what I needed to hear, but I thought she was wrong. "Recipes are written in everyday English," I assured her. "No jargon here." And just to prove it, I gave her stacks of my recipes to read. I was on the verge of making

my point when she came to the one for Yeast-Raised Coffeecake. "How can I 'proof' the yeast," she asked, "if there's nothing on it to read?"

While I scratched the recipe for reasons other than Mary's perplexity, the incident underlined the reality: Dessertmaking, like other crafts, has its own shorthand. And because it's always best to learn the lingo at the start, I've included this course. If it looks familiar, skip it; go directly to your favorite dessert and dig in. But if you're a beginner baker who needs a tutorial in pie crusts, reassurance that folding egg whites is not impossible, or an ingredient-by-ingredient run-through on measuring, read on. The sweets in this book are too good to miss because you need a cram course in dessertese.

BAKING POWDER. Double-acting baking powder is a leavening agent that produces its first salvo of gas bubbles (carbon dioxide) when liquid goes into the batter and its second when the oven's heat hits it. Baking powder is the leavening of choice in biscuits, muffins, scones, and butter cakes. Use only as much as directed and measure the powder carefully, because too much will give your desserts a metallic taste.

BAKING SODA. Baking soda is also a leavening agent (it is, in fact, a component of baking powder), but it relies on additional acid in the batter for its boost. Used more sparingly than baking powder, baking soda appears in recipes that include sour milk, sour cream, yogurt, or buttermilk, acidic liquids that complement its leavening properties.

BUTTER. I use US Grade AA unsalted butter in these recipes. Specifically, I use Land O' Lakes

butter because it is low in moisture and I think, among the nationally available brands, it has the sweetest taste and makes the best desserts and crusts.

Butter for pie crusts. I keep a few sticks of butter in the freezer for making pie crusts. I'm sure you've noticed that recipes are always warning you to keep the dough cold and not to overwork it, important advice for turning out a tender pie crust. Frozen butter gives you a head start in the cold department; ditto ice water and making the dough rapidly in a food processor, so it has little chance to warm. (See the section on CRUSTS for more information.)

Softening butter. When a recipe calls for softened butter or butter at room temperature, I mean butter that has been removed from the refrigerator enough in advance so that it is spreadable, not gooey or oily, when you start to work. The amount of time it will take for the butter to reach this consistency will depend on how warm your kitchen is. If you're in a hurry, you can beat the butter with a rolling pin to get it into shape. Keep it in its wrapper or put the sticks between sheets of waxed paper, and bash a few times with the pin. Cutting the butter in thin pieces will also hasten the softening process.

BUTTERING PANS. I always butter pans with butter, *not* shortening. In professional kitchens, bakers keep a bowl of soft butter with a pastry brush stuck in it ready for this job. Brushing is the quickest, most effective way to coat pans, particularly Bundt and other odd-shaped pans and molds, but it's impractical unless you plan to do a day's worth of baking. It's better to cut a knob of soft butter or slivers of cold butter and rub them around the pan with a sheet of paper toweling.

When a recipe calls for buttering and flouring a pan, butter the pan, then put a spoonful of all-purpose flour in the pan, shake the pan to distribute the flour evenly, turn it upside down over the sink or wastebasket, and tap out the excess flour.

The butter and flour needed to prepare pans are not included in the list of ingredients—they're extra.

When I'm making muffins, I often spray the tins with PAM, a corn oil–based product that keeps the muffins from sticking. I find this particularly convenient when I'm making mini-muffins and have dozens of tiny tins to coat.

BUTTERMILK. When I started baking more than twenty years ago, I'd read cookbook authors' laments over no-longer-available "real" buttermilk. Unable to get what they claimed was the best, I settled for what my local markets offered. Now I notice that it's harder and harder to find even this

buttermilk, inferior though it may be. I'm sure it was not a big seller—you never hear of anyone actually drinking the stuff—and store managers probably didn't have to think twice about pulling it from the shelves when Saco Powdered Buttermilk became widely available. The powdered mix is just fine—sensible too, because you can make just as much as you need for a single recipe—but I can't help being a fuddy-dud and wondering and worrying what's next to go. If neither liquid nor powdered buttermilk is on hand when you need it, an excellent substitute is yogurt thinned with milk: Use ⅔ cup plain yogurt and ⅓ cup milk for each cup of buttermilk in the recipe.

CHOCOLATE. I have tested these recipes with imported chocolate and supermarket brands and they work well with both, although I urge you to use high-quality imported chocolate, particularly when it's the principal ingredient and little else is added to interfere with its flavor. In these cases (with recipes such as Chocolate Truffles, Old-Time Creamery Hot Fudge, or Chilled Hazelnut-Chocolate Tartlets), what you bake with is what you get because the taste doesn't change much during cooking. A good rule when using sweetened chocolate is to choose a chocolate you'd enjoy eating.

I use Lindt Surfin most often when I need bittersweet chocolate. It's consistently good and readily available; and it has a deep, clear chocolate taste, a nice glossy finish, and a proper, clean snap when broken. You can substitute semisweet (a sweeter chocolate) in any recipe calling for bittersweet.

When I need unsweetened chocolate, I buy Hershey's or Baker's from the supermarket shelf.

Similarly, I buy Nestle's or Hershey's chocolate chips at the supermarket. For a change, I'll use Guittard European Morsels, extra-large unusually shaped semisweet chips. These are my choice for a chip in PB & O Snackers, peanut butter and oatmeal cookies. Whether you buy domestic or imported chocolate, make sure you buy *real* chocolate.

Melting Chocolate. I recommend two methods:

1] Break or cut the chocolate into roughly even-sized pieces and place them in the top of a double boiler over hot, *not* boiling, water. Do not let the water touch the bottom of the chocolate pot, because too much heat will burn the chocolate. Melt slowly, stirring occasionally.

2] Break or cut up the chocolate and place it in a large microwave-safe measuring cup. Cover the cup tightly with plastic wrap and cook on HIGH heat in the microwave for one minute; if it is not melted, continue to cook, checking at 30 second intervals, until melted. Often the chocolate melts but keeps its shape—check by pressing a spoon against the chocolate.

No matter which method you choose, take care not to burn the chocolate and never allow even a drop of moisture to touch it while it's melting—it will block or seize and you'll be stuck with a messy mass of unusable chocolate. (Seized chocolate can be rescued with the addition of solid vegetable shortening, but who wants Crisco in their cookies?)

White Chocolate. The white chocolate I find most unctuous (a nice quality in chocolate) and easiest to use is Tobler Narcisse. White chocolate makes a lovely glaze (see how it's used in Fudge Buttons) and a stunning baked custard (Minted White Chocolate Velvets), but it's finicky. I've never gotten the hang of melting white chocolate in the microwave—without fail, I burn it. I melt white chocolate in a double boiler over gentle heat and never take my eyes off the pot. White chocolate melts faster than dark chocolate and burns and seizes faster as well. There's nothing difficult about working with it, you just need to be alert.

COCOA. Dutch-processed cocoa powder is my recommendation for desserts in which cocoa is the primary flavoring; it is milder and darker than cocoa that is not "dutched," or treated with alkali. Look for Droste or Poulain, but if these brands are not available buy Hershey's undutched cocoa; it's a fine cocoa to bake with and one you'll have no difficulty finding.

COCONUT. I use two kinds of dried shredded coconut in my recipes: sweetened and unsweetened. The sweetened variety is easy to find on grocery shelves, but it can take a little searching to find the unsweetened kind. Look in your local health food store or the bulk bins of a large supermarket. When you find it, buy a few pounds and store it in the freezer in a double thickness of airtight plastic bags. It will keep for months.

CRANBERRIES. Cranberries have a short season but a long freezer life. Buy the berries by the bushel when they're in your market and freeze them, right in the perforated bags in which they're packed. Frozen cranberries will keep from one Thanksgiving to the next. New on the market are dried cranberries, or "craisins." These are sugar-infused and are very tart and very sweet at the same time. They make a nice change from raisins and can be substituted directly in recipes calling for raisins.

CREAMING. Beating softened, room temperature

butter until it is smooth and creamy is called *creaming*. The term also describes the process of beating butter and sugar together until they are light and fluffy.

CRUSTS. Making pie crusts can be a source of pride and joy or an ordeal to be avoided at all costs (including settling for the ready-made cardboard-like varieties found in supermarket freezers). It is probably the one thing that most clearly divides bakers from nonbakers. I think part of the fear of making pie crust, and I do think many fear it, comes from all the warnings in recipes: Don't overwork it; don't use too much flour; don't let it get soft; don't let it get hard. It's enough to make a novice give up —but don't: A homemade butter crust is too good a treat (and really too easy to make) to give up on. Here are some tips:

Use a food processor, frozen butter, and ice water to make your crusts and you won't have to worry about soft, warm dough. Follow the instructions in the recipe and process just until the ingredients hold together when pressed between your fingers. *Don't* process until the dough forms a ball and rides along the top of the blade.

Smear the dough, bit by bit, under the heel of your hand, then gather it into a compact mass, and flatten it into a ¾-inch-thick disk. In most recipes you'll be rolling the dough into a round, which is why I suggest you form the just-made dough into a disk. But if you'll be rolling a square or rectangle from the dough, form the dough into a ¾-inch-thick approximation of the shape you want in the end. You'll work the dough less if you start with the right shape.

Chill the dough before rolling to give the gluten in the flour a chance to relax, ensuring that you won't have a tough crust. If you make the dough in a processor with frozen butter and ice water, then once you get the hang of making it—and all it takes is practice—you'll probably be able to skip the 20-minute chill I recommend before rolling; you'll find the dough cold and firm enough to roll immediately.

Roll the dough gently on a well-floured work surface, working the dough on only one side but giving it a quarter-turn every now and then and lifting it frequently to make sure it's not sticking to the surface. For pie crusts, I like to use a cylindrical rolling pin that looks like a fat dowel. It doesn't have handles and I enjoy its maneuverability. Use the pin that's most comfortable for you. (I knew a wonderful baker from France who rolled all her doughs with a wine bottle.) Roll from the center out, taking care to roll just to the edge of the dough, not over it, until the dough is uniformly the thickness you want. Beginners often end up with a thick center and very thin edges. Check your progress as you roll along.

Roll the dough around your rolling pin to lift it off the work surface and unroll it (so the underside becomes the top side) onto your pan, centering it as best you can. Ease the dough down into the pan so it rests evenly against the bottom and sides. *Don't stretch the dough to fit*; it will only shrink back during baking and leave you with an uneven crust. Once you've eased it into the pan, press it against the pan gently with your fingertips. If you're making a tart, cut the edges even with the pan; if a pie, crimp the edges by pressing the tines of a fork against the dough that rests on the rim of the pie pan. Prick the inside of the crust, tart, or pie all over with the tines of a fork or the point of a knife.

Always chill the dough before baking to give it a chance to relax after it's been rolled and shaped. (You might, as I mentioned, skip the chilling period before you roll the dough, but don't skip this one.) I usually pop the crust into the freezer and let it rest there uncovered while I preheat the oven. Once the dough is firm, you can wrap it well in foil and leave it in the freezer for up to one month. *It is better to freeze an unbaked pie shell than a baked crust.*

To bake a pie or tart shell before filling it, cover with aluminum foil, pressing the foil against the bottom and sides of the pan to get a snug fit, fill with dried beans or pie weights, and bake in a hot oven (following recipe directions) for the specified amount of time, usually about 20 minutes. Remove the crust from the oven, lift off the foil and weights, and bake the crust another few minutes to give it a golden-brown finish. Fill the crust when it has cooled and continue with the recipe, either baking to cook the filling or chilling, depending on the recipe. While there are many people who bake their pie crusts and fillings simultaneously, I prefer to bake the crust blind, meaning without the filling, and then add the filling and continue to bake as needed. This method takes a bit longer but the reward is a crisp crust, one that holds its own next to any kind of filling.

DRIED FRUITS. Dried apricots, currants, raisins, and prunes add deep, winy flavors and a nice change of texture to baked goods—if the fruits are plump and moist. To keep fruits tender, pack them in tightly sealed plastic bags for extended storage. If the fruits are pleasant to eat they're fine for baking; if the fruits have become hard, steam them over boiling water or soak them in the boiling water for a minute or two. Blot the fruit dry between paper towels before using. *Hard, shriveled dried fruits will not become moist and plump in baking—they'll just spoil your recipe.*

EGGS. Each of the recipes in this book was tested with *large eggs*. For most of the recipes, it's fine to use eggs directly from the refrigerator. Some recipes call for room-temperature eggs. If you haven't planned ahead, just run the eggs under hot water for a minute or place them in a turned-off oven with a pilot light for 5 minutes. The eggs will warm up but not become so hot that their texture will change.

Separating eggs. Several recipes require just yolks, just whites, or yolks and whites in separate amounts. Cold eggs separate most easily, but room-temperature whites whip faster and fuller. Make certain when you separate eggs that no specks of yolk drop into the whites. If you have to remove a bit of yolk from whites, fish it out using the egg shell as a scoop.

Beating egg whites. The three cardinal rules for beating air into egg whites so that they lighten and leaven a batter are: Use a clean, dry bowl with clean, dry beaters (a smudge of butter or a bit of fat from cream can cause disaster); make sure your whites are free of even wisps of yolk; and stop beating before your whites form separate little puffs. An easy way to help avoid overbeating whites is to add a squeeze of lemon juice (about ½ teaspoon) or a pinch of cream of tartar to the whites just as they begin to thicken and lighten in color. Once the whites are properly beaten, use them immediately. Unlike heavy cream, which can be beaten and kept (even overnight), egg whites deflate quickly.

EXTRACTS. Pure extracts, particularly vanilla, the most frequently used flavor, are not always easy to find, but it's worth the effort to ferret out a source. For a broad selection of good extracts, look for the Wagner's brand, usually available in specialty shops and some supermarkets. Like spices, extracts should be stored in a cool, dark cupboard and checked periodically for freshness. If they've lost their deep fragrance, ditch them—they won't have the flavor you're looking for.

FLOUR. Most of these recipes call for all-purpose flour. I tested the recipes with Pillsbury and Gold Medal, nationally available brands. For the few recipes requiring cake flour, a finer, silkier flour, choose Swan's Down, Soft As Silk, or any other brand that is *not* self-rising.

FOLDING. Folding is a gentle method of blending ingredients. A recipe usually calls for folding in whipped cream or egg whites, airy ingredients you don't want to deflate. There are those who claim the best tool for folding is a hand, and they're right in many instances. But if you're new to folding, I'd suggest you use a broad, sturdy, rubber spatula. (My favorites are made by Rubbermaid Commercial Products and can be found in specialty shops.)

To fold. Place the ingredients to be folded in on top of the batter. (If the batter is very heavy, stir one-quarter of the beaten egg whites or whipped cream into the batter to lighten it. Don't try to fold airy whites or cream into a stiff batter—you'll have to work too hard and in the process you'll knock all the air out of your ingredients.) Hold the side of the bowl in one hand and the spatula in the other. Dip the narrow edge of the spatula into the center of the ingredients. Slice down through the whites or cream and then into the batter until you hit the bottom of the bowl. Now flatten the blade of the spatula against the bottom of the bowl and pull it across the bowl until it comes to the side. Twist your wrist (clockwise, if you're right-handed) while you draw the spatula up. The first part of the spatula to pop up through the ingredients should be the part that went in first. Continue to draw the spatula up as you give the bowl a quarter-turn, and repeat the entire process. Continue until the whites or cream are incorporated into the batter. Try to work as quickly and gently as you can, but don't be afraid—this stuff isn't nearly as fragile as you think.

FOOD PROCESSOR. Whenever I can cut prep and cleanup time by using the food processor, I jump at the chance. There are so many jobs this machine does well—better than the tools we used before the processor became a given in the kitchen. I always use it to make pie dough, grind nuts (I used to buy them ready-ground and worry they weren't fresh), and puree fruits for sorbets and sauces. You'll also find that I've created recipes that can be made entirely in the processor. My favorite is Fifteen-Minute Magic, a moist chocolate-amaretti torte.

Unless otherwise noted, when I direct you to *process* I mean for you to run the machine continuously. I also mean for you to use the metal blade. (I don't think I've ever used the plastic blade for anything.) *Pulse* means to turn the machine on and off for one-second intervals. Whether processing or pulsing, always stop and scrape down the sides of the bowl occasionally. (Scraping now and then is a good habit to get into whether you're blending with a processor, mixer, or rubber spatula.)

FREEZING. Many of the desserts in this book can be frozen. In fact, many should be frozen and some should even be eaten straight from the freezer—

that's the way you'll want all the great ice cream cakes and it's the way you'll enjoy the Chocolate–Peanut Butter Mousse Torte. If a dessert can be frozen successfully, you'll find a note with freezing instructions at the end of the recipe.

Always make an airtight package for freezing. I find the easiest way to do this is to pack the dessert into a plastic bag, gather the top of the bag and, holding the "neck" of the bag between the thumb and forefinger of one hand, put your mouth to the opening and draw out the air. Quickly seal the bag with a twist tie, making sure not to let in any air. If I'm going to keep something in the freezer for a few days or longer, I put this airtight package in another plastic bag and repeat the process, making a double seal. Remember to label each package with the name of the dessert and the date you tucked it into the freezer, an easy way to avoid ice-encrusted mystery food.

FRESH FRUIT. If you've got fruit that's not really ripe or as tasty as you'd like, poaching it in syrup with a vanilla bean, cinnamon stick, or some spices will improve it, but the best rule to follow in cooking or baking with fruit is to use the freshest, fullest-flavored fruits you can find. It's the rule you should heed with all ingredients—use the best and you'll turn out the best.

FROSTING. With frosting, consistency and patience are all. If the frosting is too soft it will slide off the cake; if it is too firm you may tear the cake while you're trying to get an even layer. You want a consistency not unlike that of commercial mayonnaise, one so spreadable it will tempt you to go wild with swirls and flourishes. Soft frosting should be chilled briefly and hard frosting should be

warmed to room temperature or beaten. When you're using whipped cream or buttercream as frosting and want a smooth, professional look, first spread a very thin layer of the frosting over the sides and top of the cake to seal it and put the cake in the refrigerator for 10 minutes to set. Apply the finishing layer of frosting over this undercoat. Whatever frosting you use, you'll find it easiest to spread it smoothly if you use a metal spatula, straight or offset. (Offset spatulas are angled like pancake turners and are my favorites.) Professionals use raised-platform turntables so they can swivel their cakes before them, holding their frosting spatulas stationary while the cakes turn. You can use a lazy Susan (even one from a pantry space saver) for this job, or you can just work carefully with the cake on a plate protected by waxed paper strips. It's really not hard. One tip: Frost the sides of the cake before the top. Let the frosting from the sides come up a little bit above the top of the cake. Place a dollop of frosting in the center of the cake. With your spatula, bring in the frosting from the sides to the top, smoothing it down to form a thin layer, then smooth the frosting from the center out over the top of the cake. Finish by holding the spatula above the cake at a 45-degree angle to the sides and gently blend the top and side seams. If the sides look a little scruffy, mask them with a coating of finely chopped nuts, sprinkles (or jimmies), or pulverized cake crumbs—it's what the pros do.

FRUIT SAUCES. Often, the simplest way to dress up a plain dessert is with a fruit sauce. A quick, tasty choice is a berry sauce that can be made with fresh or defrosted frozen fruit. Whether you're using frozen or fresh fruit, just puree it in a processor or

A Short Course in Dessertmaking

blender and add sugar and lemon, lime, or orange juice to taste. You may want to pass blackberry or raspberry sauce through a sieve to eliminate the little seeds, but it's not always necessary—just know your audience: Some people detest the seeds, others don't.

GELATIN. I use Knox unflavored powdered gelatin in individual packages for the recipes in this book. Each package contains a scant tablespoon of gelatin. For best results, pour the specified amount of cold liquid into a saucepan and sprinkle over the gelatin. Let the gelatin stand for a few minutes to soften and absorb the liquid. It will become whitish, thick, and gloppy. Warm the gelatin mixture over very low heat, stirring, until it dissolves and is transparent. This takes only a minute or two. Stir the gelatin into the mixture you want to thicken and continue to stir for a minute to make sure the gelatin doesn't form unpleasant strings. Chill following recipe directions.

GINGER. Several recipes call for fresh ginger, an odd-shaped root readily available in greengroceries and supermarkets. Fresh ginger should be firm— avoid any puckered or shriveled pieces—and have a very fresh smell. Ginger must be peeled before you can use it. Because of its little nooks and crannies, I like to peel it with a small, sharp knife, but you can square the ginger by cutting off the small knobs and then remove the peel with a swivel-blade vegetable peeler. If you need chopped fresh ginger, mince it with a large chef's knife or use a food processor. With the motor running, drop small pieces of fresh ginger into the machine through the feed tube. A mini-processor does a very good job of chopping or mincing small amounts of ginger.

HAZELNUTS. Also known as filberts, hazelnuts are often called a sophisticated nut, perhaps because they have been prized by fine European bakers for years. Unlike shelled walnuts, pecans, or almonds, shelled hazelnuts cannot be used straight from the bin; they must be toasted and skinned. Place the nuts on a jelly roll pan in a preheated 350° oven and bake for about 10 minutes, or until the skins separate from the nuts and the nuts are a light golden color. Turn the nuts out onto a large kitchen towel and wrap it around the nuts to cover them. Let the nuts rest and steam in the towel for a minute or two. Wearing kitchen mitts, rub the nuts in the towel until most of the skin has been removed. (Not all the nuts will come clean; that's O.K.) This is a messy, somewhat tedious job, but worth the trouble. Remove the nuts from the debris and cool to room temperature before packing into airtight plastic bags and storing in the freezer for future use. Nuts will keep in the freezer for 3 months. If hazelnuts are unavailable or you haven't the time to prepare them properly, you can substitute almonds successfully in most recipes.

HEAVY CREAM. It's hard to open a cookbook nowadays and not find the author bemoaning the dwindling availability of "real" cream—read cream that's not ultrapasteurized, a process that gives it a long shelf life and robs it of all flavor. Hunt around for a store that stocks fresh heavy cream. You'll appreciate the difference in taste and texture. I find real cream takes less time to whip, whips to a more satin-like finish and keeps this finish longer, having less of a tendency to weep (or separate) than its worked-over cousin.

To whip cream. The key to whipped cream that keeps its smooth texture and doesn't weep is nonultrapasteurized cream and slow whipping. John Clancy, a premier baking teacher, used to say that it takes 14 minutes to whip cream properly in a stationary heavy-duty mixer. Even if you don't whip the cream for a full 14 minutes, you should start whipping on low speed, moving up to medium but never to high. To avoid overwhipping—and ending up with butter—whip the cream in a mixer until it is just short of the consistency you want, then finish it by hand with a whisk.

Most heavy-duty mixers will do a good job of whipping cream no matter what the temperature. However, if you've got the time, it's good to chill the mixing bowl and beaters for a little while before whipping the cream. Unlike egg whites, which need a clean, dry, oil-free bowl and beaters to whip to their proper fullness, heavy cream can be whipped in a bowl that's just been wiped clean.

If you're serving whipped cream as an accompaniment, whip it only until it just thickens and the beaters leave tracks. This is what the French call *crème Chantilly*. If you're using the cream as a filling or frosting, you'll need to whip it to a firmer, more spreadable consistency. To pipe rosettes, you'll need very firm whipped cream. Cream for piping should always be finished by hand with a whisk.

Storing whipped cream. If you don't use ultrapasteurized cream and you whip it slowly, you'll be able to keep the whipped cream in the refrigerator overnight. Line a strainer with a double thickness of cheesecloth and pile in the whipped cream. Place the strainer over a bowl and cover the cream with plastic wrap. The next day you may find that some liquid has drained from the cream and the cream is a bit thicker. One caution: Don't store whipped cream near foods with strong odors. Cream picks up refrigerator smells quickly.

ICE CREAM—HOMEMADE. I have several recipes for made-from-scratch ice cream in this book. Each recipe was tested in two different ice cream makers: a sleek, electric Simac with a built-in freezer and an inexpensive Donvier, a do-it-by-hand machine that uses no ice or salt. The Donvier and its clones depend on an insulated tub that's kept in the freezer until needed. You fill the tub with the ice cream mix, then attach the cover and dasher. All it takes is a turn now and then and in about 20 minutes the mixture is frozen. If you've never made ice cream before but would like to try—there's nothing that tastes as good as soft, just-made ice cream licked off the dasher—I recommend you start with one of these inexpensive mechanical ice cream makers. No matter what machine you're using, follow the manufacturer's directions. You'll notice that I don't give churning times for any of the ice cream recipes but instead tell you to follow the directions that come with your machine. It has to be that way because every machine is different. It may take 40 minutes to churn ice cream in an old-fashioned, hand-cranked machine, and 20 in an electric maker. However, whatever type of machine you use, you'll probably need to put the ice cream or sorbet into the freezer to firm and ripen a bit before serving. While I love to eat ice cream straight from the tub, its soft texture won't hold up in most cases, and instead of a scoop you'll have a soup. This is particularly true with ice creams or sorbets that are flavored with alcohol, which lowers the mixture's freezing temperature and keeps it from getting very firm. On the flip side: If your ice cream or sorbet should become so hard in the freezer that it's difficult to scoop, either leave it out at room temperature for a few minutes or put it in the food processor and pulse several times to restore its creamy texture.

ICE CREAM–STOREBOUGHT. Leaf through the chapter on Adult Ice Cream and you'll find I've developed a collection of spectacular ice cream cakes made with customized storebought ice cream. For each of these desserts I've taken an off-the-shelf flavor and added something special, such as raspberry puree to vanilla or almond butter to coffee. They're great flavors and they work because I start with very high quality storebought ice cream. I tested each of these recipes with Haagen Dazs ice cream. Use it if you can find it; if not, choose a brand that's free of gums, stabilizers, emulsifiers, and any other ingredients you wouldn't use if you were making the ice cream yourself.

INSTANT ESPRESSO. An extract made from powdered instant espresso and boiling water can give a jolt to desserts. You'll see that I add instant espresso to many chocolate desserts to just tip the balance lightly toward mocha, and I use it in custards and cookies as well. I use Medaglia d'Oro brand because it's the easiest for me to find. Look for instant espresso powder in small jars in the coffee section of a supermarket or specialty shop.

JAMS AND JELLIES. Whether blending jams and jellies into a dessert or heating them to use as glazes, you should use the best-quality preserves you can find. Here's an instance in which it always pays to pay a little more and get the best: jams and jellies without several extra thickening and sweetening agents. Sugar and pectin are fine, but watch out for and avoid the corn sweeteners.

To glaze desserts with jams and jellies. Glazing tarts and small pastries with a veneer of warm jam or jelly gives them a professional polish—and it's easy to do. Bring the jam or jelly to a boil in a small saucepan over direct heat or in a microwave. To thin the jam to spreading consistency, add a few drops of water, cognac, dark rum, or liqueur. If the jam is thick with fruit, strain it first. (I know many people who puree the heated jam in a food processor and then, if necessary, reheat it and thin it a bit more. This works, but I prefer to take the time and press it through a sieve; the glaze tastes and looks smoother.) Use a pastry brush or a small paintbrush to gently brush the glaze over the dessert. Try brushing a glaze over a Bundt cake or a plain cake made in a tube pan for a touch of shine and sophistication. The rule of thumb is apricot jam over light-colored desserts, currant jelly over dark. But there's no rule that says you can't break the rule. One word of warning—a glazed dessert should not be frozen.

LIQUEURS. Liqueurs add an edge to desserts that cannot be achieved with syrups or extracts. No matter how sweet the liqueur, there's a bite and it's this bite that gives the dessert its distinctive flavor. I don't enjoy most liqueurs as drinks, but I love what they do to sweets. For an orange liqueur, I always choose Grand Marnier for its smooth, syrupy sweetness cut by good cognac. You can use Triple Sec or Curaçao, but you won't get the same fullness. Similarly, I select dark rum over white rum, finding both the color and aroma of the dark version more inviting. Most liqueurs will keep for a long time—a good thing, because you won't be using more than a tablespoon here and there. However, there are exceptions, most notably crème de cassis, which is best used within a few months of opening. Check with your dealer when buying liqueurs for baking. If you're not going to drink what you cook with, buy the smallest bottles you can find. Fortunately, many liqueurs come in airline-size bottles, just enough to make a dessert or two.

MAPLE SYRUP. Stay away from imitation pancake syrups—they're nothing but sweet and they'll spoil your good dessert. My preference is for grade B dark amber pure maple syrup; it's less expensive than its weak sister and so much lustier. Maple syrup is a pantry staple that will keep from season to season, if refrigerated, so stock up when the new tins hit the market shelves in the fall; that's also when the syrup is at its least expensive.

MEASURING. To state the obvious: Measuring is important. It is important to follow a recipe's measurements in cooking, vital in dessertmaking. A smidgen more of baking powder, a quarter teaspoon extra of cloves, and you've got a different dessert, and not usually a better one.

To measure flour and other dry ingredients. I measure with the scoop-and-sweep method and all of the recipes were tested this way. Just dip your measuring cup or spoon—a metal measuring cup or measuring spoon made for dry measuring—into the flour bin and scoop out more than you need. Hold the measuring cup or spoon over the flour bin and sweep off the excess with the flat edge of a knife. Use this method for granulated or confectioners' sugar, baking powder, baking soda, and spices.

To measure brown sugar. Brown sugar, whether light or dark, should be packed into a measuring cup. Again, use a metal cup made for dry measuring.

Dip the cup into the sugar and use your fingertips to press and pack the sugar into the cup. Level the top with your fingers or the edge of a knife. When you turn out the sugar, you'll have a moist brown sugar mold of the cup. Break up the sugar with your fingers as you add it to the batter.

To measure liquids. Small amounts of liquid, fractions of teaspoons or a few tablespoons, should be measured in the same measuring spoons you use for spices, baking powder, etc. But, for measurements of ¼ cup or more, you should use a glass cup made especially for measuring liquid. Place the measuring cup on the counter, pour in the liquid, and keep checking the amount by bending down so the measurement lines are at eye level. Holding the cup up to your eyes always results in mismeasurement; bend and you'll get it right.

To measure butter. The simplest way to measure butter is to know that a stick weighs 4 ounces and is the equivalent of ½ cup or 8 tablespoons. After that, everything else is easy to figure out. Several brands of butter mark off tablespoon measures on the wrapper. If the wrapper's on straight, use the marks.

To measure nuts and dried fruits. Use a metal measuring cup meant for measuring dry ingredients. Fill with the nuts or dried fruits and pack them down lightly. If the recipe says "¼ cup almonds, slivered or julienned, chopped," you should measure the almonds in their slivered or julienned state, then chop them. If the recipe reads "¼ cup ground almonds," you are meant to grind the almonds, then measure them.

MICROWAVE TIMESAVERS. I've come to think of the microwave as my assistant in the kitchen, there to do the little jobs that used to take time and a

A Short Course in Dessertmaking

watchful eye. For instance, I always use it to melt every kind of chocolate except white, and I no longer even think of melting butter any other way. Wherever using the microwave can cut a few minutes off preparation time, I've noted the option in the recipe.

MILK. All of my recipes were tested with whole milk. If you prefer using low-fat milk, you can do so in recipes for cakes and cookies and in ice cream recipes that also include heavy cream. However, I recommend using whole milk for custards, puddings, mousses, and creams, desserts that depend on the richness of full-fat, whole milk.

MIXERS. I use a large KitchenAid mixer for most mixing and all beating chores. It's a heavy-duty machine with a stationary bowl and a single-head beater that rotates and circles the bowl. The machine comes with a whisk, a leaf paddle, and a dough hook. I specify a whisk or paddle for most of my recipes, but everything can be made with a sturdy hand-held mixer or a standing mixer that uses rotary beaters. For small jobs, such as whipping cream for topping or beating one or two egg whites, I use a cordless handheld beater.

NONREACTIVE BOWLS AND SAUCEPANS. Recipes that include acidic ingredients instruct you to use nonreactive bowls or saucepans. Stainless steel, ceramic, glass, and nonstick coatings are nonreactive, meaning they won't affect the taste of your mixtures nor will they discolor. Avoid using aluminum and tin-lined copper.

NUTS. The same oil in nuts that gives them their full, rich flavor makes them a perishable commodity. To keep nuts from turning rancid, store them in the freezer, packed in airtight plastic bags. For most

recipes, there'll be no need to defrost the nuts before use. Buy nuts from a supplier whose turnover is rapid and always pop a nut in your mouth to check for freshness before adding them to your batter—it can save your dessert.

To toast nuts. Preheat the oven to 350°. Spread the nuts to be toasted on an ungreased jelly roll pan in a single layer. Bake for about 10 minutes, shaking the pan to turn the nuts every 3 minutes, until the nuts are lightly browned.

To pulverize nuts. You can pulverize (or grind) nuts quickly in a food processor. Always pulse, rather than process continuously, so you don't overdo it and find yourself with nut butter. For safety's sake, you can remove a spoonful of sugar or flour from the quantity specified in the recipe's ingredients and add it to the nuts before grinding. It will help keep the nuts dry and fluffy.

OATS. The oats used in all of my recipes are old-fashioned, *not* instant oats nor oat bran. Old-fashioned oats are sometimes referred to as *rolled*. They look like soft flakes and can be used straight from the box.

PIE WEIGHTS. These small metal pebbles, available in specialty shops, are used to keep pie and tart crusts from puffing during baking. (Always cover the crust with foil before adding the weights.) If you don't have weights, use dried beans or rice. You won't be able to use either for dinner after they've been baked, so let them cool and store them in a jar, at the ready for your next crust.

PIPING. In dessertmaking, *piping* refers to pushing an ingredient out through a canvas or plastic pastry bag, often one to which a decorative tip has been attached. In this book, there's just one recipe that calls for piping (Mace-Lemon Softies), and alternate directions for making the cookies with a spoon are given. But there will be times when you'll want to pipe rosettes of whipped cream on top of a dessert for an easy decorative finish, so if you've never used piping equipment you might want to practice. Pastry bags and tips are sold in kits, often in the supermarket. Drop the tip into the bag, then turn the top of the bag down to form a cuff. Hold the bag under the cuff with one hand and fill the bag, transferring the mixture from bowl to bag with a spatula. Press out the air in the top of the bag, then twist the bag to close. If you're right-handed, place your left hand around the bottom of the bag, near the tip, to guide it, and grasp the top twist of the bag between the thumb and index finger of your right hand, allowing your other fingers to circle the bulge of the pastry bag. Apply even pressure with your right hand, and what you're piping will start to flow from the tip. To stop, release the pressure and lift the bag. To pipe rosettes: Insert a star tip into the bag. Working about ½ inch from the surface you're decorating, press to form a small star, then release the pressure and lift the bag. For practice, try filling a pastry bag with storebought mayonnaise, a mixture with a wonderful piping consistency and one that can still be used for salads after your practice session.

PREHEATING. All recipes in this book are meant to be baked in a preheated oven, that is, one in which the temperature is at the prescribed level at the start of baking. Most ovens preheat in about 10 minutes.

PUFF PASTRY. Puff pastry is, perhaps, the most elegant pastry dough in the baker's repertoire. It is also the most time-consuming and, until you get the hang of it, the trickiest. A simple dough of flour, butter, and sugar is rolled into a rectangle and then wrapped around a large quantity of butter. After a series of rollings, foldings, and chillings, the dough locks the butter into layers that, when placed in a hot oven, puff into gloriously voluminous layers, pushed to remarkable heights by the water in the butter that turns to steam in the oven's heat. It's a baker's miracle and it might be something you'll want to play with when you've got a lazy afternoon ahead of you. However, when what you want is a great-looking dessert that takes just a modest amount of time to put together, turn to packaged puff pastry. I keep a box of Pepperidge Farm Puff Pastry Sheets in the freezer at all times. Left at room temperature for 20 minutes, the sheets are ready to be rolled, cut, baked and eaten. For example, a standout dessert like Apple Paper Thins can be assembled in about 20 minutes.

SIFTING. Sifting is unnecessary for most of my recipes. More often than not all you need to do is put the dry ingredients (e.g., flour, baking powder, baking soda, cocoa, salt, and/or spices) in a bowl and stir with a wire whisk to aerate and combine them thoroughly. If the recipe calls for sifting, place the sifter over a piece of waxed paper, add the dry ingredients to the sifter, and sift onto the paper or directly into the bowl, depending on the recipe.

SPICES. Spices, like extracts, should be stored in a cool, dark cupboard and checked periodically. If the scent of the spice in your tin doesn't burst forth when you open it, toss it out. You'll get pale flavor from a spice with pale aroma.

STEEPING. Steeping infuses a liquid with flavor. The liquid is warmed (or boiled, depending on the recipe) with spices or flavorings (e.g., citrus rinds, vanilla beans, cardamom pods, ginger slices, etc.), then covered and allowed to rest. It's just like making tea.

SUGAR. The sugars you'll need to have on hand to work with this book are: granulated white sugar, light brown sugar, dark brown sugar, and confectioners' sugar, also known as 10-X powdered sugar. When a recipe says "sugar," it means granulated sugar that is measured by the scoop-and-sweep method (see MEASURING). Brown sugars are always packed into the measuring cup and confectioners' sugar is sifted or sieved. Brown sugar has a tendency to become very hard, a danger because it won't soften during baking. If your brown sugar is hard, you can try bringing it back to the right consistency by warming it for a few minutes in a 350° degree oven, pressing it through a sieve, or whirling it in a food processor. The best way to store brown sugar is in airtight plastic bags.

THERMOMETER. While your oven may have a light to let you know it's reached the temperature you set it to, or you may hear the gas go off as that temperature is reached, it's always best to double check with an oven thermometer. Most oven thermometers are made to be kept in the oven at all times. Invest in a good mercury thermometer; you'll have it for years and it will save you from disaster. (Taylor is a well-known, reliable brand.)

VANILLA. Vanilla is the most frequently used flavoring in baking. It is often used in egg preparations and almost always in chocolate recipes because of the way it brings out chocolate's depth. In most recipes, using a good-quality pure vanilla extract will give you the flavor you want. (I use Nielsen-Massey, available at many specialty stores and through Williams-Sonoma's catalogue.) When you're steeping milk for custard or ice cream, a vanilla bean is preferable to extract. Cut the bean (or pod) in half lengthwise. You'll notice that inside is a moist mass of tiny little seeds, or pulp. With the tip of a small knife, scrape the pulp into the liquid (or batter, depending on the recipe). For steeping, add the bean to the liquid as well. When you are ready to use the liquid, strain out the bean (which can be reserved, rinsed and left to dry at room temperature, and buried in a jar of sugar to make vanilla sugar); the little seeds will remain, speckling your dessert and giving it a homey look and a warm, inviting flavor.

YOGURT. I like the smooth texture and tangy taste you get from yogurt in cakes and mousses. When a recipe calls for yogurt, you can use whole milk, low-fat, or even nonfat yogurt. Obviously, a whole milk yogurt will give you a richer dessert, but because each of the recipes using yogurt is so full-flavored, you won't miss the extra fat if you choose another type.

ZEST. Several recipes call for lemon, lime, orange, or grapefruit zest. The zest is the fruit's peel and you are meant to take just the thinnest top layer of colored peel from the fruit (except in the recipe for Thick-Cut Candied Citrus Peels, in which you'll take the white cottony pith as well). For long, thin strands of zest, use a zester, a little gadget with a set of tiny metal holes at the top. For broader strips of zest, use a swivel-blade peeler or a sharp knife. If necessary, flip the peel over and cut away any stubborn bits of pith that remain.

Breakfast, Brunch, and Lunch Mates

Sweets to Get You Through the Day

Soft and Spicy Fresh Plum Cake
(Mid-Morning Parfait)

Almost-Like-Grandma's Sweet-Filled Blintzes
(Blintz Beehive Cake)

Crumb-Topped Raspberry Coffeecake
(Crumb-Topped Orange Marmalade Coffeecake)

French-Fried Toast
(Pan-Fried French Toast)

Cranberry Upside-Downer
(Apple or Pear Upside-Downer)

Blueberry-Corn and Apple-Nut Mini Muffins
(Fruit and Nut Muffins)

Chockablock Bran Muffins
(Chockablock Bran Cake)

Gingered Peach Tart
(Gingered Peach Crisp)

Buttermilk Banana Waffles
(Tutti-Frutti Waffles)

Puffed Pancake
(Double Puffed Pancake)

Apple Butter Bundt Cake
(Homemade Applesauce)

Buttermilk Pie
(Buttermilk Amaretto Pie)

Directions for making sweets listed in parentheses are found at the end of each recipe in sections marked "Playing Around."

When I outlined <u>Sweet Times</u> for my editor, Maria Guarnaschelli, she said, "Don't forget breakfast — it's in with a bang." She wasn't talking about "power" breakfasts in paneled restaurants where movers and shakers close deals, but hearty food shared with family and friends, the best way to start a day. She touched my soft spot because I love A.M. meals. But while I crave something warm, cozy, and home-baked just as much as the next person, I'm not prepared to get up at dawn to make it. That's why this early-in-the-day collection is heavy on recipes that can be made ahead, frozen, or, like the Puffed Pancake (so good with maple syrup or a slice of Canadian bacon), whipped up in minutes. All of the recipes are simple — there's nothing here a novice can't master — and those that require a few extra steps or need to bake for more than 30 minutes are often the ones just right for brunch or lunch.

Soft and Spicy Fresh Plum Cake

Like pudding cakes that make their own sauce, and custardy cornbreads that separate into strata, this warmly spiced sweet performs its own sleight of hand as it bakes, alternating plums and batter, like the old hand-over-hand game, until it produces a honey-brown, sugar-crusted, soft, creamy cake over juicy, bubbling plums. In summer, when yellow, black, and red plums are plentiful, try an assortment; in fall, try small purple Italian prune plums. The cake is great both ways. § Makes 8 to 10 Servings

THE PLUMS

2 lb. ripe, tart, firm plums, pitted (about 12 medium-size plums or 30 small Italian prune plums)

¾ c. sugar

1 tsp. ground cinnamon

¼ tsp. ground ginger

¼ tsp. ground coriander

THE BATTER

1 c. sugar

1 c. all-purpose flour

2 tsp. baking powder

⅛ tsp. salt

1 c. milk, preferably at room temperature

½ tsp. pure vanilla extract

½ tsp. almond extract

½ c. (1 stick) unsalted butter, cut into 4 pieces (it can come straight from the refrigerator)

Ice cream or lightly sweetened whipped cream, optional

1] **THE PLUMS.** Position a rack in the center of the oven and preheat the oven to 350°. Cut each plum into 8 slices (if you are using prune plums, quarter them) and toss in a large nonreactive bowl with the sugar and spices. The plums will give up juice and a syrup will accumulate. Set aside while you prepare the batter, stirring occasionally to distribute the syrup.

2] **THE CAKE.** Put the sugar, flour, baking powder, and salt in another mixing bowl. By hand, whisk to combine. Add the milk and extracts and whisk just to blend. You'll have a thick batter; set aside.

3] Put the butter in a 9″ × 12″ nonreactive baking pan; good choices are Pyrex, porcelain, or stainless steel. (Don't use aluminum because it will react with the acid in the plums and give your dessert a metallic taste.) Put the pan in the oven and heat until the butter is melted, about 5 minutes. Remove from the oven.

4] Whisk the reserved batter lightly and pour it over the hot butter. Use a spatula to smooth the batter, but don't worry about getting an even layer. The batter will firm around the edges as it hits the hot butter, so it's impossible to get a perfectly even coating, but that's OK. Using a spoon or your hands, scatter the plums over the batter and drizzle on the syrup remaining in the bowl. Bake 50 to 55 minutes, until the top is golden and a toothpick inserted in the cake comes out clean. Remove to a rack and let cool in the pan for about 20 to 30 minutes before serving. You can wait longer and serve this at room temperature or chilled the next day—it is delicious at any temperature.

SERVING. Bring the cake to the table in its baking pan (it's too soft and creamy to unmold successfully) and serve it family-style, cut into generous portions, and, if you like, offered with ice cream or lightly sweetened whipped cream.

STORING. Cool the cake and cover the pan tightly with plastic wrap; refrigerate for up to 2 days. Do not freeze.

BEST MATCH. This is a good addition to a summer breakfast of granola, fruit, yogurt, and cheese or a perfect dessert after a soup, sandwich, and salad lunch. Serve with honey-sweetened lemon tea, hot or iced.

❀| **PLAYING AROUND.** (Mid-Morning Parfait) Spoon alternating layers of leftover cake and plain yogurt into a parfait glass to make an easy, but special, weekend breakfast or snack.

Almost-Like-Grandma's Sweet-Filled Blintzes

Blintzes make me think of my Russian grand-mother; they were one of her many specialties. Depending on your heritage, they might remind you of Mexican tortillas, French crêpes, or the Chinese pancakes used to encase moo-shu pork. Most cultures have a blintz-like dish, a thin pancake or crêpe wrapped around a sweet or savory filling. In this recipe, the fillings (there are two, one based on ricotta and walnuts, the other on cream cheese, farmer cheese, and coconut and each enough to fill twenty blintzes) are sweet and creamy. They're packed into the pancake, which is folded like an eggroll, then sautéed in sizzling butter. When you cut into a blintz, the filling oozes out of the crisply crusted pancake, becoming both filling and luscious sauce. These are very different from my grandmother's, but I think she'd probably like them—if she could have her scoop of thick sour cream on the side. § Makes 15 to 20 Blintzes

BLINTZ PANCAKES

1 c. all-purpose flour
4 large eggs, at room temperature
1 c. milk, at room temperature
2 tbsp. unsalted butter, melted
Pinch of salt
1½ tsp. sugar
Butter for greasing the pan and sautéing

1] THE BLINTZ PANCAKES. Place all the ingredients in a blender or food processor. Process, stopping once or twice to scrape down the sides of the container, until smooth and completely blended. Refrigerate for 30 minutes. *(The batter can be prepared ahead to this point and refrigerated, covered, for up to 3 days.)* When ready to use, pour the batter into a pitcher or measuring cup with a spout.

2] Place a 7- or 8-inch crêpe pan or skillet, preferably non-stick, over medium heat. Rub a thin film of butter over the surface of the pan, either with a paper towel or by holding a partially wrapped stick of butter at the top and rubbing the exposed end against the pan; the butter should sizzle. Pour in a small amount of batter, lift the pan off the heat, and rapidly tilt it so the batter covers the surface. Pour any excess batter back into the pitcher. Put the pan back on the heat. When the batter has just set, cut off the "tail" (the batter that stuck to the side of the pan when you poured the excess back); now you should have a round pancake. Cook for 1½ to 2 minutes, until little bubbles appear on the surface and the top looks dull. If you lift the pancake, you'll find the bottom firm and perhaps blistered; it shouldn't take on much color. Cook on one side only. Loosen an edge of the pancake with a knife and lift the pancake out of the pan (I use my fingers) and onto a sheet of waxed paper, uncooked side up. Cover with another sheet of waxed paper. Continue making pancakes until all the batter is used. *(Use the pancakes immediately or wrap them airtight and freeze for up to 2 weeks.)*

RICOTTA-WALNUT FILLING

15 oz. (1 container) part-skim ricotta
1 large egg
1 egg yolk
¾ c. walnuts
½ tsp. pure vanilla extract
3 tbsp. sugar
1 tbsp. dark rum
Pinch of salt

COCONUT–FARMER CHEESE FILLING

15 oz. (1 large pkg.) farmer cheese
2 oz. cream cheese
½ c. sweetened coconut flakes
1 large egg
1 egg yolk
½ tsp. pure vanilla extract
1 tbsp. Grand Marnier or other orange liqueur

Apricot jam, maple syrup, and/or sour cream, optional

3] THE FILLINGS. Choose a filling; each makes enough for 20 blintzes. Place all the ingredients for either filling in a food processor and process, pulsing on and off, until the mixture is smooth. (In the case of the Ricotta-Walnut Filling, you can pulse just until the mixture is blended and the walnuts are finely chopped, not ground, if you want some crunch.)

4] Lay one pancake, uncooked side up, on a sheet of waxed paper. Place about 1½ tablespoons of filling in the center of the pancake. Gently fold two opposite sides over the filling, overlapping them, and then fold the remaining sides over to form a neat oblong package. Set aside, seam-side down, while you fill the remaining pancakes. *(If the pancakes have not been frozen, you can wrap the blintzes airtight and freeze for up to 2 weeks before sautéing. Do not thaw before cooking.)*

5] Melt a small amount of butter in a large skillet. Sauté a few blintzes at a time (don't crowd them in the skillet), turning them once, until they are golden brown and heated through, about 2 minutes on a side. Transfer to a large platter and keep warm while you sauté the remaining blintzes. Serve immediately.

SERVING. Arrange the blintzes on a large serving platter (they look terrific lined up along the length of a narrow, rectangular dish) or put two or three per person on individual dessert plates. Drizzle over hot apricot preserves (thinned with a spoonful of water or the liqueur used in the filling), or maple syrup, or even both. If you'd like, follow Eastern European tradition and place a dollop of sour cream in the center of the plate.

STORING. You can freeze the unfilled pancakes for 2 weeks before filling and cooking; filled blintzes can be frozen for 2 weeks before cooking. Sautéed blintzes should be eaten immediately.

BEST MATCH. Serve blintzes as the main course of a breakfast that starts with melon or a citrus salad and features lightly smoked bacon, ham, or sausage on the side. Or serve them for dessert after a spicy Indian- or Mexican-inspired lunch; their calm and comfort is welcome after a fiery entree.

❀| **PLAYING AROUND.** (Blintz Beehive Cake) This is pretty enough for a party. Generously butter an 8-inch springform pan and dust all over with dry bread crumbs, tapping out the excess. Center a rack in the oven and preheat the oven to 350°. Place a pancake in the bottom of the pan and, if necessary, use a small, sharp paring knife to trim the pancake to fit the pan. Spread about 2 to 2½ tablespoons of filling evenly over the pancake, stopping about ½ inch from the edge. Cover with a second pancake, pressing down gently, trim the edges if necessary, and spread with filling. Continue making layers until you reach the top of the pan or exhaust your supply of pancakes and filling. Because you have not spread the filling to the edges, the cake will have a slightly domed beehive shape. Cut 1 tablespoon of unsalted butter into slivers and scatter over the cake. Bake for about 30 minutes, until the cake is hot and the filling bubbling. Sprinkle the top with confectioners' sugar and run it under the broiler for about 30 to 45 seconds to brown. Remove the sides of the springform and cool the cake for 25 minutes on a rack before serving. Place the cake, still on the springform base, on a platter. If you like, paint the top with hot apricot jam thinned with water, or dust with a fresh coat of confectioners' sugar. Cut into wedges and serve while still warm. The cake should be eaten the day it is made and is best warm or at room temperature. (If necessary, chilled slices can be reheated for 30 seconds in a microwave.)

Crumb-Topped Raspberry Coffeecake

Following a Southern tradition, this soft, moist, crumb-topped cake gets its pink color and sweet fruit taste from raspberry jam. I like the extra texture jam with seeds provides, but you can use a seedless preserve if that's your fancy. In either case, choose the best you can find, preferably one without too many sweeteners.
§ Makes 12 Servings

THE TOPPING
⅔ c. all-purpose flour
½ c. packed light brown sugar
1 c. slivered or julienned blanched almonds, toasted
½ tsp. ground cinnamon
½ c. (1 stick) cold unsalted butter, cut into 8 pieces

THE CAKE
2 c. all-purpose flour
½ tsp. baking soda
1 tsp. baking powder
½ c. (1 stick) unsalted butter, at room temperature
½ c. sugar
½ tsp. almond extract
2 large eggs, preferably at room temperature
1 c. best-quality raspberry jam, with or without seeds
½ c. buttermilk, preferably at room temperature

Fresh raspberries, optional

1] **THE TOPPING.** Place all the ingredients in a food processor. Pulse until the mixture forms curds and holds together when pressed between your fingers. Leave the topping in the processor until you're ready for it. *(The topping can be made up to 3 days ahead and refrigerated in an airtight plastic bag.)*

2] **THE CAKE.** Place a rack in the center of the oven and preheat the oven to 350°. Butter and flour a 9″ × 12″ baking pan. Measure the flour, baking soda, and baking powder into a mixing bowl and whisk just to combine.

3] In an electric mixer on medium speed, using the paddle attachment if you have one, cream the butter, sugar, and almond extract. Add the eggs, one at a time, beating for a minute after each addition. (Don't be concerned if the mixture curdles.) Mix in the jam on low speed. Keeping the mixer on its lowest speed, add half the flour mixture, beating just until the flour is incorporated. Add the buttermilk. When the liquid is incorporated, add the rest of the flour and beat just until smooth.

4] Spread the batter in the pan, using a spatula to help you get an even layer. Sprinkle the topping over the cake and pat it gently into the batter with your fingertips. Bake the cake 40 to 45 minutes, until a toothpick inserted in the center of the cake comes out clean and the cake starts to pull away from the sides of the pan. Cool the cake in the pan on a rack for 20 to 30 minutes before serving or, if you prefer, wait until it reaches room temperature.

SERVING. Cut the cake into portions in the pan and arrange them in a napkin-lined bread basket or stack attractively on a large serving platter. If they're in season, add fresh raspberries to the arrangement.

STORING. The cooled cake can be wrapped airtight and frozen for up to 1 month.

BEST MATCH. Pair this with hearty combinations such as steak and eggs or eggs, sausage, and peppers.

☀| PLAYING AROUND. (Crumb-Topped Orange Marmalade Coffeecake) Substitute best-quality orange marmalade for the jam and serve with black coffee and a liqueur-spiked orange, pineapple, and berry salad.

French-Fried Toast

When I was a teenager, my friends and I would meet on Saturday morning at what was for us the local hangout and for other older, more dignified types, a respectable neighborhood restaurant. The owner would probably have thrown us out for disrupting the dining room with our incessant table-hopping if we weren't such ardent admirers of the house breakfast special: large wedges of challah (an egg-rich bread), dipped in egg batter, deep fried until puffed and golden brown, powdered with confectioners' sugar, and topped with pats of melting butter. I loved the way the outside of the rich challah would turn crusty from frying and the inside would stay soft and eggy. My version's just like that—only better (with apologies to old times) because it's made with heavy cream and flavored with vanilla and hazelnut liqueur.
§ Makes 4 to 6 Servings

5 large eggs
1¼ c. milk
¾ c. heavy cream
2½ tbsp. sugar
Pinch of salt
1½ tbsp. Frangelico or other nut liqueur
2 tsp. pure vanilla extract
1 loaf (1 lb.) challah or best-quality white bread, unsliced, crusts removed
Safflower oil, or other almost flavorless oil, for deep frying

Confectioners' sugar
Butter, maple syrup, and/or preserves

1] Place the eggs, milk, cream, sugar, salt, liqueur, and vanilla in a shallow bowl or baking pan; whisk to combine. Cut the bread into 1-inch-thick slices and cut each slice diagonally into 4 triangles; set aside. Pour about 3 inches of oil into a deep fryer or saucepan and heat to 350°. Preheat the oven to 250°.

2] Working with 4 triangles of bread at a time, place them in the egg mixture and allow them to soak for about 1 minute on each side. Drop the triangles into the hot oil and fry, turning them so they brown evenly, for about 1½ to 2 minutes, or until they are puffed, golden, and crusty. Remove the bread from the oil with a slotted spoon and drain well on a double thickness of paper towels. Transfer to a heatproof platter and keep warm in the oven while you soak and fry the remaining bread. Serve as soon as the last piece of bread is fried.

SERVING. Sprinkle the French Toast generously with confectioners' sugar and mound attractively on a large, preheated serving platter. Serve butter, maple syrup, and jams as accompaniments.

STORING. French Fried Toast should be served as soon as it is made.

BEST MATCH. French Toast can be breakfast or brunch or the bread that accompanies omelets, eggs sunny-side up, or small portions of hash.

❀| PLAYING AROUND. (Pan-Fried French Toast) Cut and soak the bread as directed but sauté it in melted butter in a heavy skillet. If there are leftover slices of Pan-Fried French Toast, freeze them; they can be reheated in a toaster oven.

Cranberry Upside-Downer

Cranberries and Thanksgiving are an association hard to beat, but it's a shame to limit the bright fruits to a relish made once a year. Buy the berries in late October or November, when they're at their most plentiful and least expensive, and store them in the freezer, where they'll keep from holiday to holiday. That way you can make this simple sweet whenever you're in the mood to start the day with something easy and festive. No matter when you make this, if you serve it warm from the oven, it will feel like a holiday. § Makes 6 to 8 Servings

6 tbsp. unsalted butter
6 tbsp. sugar
¼ c. pecans or walnuts
2 c. cranberries, fresh or frozen (*not* thawed)
1 c. all-purpose flour
1 tsp. baking powder
1 tsp. ground cinnamon
½ c. (1 stick) unsalted butter, at room temperature
½ c. sugar
1 tsp. pure vanilla extract
2 large eggs, preferably at room temperature
⅓ c. milk, preferably at room temperature
⅓ c. red currant jelly

Vanilla ice cream or whipped cream, optional

1] Center a rack in the oven and preheat the oven to 350°. Have ready an 8-inch round cake pan. Melt the 6 tablespoons butter in a small saucepan. Add the 6 tablespoons sugar and stir until the mixture comes to a boil. Pour this evenly over the bottom of the cake pan. Sprinkle over the nuts and top with the cranberries, arranging them in an even layer by pressing them down gently with your fingers. Don't worry if the frozen berries cause the butter to congeal. Set aside.

2] In a mixing bowl, whisk together the flour, baking powder and cinnamon by hand just to combine; reserve. In an electric mixer on medium speed, using a paddle if available, cream the room-temperature butter. Add the ½ cup sugar and continue to beat on medium speed until the mixture is pale and creamy, about 3 minutes. Add the vanilla, then beat in the eggs, one at a time, stopping to scrape the bowl as needed. Continue to beat at medium speed for 2 more minutes. Set the mixer at lowest speed and add one-half of the dry ingredients, mixing only until combined. Gently mix in the milk and then the rest of the flour mixture. Spoon the batter over the cranberries and smooth the top with a rubber spatula.

3] Bake 40 to 45 minutes, or until the cake is golden and a toothpick inserted in the center comes out clean. Remove the cake from the oven. Run a knife around the sides of the pan and turn the cake out onto a serving platter. (If any of the berries stick to the pan, scrape them off with a knife and spread them on the cake.) Warm the jelly in a small saucepan, stirring until it liquifies; or you can do this in a microwave. Brush the jelly over the top of the cake.

SERVING. Serve the cake warm (about 20 minutes after it comes from the oven), when it's at its best, or at room temperature, when it's still delicious but the cranberry top is not as lush. If it's a holiday morning, trim the edges of the plate with holly leaves (discarding the pretty but poisonous berries)—it will be gorgeous. Cut into portions at the table and offer vanilla ice cream or gently whipped and lightly sweetened cream; if the cake is warm, both will melt slightly to become topping *cum* sauce.

STORING. This cake should be eaten the day it is made.

BEST MATCH. This is just the right foil for a creamy main dish such as eggs Benedict, chicken pot pie, coquilles St. Jacques, or anything topped with cheese. Lemon tea or espresso are better matches than coffee with cream.

❋| **PLAYING AROUND.** (Apple or Pear Upside-Downer) When cranberries are not in season (or not stocked in your freezer), make this cake with apples or pears, using 2 or 3 pieces of fruit, peeled, cored, and thinly sliced. Replace the currant jelly with strained apricot preserves—the color's better with pale fruits.

Two Mini-Muffin Recipes: Blueberry-Corn and Apple-Nut

These tiny, pop-in-your-mouth muffins pack a lot of flavor. The blue and yellow Blueberry-Corn Muffins, loaded with juicy berries and kernels of fresh corn, offer a bit of sweetness and crunch with each bite. The Apple-Nut are like miniature coffeecakes, slightly sweet, mildly spiced, and appealingly close-textured.

BLUEBERRY-CORN MINI-MUFFINS

1 c. all-purpose flour
1 c. yellow cornmeal, preferably a coarse, stone-ground brand
½ c. sugar
1 tbsp. baking powder
½ tsp. salt
1 c. blueberries (fresh or frozen, *not* thawed)
1 c. corn kernels (fresh; canned, and drained; or frozen, *not* thawed)
1 c. milk
1 large egg
3 tbsp. unsalted butter, melted

Butter, cream cheese, and/or jams

The trick to preparing great muffins is to combine the wet and dry ingredients with as few strokes of a wooden spoon as possible. Don't worry if the mixture is neither smooth nor completely moistened—that's just the way it's supposed to be for best results.
§ Each Recipe Makes About 48 Muffins

1] Center a rack in the oven and preheat the oven to 400°. For this recipe you'll need muffin tins with 1¾″ × ¾″ cups, each with a 1 tablespoon capacity. Butter the tins, spray with PAM (a vegetable spray), or line with paper baking cups; set aside. Put all the dry ingredients, the berries, and corn in a large mixing bowl and stir with a wooden spoon to combine. Using a whisk, mix the milk, egg, and melted butter together in another bowl or a pitcher. Make a well in the center of the dry ingredients and pour in the liquid. Mix with the wooden spoon just until combined. The mixture will be moist but there may be a few dry spots—that's OK.

2] Use a rounded teaspoonful of batter for each muffin. Bake for 15 to 18 minutes, or until the tops are lightly golden and the berries have popped. Cool in the pan for a minute. Remove the muffins from the tin and place them on a rack. Repeat until all of the batter is used. Serve immediately or cool to room temperature.

APPLE-NUT MINI-MUFFINS

2 c. all-purpose flour
1 tbsp. baking powder
¼ tsp. salt
⅓ c. granulated sugar
2 tbsp. packed light brown sugar
¾ tsp. ground cinnamon
⅛ tsp. ground allspice
1 apple, peeled, cored, and finely diced
⅓ c. raisins, light or dark
½ c. pecans, finely chopped
1 c. milk
1 large egg
3 tbsp. unsalted butter, melted
½ tsp. pure vanilla extract

Butter, cream cheese, and/or jams

1] Center a rack in the oven and preheat the oven to 400°. For this recipe you'll need muffin tins with 1¾″ × ¾″ cups, each with a 1 tablespoon capacity. Butter the tins, spray with PAM (a vegetable spray), or line with paper baking cups; set aside. Put all the dry ingredients, the apple, raisins, and pecans in a large mixing bowl and stir with a wooden spoon to combine. Using a whisk, mix the milk, egg, melted butter, and vanilla together in another bowl or pitcher. Make a well in the center of the dry ingredients and pour in the liquid. Mix with the wooden spoon just until combined. The mixture will be moist but there may be a few dry spots—that's OK.

2] Use a rounded teaspoonful of batter for each muffin. Bake for 13 to 15 minutes, or until the tops are golden. Cool in the pan for a minute. Remove the muffins from the tin and place them on a rack. Repeat until all of the batter is used. Serve immediately or cool to room temperature.

SERVING. Pile the muffins from either recipe into a napkin-lined basket and pass along with butter, cream cheese, and an assortment of jams.

STORING. Wrapped airtight, these will keep at room temperature for 1 day or frozen for 1 month.

BEST MATCH. Hot coffee and a handful of muffins grabbed from the freezer and warmed in the microwave or toaster oven make a meal. For heartier appetites, serve alongside hot cereal, scrambled eggs, or yogurt and fruit.

❀| PLAYING AROUND. (Fruit and Nut Muffins) Substitute raspberries (fresh or frozen) for blueberries in the corn recipe or pears and walnuts for apples and pecans in the Apple-Nut recipe. You can also use the recipes to make 12 regular-size muffins. Bake 20 to 25 minutes, until tops are golden and a toothpick inserted in the center comes out clean.

Chockablock Bran Muffins

These get their name from being crammed full of tastes and textures: tart and sweet, soft and chewy, mellow and bright. They're studded with bits of apricots, prunes, raisins, and bran cereal, so every bite is a high-fiber, low-fat adventure. Like most muffins, these are easy to make and freeze well. § Makes 12 Muffins

1½ c. all-purpose flour
½ tsp. baking soda
1 tbsp. baking powder
⅓ c. sugar
¼ tsp. ground allspice
1 large egg, preferably at room temperature
¼ c. safflower oil
1⅓ c. buttermilk, preferably at room temperature
1 tbsp. honey
1 tsp. pure vanilla extract
1⅓ c. Kellogg's All-Bran cereal
½ c. dried apricots, finely diced
½ c. pitted prunes, finely diced
¼ c. raisins

Butter and jams

1] Center a rack in the oven and preheat the oven to 400°. Butter a muffin tin, spray with PAM (a vegetable cooking spray), or line with paper baking cups; set aside. Put the flour, baking soda, baking powder, sugar, and allspice in a bowl and whisk to combine; set aside. In another large bowl, whisk the egg, oil, buttermilk, honey, and vanilla to combine. Add the All-Bran to the liquid ingredients, stirring with a wooden spoon to moisten. Fold in the reserved dry ingredients, taking care not to overmix. Add the fruit and stir to blend.

2] Divide the batter evenly among the muffin cups and bake 15 to 18 minutes, or until the tops are golden and a toothpick inserted in the center comes out clean. Remove the pan to a rack to cool for 5 minutes before turning out the muffins. Serve immediately or cool to room temperature.

SERVING. Serve these in a napkin-lined basket with butter and jams.

STORING. Wrapped airtight, these will keep at room temperature for 1 day or frozen for a month.

BEST MATCH. These are their own breakfast-on-the-run. Round them out nutritionally by serving with a scoop of low-fat cottage cheese or yogurt or by making them into sandwiches with low-fat cheddar cheese.

❋ | PLAYING AROUND. (Chockablock Bran Cake) Spoon the batter into an 8" × 8" baking pan, buttered or sprayed with PAM. Bake in the center of a 400° oven for 25 to 30 minutes, or until the top is golden and a toothpick inserted in the center comes out clean. Cool on a rack for 10 minutes before removing from the pan. Cut into squares with a serrated knife and serve warm or at room temperature.

Gingered Peach Tart

When I go to the market and the peaches are so ripe I catch their heady perfume even before I reach the bin, I know it's time to make this tart. For this to be a smash, you've got to use at-their-peak, mid-summer peaches because even though *this tempting tart includes a jolt of fresh ginger (to boost the lush sweetness of the fruit) and a brown sugar streusel (to add a bit of crunch), the fruit's the star. § Makes 6 to 8 Servings*

THE FILLING

2 lb. (about 5 to 6 large) ripe, fragrant peaches
1 tbsp. coarsely chopped fresh ginger
⅓ c. sugar
½ tsp. ground cinnamon
1 tbsp. all-purpose flour

THE CRUST

1½ c. all-purpose flour
1 tbsp. sugar
⅛ tsp. salt
½ c. (1 stick) unsalted butter, very cold or frozen, cut into 8 pieces
3 to 4 tbsp. ice water
1 egg white, lightly beaten with a fork

1] THE FILLING. Bring a quart of water to a boil in a medium saucepan. One by one, drop the peaches into the boiling water for 10 seconds and remove with a slotted spoon. Slip off the skins when the fruit is cool enough to handle. Stone the peaches and cut them into ½-inch chunks. Place them in a large mixing bowl. Stir in the ginger, sugar, and cinnamon. (The flour is added later.) Set aside at room temperature while you prepare the crust and streusel.

2] THE CRUST. Place the flour, sugar, and salt in a food processor. Pulse just to mix. Add the butter all at once and pulse until the mixture is grainy, about 10 to 15 times. Stop the machine, add 1 tablespoon of water, pulse, then repeat twice more with 2 more tablespoons of the water. Continue to pulse until the dough forms large curds and holds together when pressed. (If necessary, add up to 1 more tablespoon of ice water to achieve the right consistency.) Remove the dough and pat it into a disk ¾ inch thick. Wrap it in plastic and chill at least 20 minutes or up to 1 day. (Just wipe out the processor bowl and set it aside if you are going to make the streusel soon.) Roll the dough out on a floured surface to a thickness of ⅛ inch and fit it into a 9-inch tart pan with removable bottom. Prick the bottom of the crust all over with the tines of a fork. Freeze the crust, uncovered, for 30 minutes. (*The crust can be prepared ahead to this point and wrapped and frozen for up to 1 month.*) Position a rack one-third up from the bottom of the oven and preheat the oven to 425°.

3] Remove the crust from the freezer and cover with aluminum foil, pressing against the bottom and sides of the pan to get a close fit. Add pie weights or dried beans. Bake for 20 minutes. Remove the foil and weights and bake uncovered for 5 to 8 more minutes, or until lightly browned. As soon as you take the crust from the oven, brush the bottom and sides with the beaten egg white to seal it and prevent it from getting soggy. Cool in the pan on a rack. *Reduce the oven temperature to 350°.*

THE STREUSEL

¼ c. all-purpose flour
¼ c. packed light brown sugar
⅓ c. walnuts
4 tbsp. (½ stick) unsalted butter,
  cold or frozen, cut into
  4 pieces

**Ice cream, sweetened whipped
cream, or crème fraîche,
optional**

4] **THE STREUSEL.** Place the flour, brown sugar, and walnuts in the food processor. Pulse a few times to chop the nuts coarsely. Add the butter all at once. Pulse about 10 times, until the butter is evenly distributed and the mixture holds together when pressed between your fingers. (*Streusel can be prepared ahead, wrapped airtight in a plastic bag, and refrigerated for up to 3 days.*)

5] Stir the 1 tablespoon flour into the fruit mixture until evenly distributed and pile the fruit into the crust, leveling the top with a spatula. Sprinkle over the streusel and pat it down very gently with your fingertips. If you'd like, for contrast you can leave a small circle of peach filling uncovered in the center of the tart. Place the tart on a baking sheet with raised sides to catch any drips and bake 35 to 40 minutes, until the top is evenly browned and the fruit is bubbling up around the edges. Cool the tart on a rack for 30 minutes. The tart is best served warm or at room temperature but can be enjoyed chilled.

SERVING. Remove the tart from the pan, transfer to a doily-lined cake plate, and dust the streusel with confectioners' sugar. Cut the tart at table and, if you like, offer ice cream, lightly sweetened whipped cream, or crème fraîche as a topping.

STORING. The tart is best eaten the day it is made. If you prepare it ahead, keep it at room temperature or lightly covered with plastic wrap in the refrigerator.

BEST MATCH. The zip of ginger in this dessert makes it a perfect match for a lunch of assorted salads, grilled fish, chicken, or Oriental-style dishes.

❀| **PLAYING AROUND.** (Gingered Peach Crisp) For this rustic, informal crisp, double the filling and topping ingredients; bake in a buttered deep-dish pie pan until brown and bubbling, about 50 to 60 minutes.

Buttermilk Banana Waffles

There are those who believe the purpose of waffles is to catch maple syrup, butter, ice cream, or fruit sauces. They're not wrong, just half right. Waffles can stand on their own with just a gloss of syrup, provided they're as full flavored as these. To be good, waffle batter must be butter-rich; it's what gives waffles their wonderful crispness. These are rich, crisp, light, and loaded with slices of banana and shreds of coconut. They are also so easy to make there's no reason to relegate them to weekends-only status. The number of waffles you'll get from this recipe depends on the size of your waffle iron. I use a 1950s iron I got at a tag sale and usually make 6 double-size waffles, not counting the first one, which, no matter how many times I make waffles, never seems to come out right. A check among friends shows they've had the same experience. Assume the first waffle's for the cook and carry on. § Makes 6 to 8 Waffles

1¾ c. all-purpose flour
¼ tsp. baking soda
1½ tsp. baking powder
¼ tsp. salt
⅛ tsp. freshly grated or ground nutmeg, optional
½ c. packed light brown sugar
½ c. shredded unsweetened coconut
1 ripe banana, sliced very thin
1¾ c. buttermilk, at room temperature
2 eggs, separated, at room temperature
1 tsp. pure vanilla extract
7 tbsp. unsalted butter, melted

Butter, maple syrup, jam, or ice cream, hot fudge, and whipped cream, optional

1] In a large mixing bowl, whisk the dry ingredients and coconut together by hand to combine. Add the sliced banana and stir with a rubber spatula to mix. Set aside. In another mixing bowl, whisk together the buttermilk, egg yolks, vanilla, and melted butter, making sure the yolks break and blend with the other ingredients. Set aside. In a clean, dry, grease-free bowl, whip the egg whites until they are stiff and hold firm peaks.

2] Preheat the oven to 250°. Heat the waffle iron, following the manufacturer's instructions. Add the egg-and-buttermilk mixture to the dry ingredients, stirring with a rubber spatula just until the batter is blended. Using the spatula, fold in the beaten egg whites. Pour some of the batter onto the heated iron and cook, according to manufacturer's directions. (I usually use about ¾ cup of batter for each waffle, pour it across the center of my rectangular iron, and spread it to about 1 inch from the edges before shutting the top. This works for me, but you should experiment with your iron to come up with your own best method.) Place the finished waffle on a heatproof platter and keep warm in the oven while you make the rest of the waffles. Serve as soon as the last waffle comes off the iron.

SERVING. Serve waffles on preheated plates, one to a customer (unless you've got a real hungry bunch). For breakfast, offer butter, maple syrup, and preserves; for dessert, anything goes. These are delicious with ice cream, hot fudge, and clouds of whipped cream.

STORING. Waffles can be frozen for up to 2 weeks and reheated in a toaster or toaster oven, but they're best eaten as soon as they're made.

Breakfast, Brunch, and Lunch Mates

BEST MATCH. Waffles by themselves can be breakfast, or they can be the sopper-upper for a traditional bacon and eggs breakfast. For a healthy start to the day, serve waffles with cottage cheese that's been pureed for a minute in a food processor; top with fruit or Homemade Applesauce (page 59).

⚘| **PLAYING AROUND.** (Tutti-Frutti Waffles) Try substituting thinly sliced or diced peeled apple or pear for the banana or make the Tutti-Frutti Waffles, adding a combination of fruits, such as banana, pineapple, and sliced strawberries.

Puffed Pancake

A puffed pancake has everything going for it: It's made quickly and easily, the ingredients are always at hand, and it's delicious. A pancake can be whipped together in five minutes and served with a splash of maple syrup or a *spoonful of jam. It can also be dressed up with a filling or fruit topping. I've included two fillings and two toppings with this basic recipe. § Makes 2 to 4 Servings*

4 tbsp. (½ stick) unsalted butter
½ c. milk, preferably at room temperature
½ c. all-purpose flour
¼ c. sugar
2 large eggs, preferably at room temperature
Pinch of freshly grated or ground nutmeg

2 tbsp. confectioners' sugar, optional

1] Center a rack in the oven and preheat the oven to 425°. On top of the stove, melt the butter in a 10-inch ovenproof skillet (cast iron or enamel-clad cast iron is ideal), tilting the pan to coat the sides. By hand, whisk together the milk, flour, sugar, eggs, and nutmeg in a medium bowl until smooth. (This can also be done in a blender.) Pour the mixture into the skillet and cook over medium heat for 1 minute. Do not stir. Place the skillet in the oven and bake until the pancake is puffed and golden, 12 to 15 minutes. Sprinkle with confectioners' sugar or serve with one of the toppings (below).

FILLINGS

Caramelized Apple. Toss 2 cups pared diced apples with 1 tablespoon lemon juice. Melt 2 tablespoons butter in a skillet over medium-high heat. Add 2 tablespoons sugar and the apples. Cook, stirring frequently, until the apples are lightly caramelized, about 5 to 7 minutes. Add ¼ cup raisins, 1 tablespoon applejack, and ¼ teaspoon ground cinnamon and cook for a minute. Stir the apples into the batter before it goes into the skillet.

Pineapple-Kirsch. Macerate 1 cup diced pineapple, fresh or canned and drained, in ¼ cup kirsch for 20 minutes. Drain the fruit and add it to the melted butter in the skillet. Pour in the batter. Substitute sifted brown sugar for the confectioners' sugar.

TOPPINGS

Rum-Glazed Banana. Slicing on the bias, cut 2 firm, ripe bananas into 1-inch rounds. Toss them with 2 teaspoons lemon juice. Melt 2 tablespoons butter in a skillet. Add the bananas and sauté over medium heat for 30 seconds. Add 3 tablespoons dark rum and ignite carefully. Spoon the warm topping over the baked pancake. Substitute sifted brown sugar for the confectioners' sugar.

Chilled Cranberry-Orange. Heat 1½ cups fresh or frozen cranberries, ½ cup packed light brown sugar, 3 tablespoons orange juice, 1 teaspoon grated orange zest, and ½ teaspoon cinnamon in a medium saucepan until it reaches a boil. Cook over medium heat, stirring, until the mixtures thickens, about 4 to 5 minutes. Remove from heat and stir in 1½ teaspoons orange liqueur and 1 small peeled orange cut into small wedges. Refrigerate 30 minutes. Serve over the baked pancake.

SERVING. Bring the beautifully puffed and browned pancake to the table in its skillet. It deflates quickly, so have everyone seated and ready before you remove it from the oven.

STORING. You must serve the pancake as soon as it's baked.

BEST MATCH. Try this after a bagels and lox breakfast or salad Niçoise lunch. To make it the center of a festive breakfast, serve the pancake, plain, filled, or topped, with Canadian bacon or a ham steak and a few Mini-Muffins (pages 50–51).

❀| PLAYING AROUND. (Double Puffed Pancake) For 6 to 8 people, double the recipe, melting the butter in a 9″ × 12″ pan (Pyrex is fine) in the preheated oven. When the butter is bubbling, add the batter and return to the oven to bake 15 to 17 minutes.

Apple Butter Bundt Cake

This cake has "home in the country" written all over it. It's the perfect choice for a fall brunch, slightly spicy and very moist, thanks to the addition of apple butter, and bursting with the flavor and smell of fresh apples. The grated fresh apples in the batter dissolve during baking, infusing the cake with their fragrance and juiciness. I use storebought spiced apple butter for this recipe, but you can use the unspiced variety if you prefer a milder flavor.
§ Makes 12 Servings

2 c. all-purpose flour
2 tsp. baking powder
½ tsp. baking soda
½ tsp. ground cinnamon
¼ tsp. freshly grated or ground nutmeg
¼ tsp. ground ginger
½ c. plus 2 tbsp. (1¼ sticks) unsalted butter, at room temperature
1½ c. sugar
2 large eggs, preferably at room temperature
1 c. spiced apple butter
2 medium Granny Smith apples, peeled, cored, and grated
1 c. pecans, chopped
½ c. dark raisins, optional

Confectioners' sugar

1] Center a rack in the oven and preheat the oven to 350°. Butter a 10-inch Bundt pan. Place the flour, baking powder, baking soda, and spices in a mixing bowl and whisk by hand to combine; set aside.

2] In an electric mixer, using a paddle if available, cream the butter and sugar on medium speed until light and fluffy, stopping to scrape the bowl as needed, about 3 minutes. Add the eggs one at a time and beat for 1 minute after each addition. On low speed, add the apple butter and continue beating until the mixture is well combined. Add the grated apples and blend thoroughly. Add the dry ingredients, mixing only until blended. With a rubber spatula, fold in the pecans and raisins. Turn the batter into the Bundt pan and bake for 50 to 55 minutes, or until a toothpick inserted in the center of the cake comes out clean. Place on a rack and cool the cake in the pan for 5 minutes. Unmold onto a rack and cool completely. If you have the time, wrap the cake well and set it aside at room temperature for a day. Its flavor and texture will improve with this ripening.

SERVING. Dust the cake with confectioners' sugar just before serving. Cut into ¼-inch-thick slices and serve 2 slices per portion.

STORING. Wrapped airtight, the cake will keep for 5 days at room temperature or 1 month frozen.

BEST MATCH. Think of this cake when the menu is topped by any type of omelet, particularly one with cheese, a well-seasoned vegetable-filled frittata, or a hearty corned beef hash. A natural drink would be cider, mulled (page 83) or plain.

❀| PLAYING AROUND. (Homemade Applesauce) Serve slices of cake with a bowl of this delicious sauce. Quarter 10 sweet apples (if you include dark red–skinned apples, such as Empires, you'll get a pink-blushed sauce). Place the unpeeled apples, seeds included, in a large, nonreactive saucepan.

Add half a vanilla bean, split and scraped, a 2-inch piece of cinnamon stick (optional), and ¼ cup water. Cook over low heat, stirring occasionally, until the apples fall apart and most of the liquid has evaporated. Remove the vanilla bean and cinnamon stick and pass the sauce through a food mill or coarse strainer. Serve warm or chilled.

Buttermilk Pie

Buttermilk pies have a ring of the old-fashioned about them. This one retains a certain charm from yesteryear while being a not-too-sweet finish for that modern meal, brunch. In the oven, the filling forms a thin, spongy top layer; beneath, you'll find a slide-through-your-teeth, slightly tart custard (it's the buttermilk that gives it a bite). Don't be discouraged if you live in an area where blackberries are available for just a few weeks during the summer. This recipe is a success with the frozen unsweetened berries, including blueberries and raspberries, that are in supermarkets year-round.

§ Makes 6 to 8 Servings

THE CRUST

1½ c. all-purpose flour

1 tbsp. sugar

⅛ tsp. salt

½ c. (1 stick) unsalted butter, very cold or frozen, cut into 8 pieces

3 to 4 tbsp. ice water

1 egg white, lightly beaten with a fork

THE FILLING

3 large eggs, preferably at room temperature

¾ c. sugar

¼ c. all-purpose flour

2 c. buttermilk, preferably at room temperature

5 tbsp. unsalted butter, melted and cooled

2 tbsp. Grand Marnier or other orange liqueur

1 tsp. pure vanilla extract

Pinch of salt

Confectioners' sugar

1] THE CRUST. Place the flour, sugar, and salt in a food processor. Pulse twice to mix. Add the butter all at once. Pulse until the mixture is grainy, about 10 to 15 times. Stop the machine, add 1 tablespoon of the ice water, pulse, then repeat twice more with 2 more tablespoons of the water. Continue to pulse until the dough forms large curds and holds together when pressed. (If necessary, add up to 1 more tablespoon of ice water to achieve the right consistency.) Remove the dough and pat it into a disk ¾ inch thick. Wrap it in plastic and chill at least 20 minutes or up to 1 day. (Just wipe out the processor bowl and set it aside if you are going to make the rest of the pie soon.) Roll the dough out on a floured surface to a thickness of ⅛ inch and fit it into a 9-inch pie pan. Crimp the edges and prick the bottom of the crust all over with the tines of a fork. Freeze the crust, uncovered, for 30 minutes. *(The crust can be prepared ahead to this point, wrapped airtight, and frozen for up to 1 month.)* Place a rack one-third up from the bottom of the oven and preheat the oven to 400°.

2] Remove the crust from the freezer and cover with aluminum foil, pressing it against the bottom and sides of the pan to get a close fit. Add pie weights or dried beans. Bake for 20 minutes. Remove the foil and weights and continue baking for 5 to 8 more minutes, or until browned all over. As soon as you take the crust from the oven, brush the bottom and sides with the beaten egg white to seal it and prevent it from becoming soggy. Cool on a rack.

3] THE FILLING. *Increase the oven temperature to 425°.* Place the eggs, sugar, and flour in the food processor and process until creamy. Add all the other ingredients except the confectioners' sugar and process just to blend. Place the pie pan on a baking sheet and pour in the filling. Cover the edges of the crust with a shield. (To make a shield, cut a 7-inch circle out of the

THE SAUCE

½ pt. (about 1¼ c.) blackberries, fresh or frozen (unsweetened), or blueberries or raspberries

2 tbsp. sugar, or more to taste

2 tsp. Grand Marnier

Confectioners' sugar

center of a 12-inch square of aluminum foil. Place the shield on the pie shiny side up.) Bake for 10 minutes, *lower the oven temperature to 325°*, and bake 40 more minutes. Sprinkle the top of the pie with confectioners' sugar and continue baking 10 more minutes, or until the top is lightly browned and crusted and the filling puffs up in the middle. (Don't be concerned if the center of the filling cracks when it puffs or if the filling shrinks down when it cools. The pie will still look and taste terrific.) Remove the pie to a rack to cool.

4] THE SAUCE. Puree the berries, sugar, and Grand Marnier in a blender or food processor. Taste and add more sugar if you want a sweeter sauce. (Blackberries have little seeds that don't puree during processing. If you find them unpleasant, press the sauce through a sieve.)

SERVING. Serve at room temperature (when the filling is most like custard) or chilled (when the filling is firmer and the flavors slightly more pronounced). Give the pie a fresh dusting of confectioners' sugar. Serve each slice with a drizzle of sauce and pass the remaining sauce in a small pitcher.

STORING. The cooled pie can be wrapped airtight and refrigerated for 1 to 2 days, but it should not be frozen. The sauce can be kept in a tightly closed jar in the refrigerator for up to 5 days.

BEST MATCH. This soothing pie is great after spicy huevos rancheros, salty kippers, or hot chili. Serve with an aromatic tea, such as Darjeeling.

✿| PLAYING AROUND. (Buttermilk Amaretto Pie) For a mellower flavor, one better suited to coffee than tea, omit the Grand Marnier from the filling and replace with ½ teaspoon almond extract and 2 tablespoons Amaretto or Frangelico. Make the sauce without liqueur.

SNACKABLES

PB & O Snackers
(PB & C Shake)

Mocha-Almond Bars
(Mocha-Almond Ice Cream Bars)

Nutty Granola Cookies
(After-School Lassies)

Peanut Patty Cakes
(Chocolate-Tipped Peanut Patty Cakes)

Pecan Flats
(European-Style Hot Chocolate)

Olivia's Oatmeal Fruit Bars
(Dead-of-Winter Dried Fruit Compote)

Mace-Lemon Softies
(Coriander-Orange Softies)

Jelly Bellies for Kids
(Melted Chip Bellies)

Jelly Bellies for Grown-ups
(Truly Grown-up Jelly Bellies)

Cinnamon Fudge Brownies
(Kitchen Sink Fudge Brownies)

Cocoa Snaps
(New York Egg Cream)

Applesauce Spice Bars
(Mulled Cider)

Chocolate Cream Dream Pie
(Chocolate Cream Dream Pielets)

Snackables is a collection of cookies, chewy and crackly, bar cakes, brownies, and a soft, chocolate puddingish pie with a crumbly coconut and graham cracker crust — all impossible to resist. Grown-ups say these remind them of their favorite after-school treats and munch away with childish delight; kids just say "yum" and reach for seconds.

That kids can make most of these sweets on their own or with a little help from adults increases their appeal. The proof of Snackables' simplicity rests with the experiences of a friend of mine: Her entire pastry repertoire consisted of Rice Krispie–Marshmallow Bars, but she learned to bake — and taught her two daughters, aged seven and ten, how to as well — by baking through this chapter when Sweet Times was just a stack of typed sheets.

Snackables are terrific for picnics, birthday parties, school fairs, bake sales, and rewards for anyone who has to stay up late finishing homework or papers from the office. Best of all, most Snackables are freezable, so the cravings of a cookie monster or brownie fiend can be fixed in a flash.

PB & O Snackers

These bumpy, crispy, cracked-top cookies are dangerously addictive. They're delicious dunked in milk or coffee, used as a scoop for ice cream, or just grabbed by the handful from the cookie jar. Your favorite peanut butter should be fine for these Snackers, but believing there's no such thing as a cookie with too much crunch, I use a super crunchy brand and opt for chocolate chips as the add-in. § Makes About 5 Dozen Cookies

3 c. old-fashioned rolled oats, *not* quick-cooking

1 c. all-purpose flour

2 tsp. ground cinnamon

¼ tsp. freshly grated or ground nutmeg

¼ tsp. salt (if peanut butter is unsalted)

1 tsp. baking soda

1 c. (2 sticks) unsalted butter, at room temperature

1 c. peanut butter, chunky or smooth

1 c. packed light brown sugar

1 c. granulated sugar

2 large eggs, preferably at room temperature

1 tsp. pure vanilla extract

1½ c. semisweet chocolate chips or raisins

1] Position 2 racks to divide the oven in thirds and preheat the oven to 350°. Lightly butter 2 large baking sheets or set aside 2 nonstick sheets. In a large bowl, stir together the oats, flour, spices, salt, and baking soda just to combine.

2] Using an electric mixer, with a paddle if available, cream the butter, peanut butter, and brown and granulated sugars on medium speed until light and fluffy, about 3 to 4 minutes, stopping to scrape the bowl as needed. Add the eggs, one at a time, and beat for 1 minute after each addition. Beat in the vanilla. Reduce the mixer speed to low and add the dry ingredients slowly, beating only until blended. Stir in the chips or raisins. *(At this point, the dough can be wrapped and chilled for 1 hour for easy scooping or stored for up to 1 day.)*

3] If the dough is unchilled, drop by rounded tablespoonfuls onto the baking sheets. If the dough is chilled, scoop by rounded tablespoons, roll into balls between your palms, and place 2 inches apart on the baking sheets. Press the cookies gently with the heel of your hand until they are ½ inch thick. Bake for 13 to 15 minutes, until the cookies are golden and just firm around the edges. Lift the cookies onto a cooling rack with a wide metal spatula. The cookies will firm as they cool. Repeat until all the dough has been used.

SERVING. Bring Snackers to the table in a cookie jar or mounded in a basket.

STORING. The cookies will keep in a cookie jar or airtight plastic bag at room temperature for 3 days or frozen (wrapped airtight) for 1 month.

BEST MATCH. Chocolate ice cream is a favorite with these, but coffee and vanilla-fudge are super, too. Serve with coffee for the grown-ups, cold milk or frothy shakes for the kids.

✿| PLAYING AROUND. (PB & C Shake) Delight everyone and serve PB & O Snackers with a PB & C (for Chocolate) Shake. For each shake, put 1¼ cups milk, ¼ cup smooth peanut butter, and 1 large scoop chocolate ice cream in a malted machine, blender, or food processor. (You can also make this with a small hand-held beater.) Process until blended and foamy. If you want, add an extra scoop of ice cream to each shake, call it a float, and serve with long-handled fountain spoons. Don't forget the straws.

Mocha-Almond Bars

I'm reminded of Heath Bars, the chocolate-coated toffee candies sophisticates secretly crave, every time I have one of these cookies. These are put together quickly in a mixer, but take a little cajoling to spread in the pan. If you use a rubber spatula to start the job and your fingertips to finish, you'll have a thin layer in a flash.
§ Makes About 54 Bars

THE BASE

1½ tbsp. instant espresso powder
1 tbsp. boiling water
1½ c. all-purpose flour
¼ tsp. salt
½ tsp. ground cinnamon
1 c. (2 sticks) unsalted butter, at room temperature
⅓ c. packed light brown sugar
⅓ c. granulated sugar
1 tsp. pure vanilla extract
½ c. mini chocolate chips

THE FROSTING

1 c. chocolate chips, any size
¾ c. blanched almonds, toasted and coarsely chopped

1] THE BASE. Center a rack in the oven and preheat the oven to 375°. Lightly butter a 9″ × 13″ pan, or set aside a nonstick pan. Dissolve the espresso powder in the boiling water and set aside. Stir together the flour, salt, and cinnamon and reserve.

2] In the bowl of an electric mixer, fitted with a paddle if you have one, beat the butter at medium speed until it is smooth, about 2 minutes. Gradually add the brown and white sugars and beat 3 minutes more, stopping to scrape the bowl as needed, to produce a creamy mixture. Beat in the espresso and vanilla. Reduce the mixer speed to low and steadily add the dry ingredients, continuing to beat only until they are incorporated. You will have a heavy, sticky batter. Stir in the mini chips with a sturdy rubber spatula.

3] Spread the batter in the pan using the spatula and your fingertips to get a thin, even layer. Bake this base for 18 to 20 minutes, or until it is puckered and well browned.

4] THE FROSTING. Remove the pan from the oven and turn the oven off. Scatter the chocolate chips evenly over the base and return the pan to the oven for 2 to 3 minutes, until the chips are soft and spreadable. Take the pan out of the oven and immediately spread the chocolate smooth with an offset spatula or the back of a spoon. Sprinkle the chopped nuts over the chocolate and place the pan on a rack to cool.

SERVING. When the pastry reaches room temperature, refrigerate it briefly in the pan to set the frosting. Remove from the refrigerator and, using a sharp, thin-bladed knife and working in the pan, cut into 54 approximately 2″ × 1″ bars, trimming the edges if they seem too crusty. Because this frosting sets so firmly, you can overlap the bars for serving without smudging them.

STORING. Well wrapped, the bars can be stored at room temperature for 3 days or frozen for 1 month.

BEST MATCH. These are just right with espresso, cinnamon-dusted cappuccino, hot chocolate, or cold milk; tea would be a mismatch.

❀| **PLAYING AROUND.** (Mocha-Almond Ice Cream Bars) Terrific for a child's birthday party or anytime you want something simple but special. Cut the frosted pastry into 3- or 4-inch squares. Working on the frosted side, spread one-half of the bars with softened chocolate, coffee, or cinnamon (page 143) ice cream. Top with the other half of the bars, frosted-side up. Place in the freezer to re-firm the ice cream. For longer storage, wrap each bar in aluminum foil or a double thickness of plastic wrap. Let each bar soften for 5 minutes at room temperature before digging in.

Nutty Granola Cookies

These would have a shot at becoming the quintessential after-school cookie if someone could find a way to keep them around until 3:00 —they are that snackable. If you have a choice, don't buy a granola with raisins, dates, or other dried fruits. The fruits tend to become hard and dry in the box. They won't get softer and moister during baking and may end up spoiling your cookies. § Makes About 3½ Dozen Cookies

3 c. granola, preferably without dried fruit
¾ c. raisins, light or dark
½ c. unsalted roasted peanuts
½ c. blanched slivered almonds, toasted
⅓ c. wheat germ
½ c. dry unsweetened shredded coconut
14 tbsp. (1¾ sticks) unsalted butter, at room temperature
¾ c. packed light brown sugar
1 large egg, preferably at room temperature
¼ tsp. salt
1 c. all-purpose flour

1] Position 2 racks to divide the oven in thirds and preheat the oven to 375°. Lightly butter 2 large baking sheets or set aside 2 nonstick sheets. Pour the granola into a large mixing bowl and break up any clumps with your fingers. Add the raisins, peanuts, almonds, wheat germ, and coconut and mix everything together with a large spoon or your hands; set aside.

2] In an electric mixer, fitted with a paddle if available, beat the butter at medium speed for about 2 minutes. Add the sugar and continue to beat until creamy, 3 to 4 minutes, stopping to scrape the bowl. Add the egg and salt and mix until well blended. With the mixer on its lowest speed, add the flour in 2 additions. Still mixing on low speed, steadily add the granola mixture. Remove the bowl from the mixer and use a sturdy rubber spatula to blend in any dry ingredients that might be left at the bottom of the bowl.

3] Scoop out rounded tablespoonfuls of dough and mold by gently rolling or packing the scoops between your palms. Place the cookies 1½ inches apart on the prepared sheets and flatten them slightly with your fingertips. Bake 10 to 12 minutes, until the cookies are golden brown but not quite firm. Let cookies rest for a minute before lifting them with a wide metal spatula to a rack to cool. Repeat until all the dough has been used.

SERVING. Offer these straight from the cookie jar.

STORING. These will keep in a cookie jar at room temperature for 3 days or wrapped airtight in the freezer for 1 month.

BEST MATCH. Granola Cookies are made for milk but are awfully good dunked in tea.

❂| PLAYING AROUND. (After-School Lassie) Welcome home a pack of kids with a stack of these cookies and a Lassie. For each drink, put ¼ cup milk, ¾ cup plain yogurt (low or nonfat is fine), 2 teaspoons honey (more or less, to taste), 1 small, very ripe banana, and 1 ice cube in a blender. Blend on high speed for 2 minutes, or until thick and foamy. Serve in large glasses.

Peanut Patty Cakes

A nutty brown sugar shortbread-type cookie that will please grown-ups and kids alike, these are made very quickly and easily in the food processor. They're a real no-fuss treat to serve with milk, tea, coffee, or an ice cream sundae.
§ *Makes 16 Cookies*

½ c. all-purpose flour
¾ c. unsalted dry roasted
    peanuts
½ c. all-purpose flour
¼ tsp. salt
¼ tsp. ground cinnamon
½ c. packed light brown sugar
½ c. (1 stick) unsalted butter
1 tbsp. granulated sugar
¼ tsp. ground cinnamon

1] Place a rack in the center of the oven and preheat the oven to 300°. Put ½ cup flour and the peanuts in a processor. Pulse on and off for 1 minute to chop the nuts. Add all the remaining ingredients except the last 2 to the work bowl and process until the mixture forms large, moist clumps and cleans the sides of the bowl. Turn the dough out onto a work surface and knead it gently into a ball. Cut the ball in half.

2] Place both pieces of dough on an unbuttered cookie sheet. Pat each piece into a disk 6 inches in diameter and ¼ inch thick. Crimp the edges of the cakes with a fork, then use the tines to prick the dough deeply all over. Use a long sharp knife to divide each cake into 8 even wedges, cutting into, but not all the way through, the dough. Mix together the granulated sugar and ¼ teaspoon cinnamon and sprinkle it evenly over the cakes.

3] Bake the cakes for 25 to 30 minutes, until golden and still slightly soft to the touch. Take the cookie sheet from the oven and, while the cakes are piping hot, cut through the marks to form 16 wedge-shaped cookies. Carefully transfer the wedges to a rack to cool to room temperature.

SERVING. Just arrange these, pointed ends down, in a small, napkin-lined basket or in circles on a serving platter.

STORING. The cookies will keep in an airtight container for 5 days at room temperature or 1 month in the freezer.

BEST MATCH. If you want to go all out at snack time, serve these as part of a Snackable assortment including Cocoa Snaps (page 80), Mace-Lemon Softies (page 76), and Olivia's Oatmeal Fruit Bars (page 74).

❀| PLAYING AROUND. (Chocolate-Tipped Peanut Patty Cakes) The combination of chocolate and peanuts is the stuff of wake-up-in-the-middle-of-the-night cravings. When the cookies have cooled to room temperature, melt 1 cup of chocolate chips in a double boiler or microwave. Dip the pointed ends of the cookies into the chocolate so the chocolate comes up about an inch or so. Lift the cookie, scraping the bottom against the side of the pan, and allow the excess chocolate to drip back into the pan. Place the cookies on waxed paper–lined baking sheets and chill briefly to set.

Pecan Flats

Thin, semisoft Pecan Flats are more sophisticated than chunky cookie jar cookies but no less fun to munch. You'll find yourself wanting their butterscotch flavor when you reach for tea or hot chocolate. The batter is quick and easy to make in a food processor and the clean-up is minimal—always a blessing. In fact, it's only about 45 minutes from the time you put the first ingredient into the processor until the moment you take the last cookie out of the oven, so this is a recipe to grab when you need a hurry-up sweet. § Makes 6 Dozen Cookies

1¾ c. all-purpose flour
1 c. pecans
½ tsp. baking soda
¼ tsp. salt
1 c. (2 sticks) unsalted butter, at
    room temperature
1 c. packed light brown sugar
1 tsp. pure vanilla extract
2 large eggs, preferably at room
    temperature
1 tbsp. light corn syrup
2 tbsp. brewed coffee (you can
    make this with instant, if
    necessary)

1] Position 2 racks to divide the oven in thirds and preheat the oven to 350°. Butter 2 large baking sheets or have 2 nonstick pans ready; set aside. Place the flour, pecans, baking soda, and salt in a food processor. Pulse 3 times to mix the ingredients; then process for 15 seconds, or until the nuts are chopped finely, like meal. Turn the mixture out onto a large piece of waxed paper and reserve. Wipe out the processor bowl.

2] Put the butter and sugar in the processor bowl. Process until the ingredients are creamy, stopping to scrape down the sides of the bowl once or twice. Add the vanilla, eggs, corn syrup, and coffee and pulse just to mix. Process for about 15 seconds, scrape the bowl, and process 15 seconds more. When you scrape down the sides of the bowl the mixture may look curdled, but it will become smooth as you continue to process. Pour the dry ingredients over the batter and pulse 4 or 5 times. Scrape the bowl, then pulse 4 or 5 times more, until the flour is incorporated.

3] Drop the batter by teaspoonfuls onto the prepared baking sheets. Leave 2 inches between each cookie because these spread while they bake. Thanks to their spreadability, if you drop even amounts of batter you'll end up with saucer-round wafers that are all the same size. Bake the cookies for 8 to 10 minutes, until they spread and turn a deep, golden, butterscotch brown. Let them rest on the baking sheets for a minute or two before removing them with a wide metal spatula to a rack. (Slide the spatula under one end of the cookie and give a little jerk to lift it off the sheet.) Repeat until all the batter has been used. Cool the cookies to room temperature on racks.

SERVING. These are daintier and more fragile than other Snackables and are best served on a platter arranged in slightly overlapping concentric circles.

STORING. Put the Pecan Flats in an airtight container with waxed paper between the layers. They'll keep for 3 to 5 days at room temperature or up to 1 month in the freezer.

BEST MATCH. These are delicious with hot or cold tea, spiced cider, hot chocolate, or warm milk.

❁| PLAYING AROUND. (European-Style Hot Chocolate) After an ice-skating party or a round of touch football, serve Pecan Flats with a cup of this rich mix. For each serving, steam or scald 1 cup milk and, in a separate pan or a microwave, melt 1 ounce best-quality bittersweet chocolate. Serve the milk and chocolate in individual pitchers accompanied by a small bowl of superfine sugar and, for a real splurge, a bowl of softly whipped crème fraîche or heavy cream. To blend, pour the chocolate into a cup or mug and add a very small amount of hot milk, stirring to make a smooth paste. Gradually add the rest of the milk, stirring to combine. Add sugar to taste and top with cream.

Olivia's Oatmeal Fruit Bars

When my friend Olivia Brush asked if I wanted a recipe of hers for this book, I said yes without even knowing which it would be. Olivia is a great cook and a wonderful baker, someone who has a real feel for food. These are typical of Olivia's style of sweet—soft, inviting, and irresistible. (Her husband Dan used to eat these for breakfast.) They keep very well and make good pack-alongs for picnics or lunch boxes.
§ Makes About 4 Dozen Bars

1½ c. all-purpose flour
¼ tsp. salt
½ tsp. baking powder
½ tsp. ground cinnamon
⅛ tsp. ground allspice
1 c. packed moist pitted prunes, finely diced
1 c. packed moist dried apricots, finely diced
1 c. golden raisins
½ c. (1 stick) unsalted butter, at room temperature
1 c. packed dark brown sugar
1 tsp. pure vanilla extract
1 large egg, preferably at room temperature
1 c. plus 2 tbsp. old-fashioned rolled oats, *not* quick cooking

1] Place a rack in the center of the oven and preheat the oven to 350°. Generously butter a 9″ × 13″ baking pan. In a large bowl, whisk the flour, salt, baking powder, and spices together to combine; set aside. Toss the prunes and apricots with the raisins and a tablespoon of the flour mixture; reserve.

2] In an electric mixer, with a paddle if available, cream the butter and sugar, stopping to scrape the bowl as needed, until light and fluffy, 3 to 4 minutes. Add the vanilla and egg and continue to beat 2 minutes more, until the mixture is light. (It may look curdled, but it will smooth out.) With the mixer on the lowest speed, add the dry ingredients, then the oats, and finally the diced fruit. Mix only until each addition is incorporated and use a rubber spatula to help blend the mixture, which will look like a moist dough.

3] Use your hands to pat the dough evenly into the buttered pan, pressing down firmly to smooth the dough. Bake about 30 minutes, until the top is lightly browned, dryish, and feels soft to the touch; the bars will firm slightly as they cool. Place the pan on a rack to cool to room temperature.

SERVING. Cut the pastry, in the pan, into 48 approximately 1½-inch squares. Transfer to a platter or pile in a basket. For picnics and brown bag lunches, wrap each bar individually in plastic.

STORING. Wrapped airtight, these will keep for 3 to 5 days at room temperature or 1 month frozen.

BEST MATCH. These are great with a glass of cold milk or cider and slices of crisp, red apple.

❖| PLAYING AROUND. (Dead-of-Winter Dried Fruit Compote) For a filling, satisfying snack to serve when chill winds blow, offer Olivia's Fruit Bars and this Dead-of-Winter Dried Fruit Compote: In a medium, nonreactive saucepan, place 1 pound assorted dried fruit (such as pears, apricots, prunes, sour cherries, raisins, etc.), a 4-inch strip of orange zest, a

3-inch piece of cinnamon stick, a 3-inch piece of vanilla bean, 1 cup water, 1 cup apple cider, and the juice of ½ lemon in a medium, nonreactive saucepan. Bring to the boil, reduce heat to low, and simmer covered until the fruit is tender but not mushy, about 20 minutes. Remove from heat and stir in 2 tablespoons port (optional). Spoon the fruit and liquid into a bowl or storage container and cover well. Serve while still warm or cool to room temperature and chill.

Mace-Lemon Softies

Here's a simple, just-like-grandma-used-to-make butter cookie to bake by the batchful anytime you want something special in a hurry. I pipe these out into small rounds using a pastry bag and plain tip. It's speedy and I like the puffed shape I get by piping, but they're just as good when the dough is dropped from a spoon. In both cases you get a meltingly rich, pale golden cookie with a very thin crust, a soft center, and the faint taste of mace and lemon. A dunkable snackable for nibblers of all ages.
§ Makes About 3½ Dozen Cookies

2 c. all-purpose flour
½ tsp. baking powder
¼ tsp. ground mace
Pinch of salt
½ c. (1 stick) unsalted butter, at room temperature
Grated zest of one lemon
¾ c. sugar
2 large eggs
1 tsp. pure vanilla extract

1] Center a rack in the oven and preheat the oven to 400°. Lightly butter a cookie sheet and set aside. In a mixing bowl, whisk together the flour, baking powder, mace, and salt; reserve.

2] In an electric mixer, with a paddle if available, cream the butter, lemon zest, and sugar until light and fluffy, about 3 minutes, stopping to scrape the bowl as needed. Add the eggs, one at a time, and beat for a minute after each addition. Beat in the vanilla and turn the mixer to its lowest setting. Add the dry ingredients and mix just until combined.

3] Fit a large pastry bag with a plain ½-inch tip (mine's an Ateco #7) and fill the bag with the cookie dough. Pipe out 1½-inch-diameter mounds of dough onto the cookie sheet, leaving 1 to 2 inches between cookies. (It's best to pipe out each mound of dough in a continuous squeeze, keeping the bag about ½ inch above the sheet and lifting the bag as you stop squeezing. Poke down the point in the center of each cookie with your finger. If you prefer, drop the dough by rounded teaspoonfuls onto the sheets. Bake one sheet of cookies at a time for 10 to 12 minutes, until they start to color around the edges; they should remain pale. Use a wide metal spatula to lift them from the sheet to a rack. Cool to room temperature. Repeat with remaining dough.

SERVING. Serve 2 to 3 to a snacker, placing them alongside everyone's drink or arranging them on a platter.

STORING. Wrapped airtight, these will keep for 4 days at room temperature or for 1 month frozen.

BEST MATCH. Espresso is my first choice for these, but lemon tea is soothing and milk's fine if you're sharing them with kids.

❀ | PLAYING AROUND. (Coriander Orange Softies) A simple change in flavoring can turn these into a whole new cookie with a Mediterranean accent. Substitute ground coriander for the mace and the grated zest of a small orange for the lemon.

Jelly Bellies for Kids

These look like kids' cookies and taste like the stuff we all love. They're peanut butter cookies, molded into little balls, rolled around in roasted nuts, poked in the middle, baked, and filled to the brim with jelly or jam. The recipe is as much fun to make as it is to eat.
§ Makes About 5 Dozen Cookies

¾ c. (1½ sticks) **unsalted butter, at room temperature**

½ c. **peanut butter, crunchy or smooth**

½ c. **packed light brown sugar**

¼ c. **granulated sugar**

1 tsp. **pure vanilla extract**

1 **egg, separated**

1⅔ c. **all-purpose flour**

1 **egg white**

1½ c. **unsalted roasted peanuts, finely chopped**

¾ c. (approximately) **jam or jelly (black raspberry is good with these)**

1] Center a rack in the oven and preheat the oven to 375°. Lightly butter 2 baking sheets and set them aside.

2] In an electric mixer, with a paddle if available, beat the butter, peanut butter, and sugars together at medium speed until very light and fluffy, about 3 to 4 minutes, stopping to scrape the bowl as needed. Add the vanilla and egg yolk and beat well. At lowest speed, add the flour and mix only until blended.

3] Place the egg whites in a small bowl and beat with a fork just until slightly frothy. Place the chopped nuts in another bowl. Working with a teaspoonful of dough at a time, roll the dough gently between your palms to form small balls. Turn the balls in the egg whites to coat completely, then roll them in the nuts. Place the cookies 2 inches apart on the baking sheets. Steadying the cookies between the thumb and index finger of one hand, use your pinky or the end of a wooden spoon to poke a small hole in the center of each. Take care not to go all the way down to the baking sheet. Bake the cookies 15 to 18 minutes, until lightly golden. Use a wide metal spatula to transfer the cookies to a rack. Repeat with remaining dough.

4] Place the jam in a small saucepan and bring to a boil, stirring, over low heat; or you can do this in a microwave. Using a small spoon, fill each cookie with jam. Allow the cookies to cool to room temperature. The jam will form a shiny, nonsticky finish.

SERVING. Stack these in circles on a plate to form a pyramid of shiny-centered cookies or pile them into a cookie jar and let the kids dig in.

STORING. These will keep for 4 days at room temperature in an airtight container or for 1 month in the freezer.

BEST MATCH. Have cold milk on hand for kids, and coffee or tea for grown-ups who raid the kids' cookie stash.

❀| PLAYING AROUND. (Melted Chip Bellies) Omit the jam and fill the center of each cookie with chocolate, peanut butter, or chocolate and peanut butter chips before baking. Each cookie will take only a chip or two, but you'll get the taste.

Jelly Bellies for Grown-ups

An adult version of a childhood favorite, Thumbprints, these are rich, buttery, melt-in-your-mouth, agreeably sweet nut cookies with a *belly full of glistening apricot jam. They're pretty and playful at the same time.*
§ Makes About 5 Dozen Cookies

2 c. walnuts
1¾ c. all-purpose flour
1 c. (2 sticks) unsalted butter, at
room temperature
½ c. sugar
1 tsp. pure vanilla extract
½ tsp. almond extract
About 1 c. apricot jam

Confectioners' sugar

1] Position 2 racks to divide the oven in thirds and preheat the oven to 350°. Set 2 baking sheets aside. Place the nuts and about ½ cup of the flour in a food processor. Pulse on and off until the nuts are pulverized. Add the remaining flour and pulse several times to blend; reserve.

2] In the bowl of an electric mixer, fitted with a paddle if you have one, cream the butter and sugar until light and fluffy, about 3 to 4 minutes, stopping to scrape the bowl as needed. Add the extracts and beat to blend. Turn the machine to its lowest speed and gradually add the nut mixture, blending just until incorporated.

3] Working with a teaspoonful of dough at a time, mold the dough into small balls. Place the balls 2 inches apart on the unbuttered baking sheets. Steadying the cookies between the thumb and index finger of one hand, use the handle of a wooden spoon or the tip of your pinky to make an indentation in the center of each cookie. Bake for 15 to 18 minutes, until barely colored. (The cookies will be soft and fragile and look underdone, but they're fine. Don't overbake them.) While the cookies are baking, bring the apricot jam to the boil in a small saucepan over direct heat, or do this in a microwave. Remove the baking sheets from the oven and let the cookies cool on the sheets for 2 minutes before carefully transferring them to racks. Sift confectioners' sugar over the hot cookies and fill the indentation in each cookie with enough hot jam to come level with the top. Cool the cookies to room temperature. Repeat with remaining dough.

SERVING. Make a fuss over this pretty Snackable by placing the cookies on an old-fashioned, doily-lined cake plate.

STORING. These cookies will keep in an airtight container at room temperature for 3 days or in the freezer for up to 1 month.

BEST MATCH. Have coffee, cappuccino, or Earl Grey tea.

❂| PLAYING AROUND. (Truly Grown-up Jelly Bellies) Replace the walnuts with toasted, skinned hazelnuts (a very sophisticated nut prized in Europe and never thought of as anything younger than grown-up); substitute raspberry jam or orange marmalade for the apricot jam.

Cinnamon Fudge Brownies

Soft, dense, deeply chocolaty, and first-quality lick-the-bowl material, these brownies fall definitively on the fudgy side of the cakelike-fudgelike brownie divide. They are mixed in a saucepan in under 15 minutes and are great plain or with ice cream. You can even eat them straight from the freezer—a lifesaver for those with serious chocolate cravings.

§ Makes 16 Brownies

½ c. all-purpose flour
Pinch of salt
1½ tsp. ground cinnamon
⅓ c. (5⅓ tbsp.) **unsalted butter**
2 tbsp. brewed coffee (you can make this with instant)
½ c. plus 2 tbsp. **sugar**
6 oz. high-quality bittersweet chocolate, such as Lindt or Tobler, coarsely chopped
1 tsp. pure vanilla extract
2 large eggs
½ c. **walnut pieces**

Sweetened whipped cream or ice cream, optional

1] Center a rack in the oven and preheat the oven to 325°. Butter an 8-inch square baking pan, flour the bottom, and tap out the excess; set aside. In a small bowl, whisk together the flour, salt, and cinnamon; reserve.

2] In a medium saucepan over direct heat, or in a bowl in a microwave, bring the butter, coffee, and sugar just to the boil, stirring occasionally. Remove from heat, add the chopped chocolate, and stir with a small whisk until smooth. Stir in the vanilla and allow the mixture to cool for a minute or two.

3] Still working in the saucepan with the small whisk, beat in the eggs, one at time, until you have a thick, glossy batter. Switch to a rubber spatula and gradually stir in the reserved dry ingredients, stirring only until the flour is incorporated. Fold in the nuts and scrape the batter into the prepared pan.

4] Bake for 33 to 35 minutes, until the top is dry and crackly. Place the pan on a rack to cool for 10 minutes. Unmold the brownies onto the rack, then invert onto another rack to finish cooling to room temperature right-side up.

SERVING. Cut the brownies into sixteen 2-inch squares and serve from a platter or basket. For a sit-down, spoon-and-fork snack, top each square with sweetened whipped cream or a scoop of ice cream. A drizzle of Old-Time Creamery Hot Fudge (page 143) can only make it better.

STORING. These brownies will keep for 3 days at room temperature wrapped in plastic or up to 1 month in the freezer.

BEST MATCH. Purists will want only milk with these, but I think they're best with espresso. They overpower tea.

❀| **PLAYING AROUND.** (Kitchen Sink Fudge Brownies) Reduce the sugar to ⅓ cup and mix in 1½ cups of assorted sweet crunchies, such as semisweet, white milk chocolate, and peanut butter chips. (Keep the ½ cup of walnuts, you'll need them for balance.)

Cocoa Snaps

I think of these dark, crispy, very chocolaty cookies as "now and later" treats. They can be baked as soon as they're mixed—now—or shaped into rolls and packed in the freezer waiting to be sliced and baked—later.
§ Makes 3 Dozen Cookies

½ c. cocoa, preferably a Dutch-processed brand, such as Droste or Poulain

1¼ c. all-purpose flour

¾ tsp. ground allspice

Pinch of salt

½ c. sugar

1 large egg

½ tsp. pure vanilla extract

½ c. (1 stick) unsalted butter, at room temperature, cut into 4 pieces

½ c. mini chocolate chips

1] Place the cocoa, flour, allspice, and salt in a food processor and pulse several times to mix. Turn the ingredients out onto a sheet of waxed paper and reserve.

2] Put the sugar, egg, and vanilla in the work bowl and process for 30 seconds. Scrape down the bowl. Add the butter all at once and process the mixture for 1 minute, stopping to scrape down the bowl after 30 seconds. Pour the reserved dry ingredients over the mixture and pulse 10 to 15 times, until the flour is incorporated and the dough starts to leave the sides of the bowl. Add the mini chips and pulse 2 or 3 times, just to incorporate. Turn the dough out onto a large sheet of waxed paper and form it into a log about 9 inches long and 1½ inches in diameter.

3] **If You Want to Make the Cookies Now.** Position 2 racks to divide the oven into thirds and preheat the oven to 350°. Cut the log into 18 slices, then cut each slice in half. Roll the pieces of dough between your palms to make balls the size of small walnuts. Place the balls about 2 inches apart on unbuttered baking sheets. Put a piece of waxed paper over the cookies and, with the bottom of a small glass, press each cookie until it is approximately ¼ inch thick. Remove the waxed paper. Bake for 10 to 12 minutes, or until the tops are firm. Transfer the cookies to a rack and cool.

4] **If You Want to Make the Cookies Later.** Wrap the log of dough in a double thickness of plastic wrap and freeze until needed. *(The dough will keep in the freezer for up to 1 month.)* Use a serrated knife to carefully cut as many ¼-inch-thick cookies at a time as you need. Bake in a preheated 350° oven on unbuttered baking sheets for 12 to 14 minutes, or until the tops are firm. Transfer the cookies to a rack and cool.

SERVING. Offer these in a cookie jar or tin with a mouth wide enough to make plucking a handful easy.

STORING. These can be kept in a tin or wrapped airtight for 4 days at room temperature or 1 month (wrapped airtight) in the freezer.

BEST MATCH. These are a model milk-and-cookies cookie; however, because of the touch of allspice, they're exceptionally good with black coffee or espresso.

◉| **PLAYING AROUND.** (New York Egg Cream) This is a classic that uses neither eggs nor cream. Put 1½ to 2 tablespoons chocolate syrup in a 12-ounce glass. (Old-time New Yorkers swore the only real egg cream was one made with Fox's U-Bet Syrup, a product almost impossible to find outside New York City, but modern-day mavens agree Hershey's is fine.) Add ¼ cup milk and stir with a spoon to combine. Pour in about 1 cup seltzer, stirring up a froth. Stop just when the bubbles are ready to spill over the side of the glass.

Applesauce Spice Bars

Soft, appley sweet, and packed with pecans, raisins, and bits of baking apple, the batter for these bars is mixed in a saucepan. I created these for an article about apples for Food & Wine *magazine, which photographed them beautifully,* *showing them to advantage in a kitchen setting. But in real life, these show up most often in kids' fists or at the edge of the desk when grown-ups are burning the midnight oil and need a little extra fuel. § Makes 3 Dozen Bars*

THE BARS

1¼ c. all-purpose flour
1 tsp. baking powder
¼ tsp. baking soda
1 tsp. ground cinnamon
¼ tsp. ground allspice
½ c. (1 stick) unsalted butter
1 c. packed light brown sugar
2 large eggs
½ c. unsweetened applesauce
1 tsp. pure vanilla extract
1 tbsp. applejack or brandy
1 baking apple, such as Rome or Cortland, peeled, cored, and finely diced or chopped
½ c. raisins
½ c. chopped pecans

THE GLAZE

2½ tbsp. heavy cream
⅓ c. packed light brown sugar
2½ tbsp. unsalted butter
1 tsp. light corn syrup
½ tsp. pure vanilla extract

Fresh apple slices (rubbed with lemon juice) or dried apple rings, optional

1] THE BARS. Center a rack in the oven and preheat the oven to 350°. Butter a 9″ × 13″ baking pan, line the bottom with parchment or waxed paper, and butter the paper. Dust the pan with flour and tap out the excess. In a bowl, whisk the flour, baking powder, baking soda, cinnamon, and allspice to combine; set aside.

2] In a heavy-bottomed saucepan, melt the butter over low heat. Whisk in the brown sugar and stir until the sugar is melted and the mixture is smooth, about 1 minute. Remove the pan from the heat.

3] Still working in the saucepan, whisk in the eggs, one at a time, until well blended. Blend in the applesauce, vanilla, and applejack. Stir until the mixture is smooth. Switch to a rubber spatula and add the dry ingredients, one half at a time, stirring to incorporate. Mix in the diced apple, raisins, and pecans. Pour the batter into the prepared pan and smooth the top with the spatula.

4] Bake for 23 to 25 minutes, until the cake starts to pull away from the sides of the pan and a toothpick inserted in the center comes out clean. Let the cake cool in the pan for 10 minutes while you make the glaze.

5] THE GLAZE. Combine the cream, sugar, butter, and corn syrup in a small saucepan. Bring to a boil over medium heat and simmer, whisking frequently, for 5 minutes. Remove from heat and stir in the vanilla.

6] Run a knife around the sides of the partially cooled cake and invert it onto a rack. Remove the paper and turn the cake right-side up onto a rack set over a sheet of waxed paper. Pour the hot glaze over the top of the cake, spreading if necessary to get an even coating. Let the cake cool completely.

SERVING. Cut the cake into bars, each approximately 1½″ × 2″. Serve on a large platter decorated, if desired, with slices of fresh, red apple (rubbed with lemon juice so as not to darken) or rings of dried apple.

STORING. Because of their glaze, these bars cannot be frozen. Store them for 3 to 4 days at room temperature in an airtight tin with waxed paper between the layers.

BEST MATCH. Almost anything goes with these cookies: milk, tea (hot or cold), coffee, or cider. The only beverage I'd hesitate to have would be one with chocolate.

❀| PLAYING AROUND. (Mulled Cider) For after-ski, to cap an autumn walk, or just because spirits need a lift. Put 1 quart apple cider, 1 thinly sliced, unpeeled orange, a 3-inch piece of cinnamon stick, a 3-inch piece of lemon zest, and 6 whole cloves into a medium saucepan. Bring to the boil, reduce heat, and simmer gently, uncovered, 10 minutes. Strain and serve immediately or chill and reheat when needed.

Chocolate Cream Dream Pie

Anyone who doesn't love this dessert is missing a sweet tooth or a childhood. The crust is an old-fashioned graham cracker liner with coconut tossed in for crunch, and the topping is fresh, snowy, lightly sweetened whipped cream. And, the filling . . . that's the dream. A not-so-sweet, *soft chocolate cream, just enough of it to form a cushion and more than enough for a mouthful of memories: This is the pie we all hoped would be waiting for us after school. Pure happiness, and it's made in minutes. § Makes 6 to 8 Servings*

THE CHOCOLATE CREAM
1 c. milk
¼ c. sugar
2 egg yolks
1 tbsp. all-purpose flour
2 tsp. cornstarch
2 oz. unsweetened chocolate, chopped
1 tsp. pure vanilla extract

THE CRUST
1⅓ c. graham cracker crumbs (from 11 double crackers)
⅔ c. sweetened shredded or flaked coconut
4 tbsp. (½ stick) unsalted butter, melted

THE TOPPING
¾ c. heavy cream
1 tbsp. confectioners' sugar, pressed through a sieve
½ tsp. pure vanilla extract

1] **THE CHOCOLATE CREAM.** Bring the milk and sugar to a boil in a medium saucepan. Meanwhile, whisk the egg yolks, flour, and cornstarch together by hand until thick, smooth, and pale. Very gradually add the hot milk, whisking constantly. Pour this mixture through a strainer and back into the pan and cook over medium heat, stirring vigorously with a wooden spoon, until the cream thickens and one bubble comes to the top and pops, about 1½ to 2 minutes. Remove from heat and blend in the chocolate and vanilla. Scrape the cream into a clean bowl, lay a sheet of plastic wrap against the top of the cream, and chill for at least 1 hour. *(The cream can be made up to 2 days ahead and kept covered in the refrigerator.)*

2] **THE CRUST.** Center a rack in the oven and preheat the oven to 350°. In a medium bowl or a food processor, mix together the crumbs, coconut, and melted butter until the ingredients are uniformly moistened. Press the mixture evenly into a 9-inch pie plate, bringing the crust up to the top of the plate around the sides. Bake for 5 to 8 minutes, until lightly browned. Cool on a rack. *(The crust can be made in advance, covered, and refrigerated for 2 days or wrapped airtight and frozen for 1 month.)*

3] **THE TOPPING.** Whip the cream until it holds soft peaks. With a rubber spatula, fold in the sugar and vanilla.

4] Fill the crust with the chocolate and top with the whipped cream.

SERVING. Serve this immediately or refrigerate it for up to 3 hours.

STORING. Each part of the pie can be made ahead as indicated above, but once assembled the pie should be eaten within 3 hours.

BEST MATCH. Milk and Chocolate Cream Dream Pie is a marriage made in heaven, but the pie's awfully good with coffee as well.

❀| **PLAYING AROUND.** (Chocolate Cream Dream Pielets) For a different look, press the crust into six 3-inch tartlet pans, then bake and fill as directed.

TEATIME TREATS

Sweets for the Afternoon

Round Pound Cake with Blueberry Jam
(Whipped Cream Trifle)

Chocolate-Dipped Walnut Wafers
(Hazelnut or Fruit-Filled Sandwiches)

Coconut Tea Cake
(New Sweets from Stale Cake)

Burnt Butter Baby Cakes
(Burnt Butter Toddler Cakes)

Made-in-a-Bag Espresso–Chocolate Chip Shortbreads
(Subtle Coconut and Oatmeal-Spice Shortbreads)

Cream Scones
(Savory Cheddar Cheese Scones)

Lucky Devil's Cake
(Luckiest Devil's Double Decker)

Flaky Cinnamon Twists
(Flaky Ginger Twists)

Orange Custard Bars
(Lime Custard Bars)

Gently Spiced Carrot-Pecan Torte
(Layered Carrot-Pecan Ice Cream Cake)

Chocolate Swirl Sour Cream Bundt Cake
(Chocolate Swirl Cupcakes)

Lemon-Drenched Zucchini Loaves
(Orange-Drenched Zucchini Loaves)

Buttermilk–Brown Sugar Pound Cake
(Toasted Almond Pound Cake)

While few of us can settle down daily to a proper tea, all of us need something special in the middle of the afternoon, that time when we feel as though we've finished a full day's work but know there's still lots more to do. These pound cakes, loaves, scones, twists, tortes, wafers, and devilishly delicious devil's food cake are the kinds of sweets that can make four o'clock a favored hour.

Any one of these sweets makes a perfect pick-me-up; two or three make a party. Teatime Treats includes elegant sweets to serve at a fancy tea, homey cakes to have on hand when friends drop by for a "cuppa," and substantial cakes to take to work for a midday at-your-desk indulgence.

Round Pound Cake with Blueberry Jam

I love everything about this cake: its look, solid, golden, and homey (it's baked in a springform pan and grows to be over 2 inches high); its texture, just a little more open than the tightly packed crumb of classic pound cakes (the better to absorb fruit sauces, ice cream, or wonderful Blueberry Jam); and its taste, buttery, satisfying, and sweet (but not too). Cut in wedges and paired with Blueberry Jam, a preserve you'll want to make by the potfull, this will become a regular in your repertoire.
§ Makes 10 to 12 Servings

THE CAKE
2 c. all-purpose flour
2 tsp. baking powder
½ tsp. baking soda
¼ tsp. salt
1 c. (2 sticks) unsalted butter, at room temperature
1 c. sugar
4 large eggs, at room temperature
1 tsp. pure vanilla extract
¼ tsp. almond extract
½ c. plain yogurt, at room temperature

THE JAM
1 pt. blueberries
½ tsp. cinnamon
3 tbsp. sugar
1½ tsp. lemon juice
½ pt. blueberries

1] THE CAKE. Position a rack one-third up from the bottom of the oven and preheat the oven to 325°. Generously butter an 8-inch springform pan, dust with flour, and tap out the excess. Place the flour, baking powder, baking soda, and salt in a bowl and whisk just to combine; set aside.

2] Put the butter and sugar in the bowl of an electric mixer with the whisk attachment in place. Beat at medium-high speed, stopping to scrape the bowl as needed, for about 3 to 4 minutes, until the mixture is light and fluffy. Add the eggs, one at a time, and beat for 1 minute after each addition. Beat in the vanilla and almond extracts. Reduce the mixer speed to low and add one-third of the reserved dry ingredients, mixing just until the flour is incorporated. Don't overmix. Mix in half of the yogurt. Repeat with half of the remaining dry ingredients, the rest of the yogurt, then the last of the dry mixture.

3] Give the batter a last turn with a rubber spatula and scrape it into the prepared pan. Bake the cake for 1 hour and 10 to 20 minutes, or until beautifully golden and a toothpick inserted in the center of the cake comes out clean. Remove the cake to a rack and cool for 10 minutes before unmolding. Release the sides of the pan, and turn the cake upside-down onto a rack; lift off the bottom of the springform. Invert onto another rack and let the cake come to room temperature right-side up.

4] TO MAKE THE JAM ON A STOVETOP. Place the pint of blueberries, the cinnamon, sugar, and lemon juice in a heavy saucepan and bring to a boil over medium heat, stirring constantly. Reduce the heat and simmer, stirring frequently, until the mixture thickens to a runny jam, from 15 to 20 minutes. Scrape the jam into a bowl, stir in the remaining berries, and allow to cool. The jam will thicken as it cools. Refrigerate the jam, covered, when it reaches room temperature.

TO MAKE THE JAM IN A MICROWAVE. Place the pint of blueberries, the cinnamon, sugar, and lemon juice in a 2-quart microwave-safe bowl or measuring cup. Stir to blend. Microwave on high, uncovered, for 5 to 8 minutes, checking often. Remove from the oven when most of the berries have popped. The jam will be quite thin but will thicken as it cools. Fold in the remaining berries. Refrigerate the jam, covered, when it reaches room temperature.

SERVING. The cake should be served at room temperature. It is most easily cut with a finely serrated knife. Cut some slices, each about ¼ inch thick, and present them fanned out on the serving plate around the uncut portion of cake. Pass the jam.

STORING. Well wrapped in plastic, the cake will keep 3 days at room temperature or 1 month frozen. The jam will keep in a tightly covered jar in the refrigerator for 2 weeks.

BEST MATCH. Because the texture and taste of this cake are so straightforward, it's a fine match with coffee or tea, and a most civilized companion to sherry.

❀| PLAYING AROUND. (Whipped Cream Trifle) Use slices of this cake as the base for a trifle. Sprinkle the cake with a small amount of sherry or liqueur and, in a glass bowl, build up layers of cake, cut soft fruit and berries, and whipped cream, ending with rosettes of cream decorated with fruit.

Chocolate-Dipped Walnut Wafers

These meltingly rich cookies have the look of fancy wafers bought from a fine pastry shop. They are delicate, pale, dipped in chocolate to their halfway points, and surprisingly fuss-free because they need no rolling.
§ Makes About 4 Dozen Cookies

THE WAFERS

1 c. walnuts, toasted and very finely chopped
1¾ c. all-purpose flour
¼ tsp. ground cloves
Pinch of salt
1 c. (2 sticks) unsalted butter, at room temperature
½ c. sugar
½ tsp. almond extract

THE GLAZE

1 c. semisweet chocolate chips

1] THE WAFERS. Whisk the nuts, flour, cloves, and salt together and set aside. In an electric mixer, with the paddle if you have one, beat the butter on medium speed until it is light colored, about 2 minutes. Add the sugar and almond extract and continue to beat 3 more minutes, until fluffy. Reduce the mixer speed to low and gradually add the nut and flour mixture, beating until the dough is well combined and starts to gather around the paddle. *(You can make the dough to this point, wrap it well, and keep it refrigerated for 2 days.)*

2] Adjust the racks to divide the oven in thirds and preheat the oven to 350°. Have ready 2 baking sheets, preferably nonstick. Working with a teaspoonful of dough at a time, roll the dough between your palms into balls about 1 inch in diameter. Place 1½ inches apart on the unbuttered sheets. Cover with waxed paper and, using the bottom of a glass, gently flatten each ball until it is ¼ inch thick. Remove the waxed paper. Bake for 13 to 15 minutes, or until the cookies are very lightly colored. (They should remain pale.) Use a wide metal spatula to transfer the cookies to a rack to cool. Repeat until all the dough has been used.

3] THE GLAZE. Melt the chocolate in the top of a double boiler over hot water, or in a bowl in a microwave. When the chocolate is melted and smooth, place the top of the double boiler, or the bowl, on the counter. Tilt the pot or the bowl so the chocolate pools, and dip each cookie into it just until half of the cookie is coated with chocolate. Lift the cookie and let the excess chocolate drip back into the pot. Gently run the edge of each wafer against the rim of the pot to remove the last of the dripping chocolate. If the chocolate becomes too thick to dip the cookies easily, return the pot to the heat for a minute (or rewarm briefly in the microwave). Place the dipped wafers on baking sheets lined with waxed paper and refrigerate 5 to 10 minutes to set the chocolate.

SERVING. These should be served at room temperature. They are inviting arranged on an oblong platter, chocolate half on top, plain walnut half on bottom, each cookie overlapping the preceding one slightly.

STORING. The wafers can be well wrapped and kept at room temperature for 3 days or frozen for 1 month.

BEST MATCH. These are good plate-mates to Flaky Cinnamon Twists (page 101), Made-in-a-Bag Espresso–Chocolate Chip Shortbreads (page 96), and Coconut Tea Cake (page 92), and they are equally well suited to coffee or tea.

❂│ PLAYING AROUND. (Hazelnut or Fruit-Filled Sandwiches) These cookies are lovely made with toasted, skinned hazelnuts rather than walnuts and are doubly good sandwiched with a thin layer of warmed jam; try raspberry or apricot jam or citrus marmalade.

Coconut Tea Cake

Each of the recipes in this book is a favorite of mine, but this one is in the ranks of most favorite. For me, it is the perfect tea cake. It has a finely textured crumb, a firm, sugary crust, and a light, but lingering, coconut flavor and aroma. It can stand up to dunking (when no one's watching, of course) and can be kept fresh for days. This is the kind of cake you make once and get requests for again and again. § Makes 12 Servings

2 c. all-purpose flour
1 tsp. baking powder
¼ c. (½ stick) unsalted butter
1 c. canned unsweetened coconut milk (available at Asian and specialty shops as well as some supermarkets), measured after the top cream has been stirred into the liquid
4 large eggs
2 c. sugar
1 tsp. pure vanilla extract
¾ c. dry unsweetened shredded coconut

Confectioners' sugar

1] Position a rack one-third up from the bottom of the oven and preheat the oven to 350°. Generously butter a 9-inch kugelhopf or tube pan. Dust with flour and shake out the excess.

2] Sift the flour and baking powder together onto a sheet of waxed paper; reserve. Heat the butter and coconut milk in a small saucepan until the butter is melted and the milk hot; or you can do this in a microwave. Keep warm while preparing the batter.

3] Put the eggs and sugar in the bowl of an electric mixer fitted with a whisk attachment. Beat at medium-high speed until the mixture is thick and pale, about 2 minutes. Beat in the vanilla. Reduce the mixer speed to low and gradually add the flour and baking powder. Beat until well combined. Scrape down the sides of the bowl and add the coconut, mixing only until it is incorporated. Still on low speed, carefully and steadily pour the hot milk and butter into the batter. Stop mixing when the batter is smooth. Make sure the ingredients at the bottom of the bowl have been well incorporated by stirring the batter gently with a rubber spatula.

4] Pour the batter into the prepared pan. Rotate the pan briskly once or twice to settle the batter and bake 60 to 65 minutes, until a toothpick inserted in the center of the cake comes out clean. Transfer to a rack to cool for 10 minutes. Unmold onto a rack and cool to room temperature.

SERVING. The shape of the kugelhopf mold and the cake's honey-brown crust make it a pretty offering for a tea table. Just before serving, place the cake on a doily-lined platter and dust with confectioners' sugar. Cut into thin slices and serve at room temperature. This is delicious—and elegant—served with Grand Marnier Custard Sauce (page 193).

STORING. The cake can be wrapped airtight and stored at room temperature for 3 to 5 days or frozen for 1 month.

BEST MATCH. Pair this with a light tisane, a fragrant herbal tea, or a glass of sherry. (This cake is out of this world dipped in sherry.) And, because Coconut Tea Cake is not very sweet, it is also lovely matched with champagne.

❀| **PLAYING AROUND.** (New Sweets from Stale Cake) Serve a slice of lightly toasted cake as the base for a scoop of ice cream and a bath of Old-Time Creamery Hot Fudge Sauce (page 143) or the sponge for Pineapple en Papillote (page 127).

Burnt Butter Baby Cakes

The tops of these little sweets are golden, domed, dark-rimmed, and crisp. When you bite through, you find a dense, soft, fragrant almond cake. Like their foreign cousins, the famous French pastries called financiers, *these get extra flavor and aroma from* beurre noisette, *butter that's* heated until it turns a rich brown and gives off the scent of hazelnuts. That anything this good can be this easy to make should be an inspiration to every fledgling baker.*
§ Makes About 3 Dozen Cakes

6 tbsp. (¾ stick) unsalted butter
½ c. (rounded) slivered or julienned blanched almonds
½ c. sugar
3 egg whites
¼ c. plus 2 tsp. cake flour
2 tsp. dark rum or 1 tsp. pure vanilla extract

1] Place the butter in a small saucepan over medium heat. Heat, swirling the pan occasionally, until the butter turns a deep brown. Keep a constant watch because the time between brown and black can be short. Remove from heat and place in a warm spot while preparing the batter.

2] Pulverize the almonds and sugar in a food processor. Transfer them to a metal mixing bowl that can go on top of a burner, or a saucepan. Add the egg whites and stir with a wooden spoon. Place the bowl over very low heat and, stirring constantly, heat until the mixture is hot to the touch, runny, and slightly white, about 2 minutes. (To avoid burning the egg whites, lift the bowl from the heat now and then.) Remove from heat and stir in the flour. Gradually add the hot brown butter and the rum or vanilla. (The aroma as you do this is incomparable.) The batter will look shiny and glazed. Press a piece of plastic wrap against the top of the batter and chill the mixture for at least 1 hour before baking. *(The batter can be made to this point and refrigerated for up to 3 days before baking.)*

3] Place a rack in the center of the oven and preheat the oven to 400°. Butter the insides of 3 mini-muffin tins, each with 12 cups with capacities of 1 tablespoon each. (If you don't have enough tins to make all of the Baby Cakes in one batch, make as many as you can, cool the tins, wash, and repeat.) Use a half teaspoonful of batter for each cake. Don't worry if the batter isn't even; it will smooth out in the oven. Bake for 12 to 13 minutes, until the tops are crowned and golden. Pry the cakes from the tins with a small butter knife and cool to room temperature on a rack.

SERVING. For an informal teatime pick-me-up, serve Baby Cakes mounded in a napkin-lined basket. For a slightly dressier look, place the cakes in paper or foil cups and arrange on a platter or tiered cake stand.

STORING. The cakes will keep for 3 days at room temperature in an airtight tin. In a pinch, they can be frozen for 1 week, but they are really at their best fresh.

BEST MATCH. This is a tea cake if ever there was one.

❀| **PLAYING AROUND.** (Burnt Butter Toddler Cakes) Burnt Butter Baby Cakes Grown-up. Make the batter as directed and divide it evenly among the 12 cups of a well-buttered standard-size muffin tin. Bake 15 minutes, until golden and crowned. Serve on small dessert plates with a fan of pineapple, mango, or plum slices and a spoonful of lightly whipped cream.

Made-in-a-Bag Espresso–Chocolate Chip Shortbreads

Everyone loves shortbread's sandy texture and buttery richness. I've always adored it but hated to roll it—all that butter makes the dough difficult to work. My friend Bonnie Lee Black, a New York caterer, solved the problem by suggesting the dough be popped into a Ziploc plastic bag right after it's mixed, rolled in the bag, chilled, cut, and baked. Easy! To match this untraditional method, I've created this wonderful flavor combination not often associated with old-fashioned shortbread.

§ Makes 3½ Dozen Cookies

1 c. (2 sticks) unsalted butter, at room temperature

⅔ c. confectioners' sugar

½ tsp. pure vanilla extract

1 tbsp. espresso powder dissolved in 1 tbsp. boiling water

2 c. all-purpose flour

¾ c. mini chocolate chips

Confectioners' sugar, optional

1] In an electric mixer, fitted with a paddle if you've got one, beat the butter and sugar together on medium speed, stopping to scrape the bowl frequently, until light and fluffy, about 3 minutes. Beat in the vanilla and espresso. On low speed, stir in the flour, mixing only until combined. Fold in the chocolate chips with a sturdy rubber spatula.

2] Use the spatula to transfer the soft, sticky dough into a ziploc plastic bag. Place the bag on a flat surface, keep the top open, and roll the dough into a 9″ × 10½″ rectangle that's ¼ inch thick. As you roll, turn the bag occasionally and lift the plastic from the dough so it's free of creases. When you get the right size and thickness, seal the bag, pressing out as much air as possible, and chill the dough for 1 hour. *(The dough can be made ahead and refrigerated for 2 days.)*

3] Center a rack in the oven and preheat the oven to 325°. Place the plastic bag on a cutting board and slit it open around the edges; discard the bag. Turn the firm dough out onto the board and, using a ruler and a sharp, thin-bladed knife, cut the dough into 1½-inch squares. Transfer to an unbuttered baking sheet and carefully prick each cookie twice with the tines of a fork, gently pushing the tines through the cookie until they hit the sheet. Bake for 18 to 20 minutes, until the shortbreads are very pale; they should not take on much color. Transfer the cookies to a rack to cool. If you want, while the shortbreads are still hot, dust with confectioners' sugar.

SERVING: These can be arranged on a small serving plate, but it's nice to put one or two on the side of each guest's saucer.

STORING. When cool, these cookies can be packed airtight in plastic bags and frozen for 1 month.

BEST MATCH. Without question, the best match is coffee served in cups wide enough for dunking.

❂| **PLAYING AROUND.** (Subtle Coconut and Oatmeal-Spice Shortbreads) Once you've got such a terrific technique down pat, it's a shame not to play around with the possibilities. Here are two more of my favorite shortbread flavors. Subtle Coconut: Combine 2 cups all-purpose flour and 1 cup shredded unsweetened coconut; set aside. Following the directions for Espresso–Chocolate Chip Shortbreads, beat together 1 cup butter and ⅔ cup confectioners' sugar. Add ½ tsp. pure vanilla extract and then the dry ingredients. And for Oatmeal-Spice: Combine 1½ cups all-purpose flour, ⅔ cup old-fashioned rolled oats, 1 tsp. ground cinnamon, ½ tsp. ground ginger, ¼ tsp. grated or ground nutmeg, and ⅛ tsp. ground cloves; set aside. Following the directions for Espresso–Chocolate Chip Shortbreads, beat together 1 cup butter and ⅔ cup confectioners' sugar, then add the dry ingredients. Serve these with tea.

Cream Scones

Scones, once quintessentially British, have become a popular American food. In fact, they, like croissants, have been so thoroughly adopted stateside they're found in corner coffee shops and not-so-fancy takeout stores. Unfortunately, most of the commercially available scones are a pale substitute for the real thing. Taste these—rich, tender, flaky, comfortably filling, and quick to make—and you may never eat storebought scones again. § Makes 1 Dozen Scones

2 c. all-purpose flour
1 tbsp. baking powder
2 tbsp. sugar
¼ tsp. salt
½ c. (1 stick) cold unsalted butter, cut into small pieces
¾ c. plump currants
1 large egg
⅔ c. heavy cream
About 1 tbsp. unsalted butter

Marmalade, butter, and/or Devonshire cream, optional

1] Center a rack in the oven and preheat the oven to 375°. Place the flour, baking powder, sugar, and salt in a large mixing bowl. Stir to combine. Add the cold butter to the bowl. Using your fingers (my favorite tools), two knives, or a pastry blender, work the butter into the dry ingredients until the mixture is crumbly and looks like fine meal. Add the currants and toss to mix. Mix the egg and heavy cream together to blend. Pour this over the dry ingredients and stir with a fork just until a dough forms. Don't overdo it.

2] Gently knead the dough in the bowl just until it comes together, about 8 times. The dough will be so pleasantly malleable you'll be tempted to knead more than you should. Resist! Turn the dough out onto a smooth, lightly floured surface. Divide it in half and shape each half into a 6-inch disk about ½ inch thick. Cut each disk into 6 wedges. Transfer the wedges to an unbuttered baking sheet using a flapjack or offset spatula.

3] Bake the scones for 20 to 22 minutes, until golden. Transfer them to a rack and immediately brush the tops with butter. (You can do this easily by rubbing the tops with the end of a stick of butter.) Cool for 10 minutes before serving, or wait until they reach room temperature.

SERVING. Put these in a basket or silver bread platter lined with a linen napkin large enough to wrap over the scones. Serve with an assortment of marmalades (you could include Blueberry Jam, page 88), sweet butter, and, if you like, Devonshire cream, a double cream now available in many specialty shops.

STORING. Well wrapped, the scones will keep in the freezer for a month. Reheat in a conventional or toaster oven before serving.

BEST MATCH. Serve with a full-bodied tea brewed in a proper teapot with, as the British say, a good pour.

◉| **PLAYING AROUND.** (Savory Cheddar Cheese Scones) A soothing, somewhat more substantial scone. Reduce the sugar to 1½ teaspoons, omit the currants, and add ¾ cup shredded good-quality sharp Cheddar cheese.

Lucky Devil's Cake

Light, moist, and satanically tempting, this is the ultimate all-American chocolate cake, made doubly delicious with bittersweet chocolate and fine cocoa powder. For 3 o'clock milk or 4 o'clock tea I make this in a single layer, covering it with a chocolate glaze that sets firm, then melts when it hits your tongue. But for anyone who's been angelic, or for a kid on his birthday, I make two layers, a demon double-decker sandwiched with whipped cream.
§ Makes 8 to 10 Servings

THE CAKE

¼ c. cocoa, preferably a Dutch-processed brand, such as Droste or Poulain

⅓ c. boiling water

2 oz. high-quality bittersweet chocolate, such as Lindt or Tobler

1 c. all-purpose flour

½ tsp. baking soda

¼ tsp. salt

6 tbsp. (¾ stick) unsalted butter, at room temperature

¾ c. sugar

2 large eggs, preferably at room temperature

½ tsp. pure vanilla extract

½ c. plain yogurt, preferably at room temperature

THE GLAZE

4 oz. high-quality bittersweet chocolate, such as Lindt or Tobler

3 tbsp. confectioners' sugar

3 tbsp. unsalted butter, at room temperature

1] THE CAKE. Place a rack in the center of the oven and preheat the oven to 350°. Butter a 9-inch round cake pan, line the bottom with a circle of waxed paper, butter the paper, and dust the inside of the pan with flour, tapping out the excess.

2] Dissolve the cocoa in the boiling water, stirring to make a smooth paste. Melt the chocolate in the top of a double boiler over hot water, or in a bowl in a microwave. Stir the chocolate into the cocoa paste and set aside to cool. Whisk together the flour, baking soda, and salt; reserve.

3] In an electric mixer, fitted with a paddle if available, cream the butter and sugar at medium speed until light and fluffy, about 3 minutes. Add the eggs one at a time and beat for a minute after each addition, stopping to scrape the sides of the bowl as needed. Beat in the vanilla. Turn the mixer speed to low and add half the dry ingredients, mixing just until the flour is incorporated. Scrape the bowl and mix in the yogurt. Add the remainder of the dry ingredients and mix to combine. Scrape the chocolate into the bowl and mix only until blended. (To be sure to avoid overmixing, you can mix in the chocolate with a rubber spatula.)

4] Pour the batter into the prepared pan and bake for 30 to 35 minutes. The cake will dome slightly and feel springy when you touch it. Remove it from the oven and cool on a rack for 5 minutes. Run a blunt knife around the edge of the cake and unmold onto a rack; peel off the paper. Invert onto another rack and let the cake cool to room temperature right-side up.

5] THE GLAZE. Melt the chocolate in the top of a double boiler over hot water or in a bowl in a microwave. With a rubber spatula, stir in the sugar. Blend in the butter a little bit at a time. Allow the glaze to cool for 10 minutes at room temperature before using.

6] Pour the glaze on top of the cake and spread it evenly across the top and sides with a long metal spatula. The glaze needs to set for 30 minutes at room temperature.

Teatime Treats

**Lightly whipped, lightly
sweetened cream**

SERVING. Once the glaze is set, you can cut and serve the cake. This deserves a beautiful cake plate and a lacy white or gold doily. Cut the cake in generous wedges and serve a dollop of lightly whipped cream on the side.

STORING. Covered with plastic wrap the cake will keep at room temperature for 3 days, or it can be frozen for 1 month. Place the unwrapped cake in the freezer for 1 hour to firm before wrapping it airtight for longer storage.

BEST MATCH. Choose coffee, tea, or milk; this cake is a pleaser with anything.

❀ **PLAYING AROUND.** (Luckiest Devil's Double Deckers) Double the recipes for both the cake and glaze. When the cakes are cool, top one with swirls of lightly sweetened whipped cream. (Play around—you can add a bit of spice, ginger, or cinnamon, for instance, to the whipped cream.) Place the other layer upside-down on top of the cream. Glaze the cake, let it set, then enjoy.

Flaky Cinnamon Twists

These impossible-to-resist cookies are made with cream cheese dough, a boon to bakers who haven't the patience to pamper pie dough. You can punch the dough, pound it, work it over and over, and still end up with a flaky, tasty, crispy cookie. *These get all their flavor from the dough and a rolling in cinnamon and sugar, perfect partners to the tang of cream cheese.*
§ *Makes 20 to 24 Cookies*

4 oz. cold cream cheese, cut into 4 pieces
½ c. (1 stick) cold unsalted butter, cut into 8 pieces
1 c. all-purpose flour
1 c. sugar
⅓ c. ground cinnamon

1] Let the cold cream cheese and butter stand at room temperature for 10 minutes. Put the flour in a food processor. Scatter the cream cheese and butter over the flour and pulse 6 to 8 times. Now let the machine run, stopping to scrape the sides of the bowl frequently, until the dough forms large curds. Stop before the dough forms a ball on the blade.

2] Turn the dough out onto a work surface and gather it into a ball. Divide the dough in half and shape each half into a square. Wrap the dough tightly in plastic wrap and chill for at least 2 hours before using. *(The dough can be refrigerated for up to 3 days.)*

3] Remove one package of dough from the refrigerator and let stand at room temperature until malleable, about 10 minutes. In a small bowl, combine the sugar and cinnamon. Butter 2 baking sheets and set them aside.

4] Sprinkle ¼ cup of cinnamon-sugar on a work surface. Put the dough on the sugared surface and sprinkle the top of the dough with about 2 tablespoons of the mixture. Roll the dough out to a 10- to 12-inch square, sprinkling with more cinnamon-sugar and turning the dough several times as you work.

5] Trim the edges of the dough and, with a ruler, mark the top and bottom edges of the square at 1-inch intervals. Cut the dough into 1-inch-wide strips and then cut the strips in half crosswise. Work with two strips at a time. Press the tops of the strips together with light pressure so they form an upside-down "V". Twist the strands one over the other loosely, turning the strips so they cross on their thin edges rather than their broad sides. Finish the twist by pressing together the bottom ends. Place the twists on a buttered baking sheet and chill, uncovered, for at least 30 minutes before baking. Repeat with the other package of dough.

6] Arrange 2 racks to divide the oven in thirds and preheat the oven to 400°. Bake the cookies for 10 to 12 minutes, until the tops are deeply golden and the bottoms caramelized (like the French cookies called *palmiers*). Transfer the cookies to a rack to cool to room temperature.

SERVING. These are pretty served like bread sticks, standing on end in a crystal tumbler.

STORING. These are best eaten the day they are made, but they can be wrapped and stored in the freezer for up to 1 month.

BEST MATCH. Twists are lovely with tea and make good plate-mates to Chocolate-Dipped Walnut Wafers (page 90) and Made-in-a-Bag Espresso–Chocolate Chip Shortbreads (page 96).

❀ **PLAYING AROUND.** (Flaky Ginger Twists) For a twist on a Twist, change the cinnamon to ground ginger and carry on.

Orange Custard Bars

A lovely combination of tart and sweet, these little pastries have a buttery brown sugar crust and a very thin layer of creamy baked custard. You may want to double this recipe and bake the sweets in a 10″ × 15″ jelly roll pan. If you do, cut the pastries into 100 small squares and freeze them—you'll never be caught short by unexpected guests. § Makes 18 Bars

THE DOUGH

1 c. all-purpose flour
3 tbsp. packed light brown sugar
½ c. (1 stick) cold unsalted butter, cut into 8 pieces

THE CUSTARD

½ c. sugar
2 tbsp. all-purpose flour
¼ tsp. baking powder
⅓ c. frozen orange concentrate, thawed
2 large eggs
1½ tsp. Grand Marnier or other orange liqueur
1½ tsp. fresh lemon juice
Grated zest of 2 oranges

Confectioners' sugar

1] THE DOUGH. Center a rack in the oven and preheat the oven to 350°. Set aside a 9″ × 9″ baking pan. Place 1 cup flour and the brown sugar in a food processor and pulse 3 to 4 times, just to mix. Scatter the butter over the mixture. Pulse several times and then process for about 30 seconds, or until the dough cleans the sides of the bowl and forms curds. Press the dough into the baking pan and bake for 15 to 18 minutes, or until the crust firms and starts to take on color.

2] THE CUSTARD. While the crust is baking, wipe out the bowl of the processor (it's not necessary to wash it) and put in all the custard ingredients. Just before the crust is ready, process the ingredients for 1 minute, stopping once to scrape down the sides of the bowl. When the crust is ready, take the pan out of the oven, pour the custard over, and tilt the pan to smooth the top.

3] Return the pan to the oven and bake for about 15 minutes, until golden and set. Place the pan on a rack to cool to room temperature.

SERVING. When the pastry is cool, run a knife around the edges of the pan, turn the pastry out onto a rack, and turn it right-side up onto a cutting board. Trim the edges if they are very brown and cut the pastry into eighteen 1½″ × 3″ bars. Just before serving, dust with confectioners' sugar.

STORING. Well wrapped, the bars will keep in the refrigerator for 3 days or up to 1 month in the freezer. Bring to room temperature before serving.

BEST MATCH. These are equally irresistible with tea or strong black coffee.

❀| PLAYING AROUND. (Lime Custard Bars) Replace the orange concentrate with freshly squeezed lime juice and the grated orange zest with lime zest and you'll turn out a tart, tasty treat.

Gently Spiced Carrot-Pecan Torte

This is a carrot cake more familiar to Europeans than Californians. The mixture relies on ground nuts rather than flour for its binding and bakes to a delicate, spongy finish. It's neither dense nor very sweet, like its West Coast cousin, nor would it take to a cream cheese frosting. It's meant to be served with a dusting of sugar or a spoonful of whipped cream and a cup of strong tea, accompaniments that let the soft spices and natural sweetness of the ingredients shine through. § Makes 6 Servings

1 c. pecans
2 tbsp. all-purpose flour
2 tsp. baking powder
½ tsp. ground ginger
¼ tsp. ground cinnamon
⅛ tsp. freshly grated or ground nutmeg
2 medium carrots, scraped, trimmed, and cut into chunks
4 eggs, separated
⅔ c. sugar
2 tbsp. lemon juice

Confectioners' sugar

Lightly sweetened whipped cream

1] Place a rack in the center of the oven and preheat the oven to 350° Butter an 8-inch springform pan, line the bottom with waxed paper, and butter the paper. Dust the inside of the pan with flour, tap out the excess, and set aside. Place the pecans, flour, baking powder, and spices in a food processor and pulse and process until the nuts are finely ground. Turn the mixture out onto a sheet of waxed paper and reserve. Put the carrots in the machine and pulse and process to mince. You will have ⅔ cup. Set aside.

2] In a large bowl, by hand, whisk together the egg yolks and sugar until the mixture turns pale, about 1 minute. Switch to a large rubber spatula and blend in the lemon juice, carrots, and nut mixture. Beat the egg whites in an electric mixer with the whisk attachment until they stand in stiff peaks. Gently fold the whites into the carrot mixture, taking care not to overmix. Turn the batter into the prepared pan and smooth the top.

3] Bake the cake for 60 to 65 minutes, until it just starts to pull away from the sides of the pan and the top is golden. The cake rises during baking, then sinks a bit in the center. It's all right—nut tortes do this. Put the pan on a rack and let the cake cool for 10 minutes. Carefully run a blunt knife around the sides of the pan and remove the sides of the springform. Invert the cake, remove the pan bottom and the paper, then turn the cake right-side up onto another rack to cool to room temperature.

SERVING. Just before serving, dust the cake with confectioners' sugar. Bring to the table on a cake platter, cut with a serrated knife using a sawing motion, and serve with a spoonful of whipped cream on the side.

STORING. The cooled cake will keep, wrapped in plastic, for 3 days at room temperature.

BEST MATCH. This cake is made for tea. It would make a good tea-table companion to Orange Custard Bars (page 103), Flaky Cinnamon Twists (page 101), and Burnt Butter Baby Cakes (page 94).

✿| **PLAYING AROUND.** (Layered Carrot-Pecan Ice Cream Cake) Thin layers of this torte make an unusual, and quite beautiful, ice cream cake. Spray an 8-inch springform pan with PAM. Cut the cake horizontally into ½-inch-thick layers. Place a layer of cake on the bottom of the pan; top with a layer of softened vanilla ice cream. Continue making layers, ending with ice cream, until the cake is the height you want. If the ice cream becomes too soft to work with, return the cake and ice cream to the freezer for 20 minutes before continuing. Sprinkle chopped toasted pecans over the top of the cake. Freeze until firm before serving or cover tightly and freeze for up to 1 month.

Chocolate Swirl Sour Cream Bundt Cake

Here's a sour cream Bundt cake with a swirling ribbon of crunchy chocolate-nut filling and a fragrance that warms the kitchen. It's pretty just the way it is, plain, golden-crusted, and marked here and there by dark bands of filling, but you can dress it up with a drizzle of chocolate glaze.

Either way, it's what farm bakers call "a good keeper." It can be frozen, but it will stay fresh and at-the-ready for several days at room temperature and, in fact, improves with a 24-hour rest after baking. § Makes 12 Servings

THE CAKE

1 c. pecans
⅓ c. packed light brown sugar
1 tsp. ground cinnamon
1 tbsp. cocoa
½ oz. semisweet chocolate
2 c. all-purpose flour
1½ tsp. baking powder
½ tsp. baking soda
1 c. (2 sticks) unsalted butter, at room temperature
1½ c. granulated sugar
2 large eggs, preferably at room temperature
1 c. sour cream, preferably at room temperature
1½ tsp. pure vanilla extract

THE GLAZE (OPTIONAL)

1½ oz. semisweet chocolate
2 tsp. strong brewed coffee (can be made with instant)
1½ tsp. unsalted butter, at room temperature
1 tbsp. confectioners' sugar

1] THE CAKE. Place a rack in the center of the oven and preheat the oven to 325°. Butter a Bundt pan and dust it all over with flour, tapping out the excess. (A 9-inch tube pan also works well for this cake.) Place the pecans, brown sugar, cinnamon, cocoa, and chocolate in a food processor and pulse to pulverize. (Don't worry if a few chunks of nuts and chocolate remain.) Leave the mixture in the machine until you need it. Whisk together the flour, baking powder, and baking soda in a mixing bowl; set aside.

2] In the bowl of an electric mixer, fitted with a paddle if you have one, cream the butter and sugar together until very light and fluffy, about 4 minutes, scraping the bowl occasionally. Add the eggs 1 at a time and beat at medium speed for 2 minutes after each addition, scraping as needed. Add the sour cream and vanilla and beat 2 minutes longer. On lowest speed, mix in the dry ingredients, mixing only until blended.

3] Spoon half of the batter into the prepared pan, smooth the top, and sprinkle over half of the reserved chocolate mixture. Top with the remaining batter and then the rest of the chocolate. Swirl the chocolate mixture by running a blunt knife in circles through the batter. You'll notice that a lot of the chocolate remains on top of the cake—that's just the way it's supposed to be. Bake the cake for 1 hour and 15 to 20 minutes, until a toothpick inserted in the center of the cake comes out clean. Cool on a rack for 5 minutes before unmolding. (When you turn the cake over, some of the filling will go flying—be prepared.) Cool to room temperature on a rack before glazing.

4] THE GLAZE. Melt the chocolate with the coffee in the top of a double boiler over hot water, or in a bowl in a microwave. Remove from heat and beat in the butter and then the sugar. Drizzle the glaze over the cake in a

Confectioners' sugar, optional

zigzag pattern, going from the inside to the outside of the cake, by allowing it to drip onto the cake from the tip of a spoon. Let the glaze set for about 20 minutes before serving.

SERVING. If you haven't glazed the cake, dust it with confectioners' sugar before serving. Place the cake on a large serving platter and bring to the table whole. Cut in thin slices and serve two to a guest.

STORING. The cake will keep for at least 3 days well wrapped at room temperature or it can be frozen for up to 1 month.

BEST MATCH. While tea is usually the first choice with a sour cream cake, the chocolate filling in this cake makes coffee an equally pleasing partner.

❂| PLAYING AROUND. (Chocolate Swirl Cupcakes) Cut the recipe in half (omitting the glaze) to make these cupcakes. Fit 18 cups of standard-size muffin tins with cupcake liners. Fill the cups with half the batter, top with half the chocolate, and repeat with remaining batter and chocolate filling. Swirl the batter with a knife. Bake in a preheated 350° oven for 30 minutes, until a toothpick inserted in the center of a cupcake comes out clean. Cool to room temperature on racks.

Lemon-Drenched Zucchini Loaves

This is a simple, one-bowl recipe that turns out loaves bursting with flavor. Each slice of cake is lightly spiced, flecked with shreds of zucchini, and soaked through and through with a lemon syrup made from fresh lemons—a refreshing change from butter cakes and a delightful treat you can make year-round.
§ *Makes 2 Loaves, 8 to 10 Servings Each*

THE LOAVES

3 c. all-purpose flour
1 tbsp. baking powder
1¼ tsp. ground cinnamon
1 tsp. ground ginger
½ tsp. ground allspice
¼ tsp. freshly grated or ground nutmeg
3 large eggs, preferably at room temperature
1 c. safflower oil
1½ c. sugar
1 tsp. pure lemon extract
1 whole zucchini (about ¾ lb.), unpeeled, scrubbed and grated
Grated zest of 2 lemons

THE SYRUP

¼ c. freshly squeezed lemon juice
½ c. sugar

1] THE LOAVES. Place a rack in the center of the oven and preheat the oven to 350°. Butter 2 loaf pans, each 8½″ × 4½″ × 2½″. Dust them all over with flour and tap out the excess. Place the flour, baking powder, and spices in a mixing bowl and whisk by hand to combine; set aside.

2] In an electric mixer, using the whisk attachment, beat the eggs, oil, sugar, and lemon extract on medium-high speed until well blended, about 3 minutes. Stop and scrape the bowl as needed throughout mixing. On low speed, add the grated zucchini and lemon zest. Still on low speed, add the dry ingredients and mix only until combined. Divide the batter between the 2 pans, smooth the tops with a spatula, and bake for 50 to 60 minutes, or until a toothpick inserted in the center of the cakes comes out clean.

3] THE SYRUP. Prepare the syrup as soon as you put the pans in the oven. Put the juice and sugar in a small nonreactive saucepan. Heat, stirring, until the sugar dissolves. Remove from heat and set aside.

4] Remove the cakes from the oven and allow them to cool on a rack for 5 minutes. Unmold the cakes, then turn them right-side up onto racks. Place the racks over a baking sheet or waxed paper. With a toothpick or cake tester, poke holes all over the top crusts of the cakes. (There's no need to make holes in the sides, the syrup will seep in everywhere.) Brush the tops and sides of the cakes with the syrup, using most of the syrup for the tops. Allow the cakes to cool to room temperature before serving.

SERVING. Because these loaves are so moist, they must be cut into rather thick slices. Work with a knife and a broad or wedge-shaped cake server to cut and lift slices onto cake plates.

STORING. Wrapped in plastic, the loaves will keep for 4 days at room temperature or frozen for 2 weeks.

BEST MATCH. These moist, citrusy cakes are best with tea, either icy lemon tea or strong hot tea without milk.

❀ PLAYING AROUND. (Orange-Drenched Zucchini Loaves) Give the loaves a new flavor by highlighting orange instead of lemon. Substitute 1 teaspoon orange extract for the lemon extract, and the grated zest of 1 orange for the lemon zest; make the syrup with ¼ cup freshly squeezed orange juice, 2 teaspoons freshly squeezed lemon juice, and ½ cup sugar. Before using the cooled syrup, add 1 tablespoon Grand Marnier or other orange liqueur.

Buttermilk–Brown Sugar Pound Cake

You'd expect to find this cake tagged with a blue ribbon at a country fair. Its look is plain home-baked, its aroma warm and gentle. The surprise is the taste. A drop of anise, some fresh orange zest, vanilla, and smooth buttermilk blend to produce a flavor that is slightly exotic, mildly mysterious, and very pleasing.
§ Makes 12 Servings

2½ c. all-purpose flour
1 tsp. baking powder
½ tsp. baking soda
⅛ tsp. salt
1 c. (2 sticks) unsalted butter, at room temperature
2 c. packed light brown sugar
3 large eggs, preferably at room temperature
1 tsp. pure vanilla extract
¼ tsp. pure anise extract or 1½ tsp. Pernod
1 c. buttermilk, preferably at room temperature
Grated zest of 1 orange
½ c. plump currants

Confectioners' sugar

1] Place a rack in the center of the oven and preheat the oven to 350°. Butter a 10-inch tube or Bundt pan. If you're using a tube pan, line the bottom with waxed or parchment paper and butter the paper. Dust either pan with flour, tapping out the excess. In a large bowl, whisk together the flour, baking powder, baking soda, and salt to combine.

2] In an electric mixer, with a paddle if you have one, beat the butter and sugar together on medium speed until the mixture is light and fluffy, about 3 minutes. Stop and scrape down the sides of the bowl as needed. Add the eggs, one at a time, beating well for 1 minute after each addition. Add the extracts and beat for another minute. On the lowest speed, add one-third of the dry ingredients, beating just until they are blended. Pour in half of the buttermilk and beat until mixed. Repeat, adding half of the dry ingredients, the remaining buttermilk, and then the last of the flour mixture. Beat only until the mixture is combined. Fold in the orange zest and currants with a large rubber spatula.

3] Spoon the batter into the prepared pan. Rotate the pan briskly once or twice to even and settle the batter. Bake the cake for 60 to 65 minutes, until a toothpick inserted in the center of the cake comes out clean. Transfer to a rack to cool for 15 minutes. Turn the cake over onto another rack, lift off the pan, and peel away the paper. Invert the cake so the top side is up, and cool to room temperature.

SERVING. Dust the top of the cake generously with confectioners' sugar just before bringing the cake to the table. Serve cut in thin slices, two to a plate.

STORING. This cake keeps very well and, in fact, the flavor deepens with a day's rest. Wrap the cake in plastic and store at room temperature for 4 to 5 days or freeze for up to 1 month.

BEST MATCH. Tea, orange, and anise are made for each other.

❀| **PLAYING AROUND.** (Toasted Almond Pound Cake) For a warm, soul-satisfying cake that's more mainstream but no less delicious, use this recipe to make a Toasted Almond Pound Cake. Omit the orange rind, currants, and anise extract and reduce the vanilla extract to ½ teaspoon; add 1 teaspoon almond extract. Add ½ cup finely ground blanched toasted almonds to the dry ingredients mixture, and fold ½ cup coarsely chopped blanched toasted almonds into the batter before pouring it into the pan.

COMFORT ON A SPOON

Sweets to Snuggle Up with

Triple Chocolate Old-Fashioned Pudding
(Chocolate Pudding Pie)

Chocolate-Laced Cinnamon Pudding
(Peanut Butter–Cinnamon Pudding)

Rich Bread Pudding with Buttery Apples
(Apple Butter or Sugary Rum-Banana Bread Pudding)

Prune Bread Pudding Cups
(Apricot-Ginger Bread Pudding Cups)

Summer Pandowdy
(Apple Pandowdy)

Raspberry Peach en Papillote
(Pear, Nectarine, or Pineapple en Papillote)

Sweet Plums with Tart Cream
(Fruit Variations)

Pear-Cranberry Crisp
(Pineapple-Banana Crisp)

Honey-Yogurt Mousse
(Almond-Crusted Honey-Yogurt Mousse Tart)

Slippery Slidey Lemon-Clove Cup Custard
(Vanilla-Ginger and Espresso-Cinnamon Cup Custard)

Outrageous Rice Pudding
(Rice Pudding Ring with Berry Sauce)

Thoroughly Modern Betty
(Old-Fashioned Apple Brown Betty)

These soft, soothing, slide-through-your-teeth custards, creams, puddings, mousses, and fruit desserts are the sweets we crave when we want to be especially nice to ourselves and those we care about. Reach for these to chase away the blues, bring sunshine to a dreary day, and let family and friends know you're glad they're around. Spoon Desserts are easy enough to make on weekdays (when we need comforting most), and special enough to share with treasured co-snugglers. They're not sweets that can be stored in the freezer, but many can be made in advance in preparation for a need for their warmth and goodness.

Triple Chocolate
Old-Fashioned Pudding

What's old-fashioned about this pudding is its rich, creamy smoothness and its deep chocolate flavor. What's neither old-fashioned nor remembered from the boxed stuff of childhood is the grown-up bittersweet edge, the intensity of flavor you get only from fine chocolate and

mellowing imported dutched cocoa, and the booster shot of liqueur. You can serve this with whipped cream or heavy cream poured over the top, but it's mighty fine just the way it is.
§ Makes 6 Servings

4 oz. high-quality bittersweet chocolate, such as Lindt or Tobler

1 oz. unsweetened chocolate

2 c. milk

¼ c. sugar

⅛ tsp. salt

2 tbsp. cornstarch

3 tbsp. cocoa, preferably a Dutch-processed type, such as Droste or Poulain

½ tsp. instant espresso powder

1 large egg

2 egg yolks

3 tbsp. sugar

¼ c. milk

2 tbsp. (¼ stick) unsalted butter, at room temperature

1 tsp. pure vanilla extract

1 tbsp. Frangelico or Amaretto

1] Melt the bittersweet and unsweetened chocolates in the top of a double boiler over hot water or in a bowl in a microwave. Set aside. Bring the 2 cups of milk and the ¼ cup of sugar to the boil in a heavy medium-size saucepan.

2] While the milk is heating, place the salt, cornstarch, cocoa, and espresso powder in a food processor and pulse to blend. Turn the ingredients out onto a piece of waxed paper and reserve. Place the egg, egg yolks, and the 3 tablespoons sugar in the processor and process for 1 minute, stopping to scrape the bowl once. Add the ¼ cup of milk, process for a few seconds, and pour in the dry ingredients, pulsing just until they are incorporated.

3] With the machine running, slowly pour in the hot milk and sugar and process until the mixture is combined. It will be foamy, but the bubbles will disappear when the pudding is cooked. Pour it back into the saucepan and set over medium-high heat. Use a wooden spoon to stir the mixture energetically, without stopping, for about 2 minutes, or until the pudding thickens and one bubble rises to the surface. The pudding should not boil. Pour the thickened pudding back into the processor. (Don't scrape up any pudding that may have scorched.) Add the melted chocolate and the remaining ingredients except the cream, and pulse just until everything is mixed. Pour the pudding into six ½-cup bowls. If you don't want a skin to form on the tops of the puddings, place a piece of plastic wrap directly against the top of each pudding until ready to serve. Chill at least 4 hours.

SERVING. The pudding is ready to serve straight from the bowl when it is well chilled and set. It is scrumptiously satisfying served as is and super-

Heavy cream or lightly whipped cream, optional

special with a thin layer of heavy cream poured over the top or a spoonful of softly whipped cream (unsweetened is fine) mounded in the center.

STORING. You can keep the pudding, covered with plastic wrap, in the refrigerator for 2 days.

BEST MATCH. A glass of cold milk and a bowl of this Old-Fashioned Pudding is a classic match. Even people who haven't had a glass of milk since grade school agree the combination is a recipe for happiness.

❋| **PLAYING AROUND.** (Chocolate Pudding Pie) For a treat to warm the heart of any red-blooded American, use Triple Chocolate Old-Fashioned Pudding to make a pie. You can pour the pudding into a prebaked pie or tart shell (page 61 or 53), a storebought or homemade graham cracker crust (follow the instructions on the back of any box of graham crackers), or a crunchy toasted almond crust (page 150). No matter which crust you choose, top the pie with swirls of lightly sweetened whipped cream.

Chocolate-Laced Cinnamon Pudding

This is comfort food and kid food, a Sunday supper's finish or fare for a birthday party. The flavors are clear, the texture smooth, and the chocolate lacing a luscious layer of cream. The most sophisticated foodies find it impossible to pass up this pudding. § Makes 6 Servings

THE CHOCOLATE CREAM

⅓ c. heavy cream

2 oz. high-quality bittersweet chocolate, such as Lindt or Tobler, finely chopped

THE PUDDING

2¼ c. milk

⅓ c. sugar

Pinch of salt

3½ tbsp. cornstarch

2 tsp. ground cinnamon

3 egg yolks

2 tbsp. sugar

¼ c. milk

2 tbsp. unsalted butter, at room temperature

1 tsp. pure vanilla extract

1] THE CHOCOLATE CREAM. Bring the heavy cream to a boil in a small saucepan over medium heat or in a bowl in a microwave. Remove from heat and add the chocolate, stirring until the chocolate melts and the mixture is smooth and glossy. Set aside.

2] THE PUDDING. Bring the 2¼ cups milk and the ⅓ cup sugar to a boil in a heavy medium saucepan.

3] While the milk is heating, place the salt, cornstarch, and cinnamon in a food processor. Pulse to blend, then turn the ingredients out onto a piece of waxed paper; reserve. Place the yolks and the 2 tablespoons sugar in the machine and process for 1 minute, stopping to scrape down the sides of the bowl once. Add the ¼ cup milk and process briefly. Add the dry ingredients and pulse just until they are incorporated.

4] With the machine running, gradually pour in the hot milk and sugar. Process until the mixture is combined. It will be foamy, but the bubbles will disappear when the pudding is cooked. Pour the pudding back into the saucepan and set over medium-high heat. Use a wooden spoon to stir the mixture energetically, without stopping, for about 2 minutes, or until the pudding thickens and one bubble rises to the surface. The pudding should not boil. Pour the pudding back into the processor (don't scrape up any pudding that may have scorched), and add the butter and vanilla. Pulse to blend and give the pudding a lumpless finish.

5] Divide half of the pudding evenly among six 6-ounce bowls. Top with the warm chocolate. Fill the cups with the remaining pudding. The chocolate will rise up around the edges and form a lacy halo. If you don't want a skin to form on the tops of the puddings, place a piece of plastic wrap directly against the top of each pudding until ready to serve. Chill at least 4 hours.

SERVING. The puddings are ready to serve when chilled and well set. Just place the little bowls on saucers and serve.

STORING. This pudding will keep for 2 days covered with plastic in the refrigerator.

BEST MATCH. Hands-down, the most popular sip-along is anything milky: cold milk, chilled chocolate milk, or hot chocolate; but you can play up the chocolate-cinnamon connection by serving this pudding with espresso or cappuccino.

❀ PLAYING AROUND. (Peanut Butter–Cinnamon Pudding) Add ⅓ cup creamy peanut butter to the pudding when you blend in the butter and vanilla. This version becomes a little thicker than the plain cinnamon, less spicy, and an instantaneous family favorite. For relaxed dinners, pour either version into a graham cracker or chocolate wafer crust and top with chocolate shavings.

Rich Bread Pudding with Buttery Apples

Buttery, caramelized apples are sandwiched between layers of custard-soaked bread and plump raisins to give this pudding extra appeal. While brioche and challah are the best sponges for custard and lend their own richness to the pudding, don't hesitate to use a premium brand white bread—the result will still be superb.
§ Makes 6 Servings

3 tart apples, such as Granny Smith or Golden Delicious, peeled, cored, quartered, and thinly sliced
2 tsp. fresh lemon juice
2½ tbsp. unsalted butter
2½ tbsp. sugar
1 tbsp. Calvados or applejack
½ c. raisins or currants
¾ lb. egg bread, such as brioche or challah, crusts removed, sliced
3 c. milk
1 c. heavy cream
¾ c. sugar
3 large eggs, at room temperature
3 egg yolks, at room temperature
1½ tsp. ground cinnamon
1½ tsp. pure vanilla extract
2 tbsp. sugar

1] Toss the apples with the lemon juice. Melt the butter in a heavy skillet. Sauté the apples in the butter, shaking and turning them frequently, for about 4 minutes over medium-high heat or until they start to brown. Sprinkle over the 2½ tablespoons sugar and cook about 2 to 4 minutes more, until the apples are lightly caramelized. Pour in the Calvados and cook 1 minute longer. Remove the skillet from the heat and set aside.

2] Position a rack in the center of the oven and preheat the oven to 400°. Butter a shallow baking dish—an 8″ × 14″ oval gratin dish is best, but a standard 11″ × 7″ rectangular Pyrex pan is fine. Set aside another pan that is large enough to hold the baking dish.

3] Sprinkle half the raisins over the bottom of the buttered baking dish. Cut the bread slices in half diagonally. Lay bread triangles, slightly overlapping, around the edges of the pan. Fill in the center of the pan with bread. Sprinkle over the rest of the raisins and spoon on the caramelized apples. Top with another layer of bread.

4] Heat the milk, cream, and ¾ cup sugar in a saucepan, or in a bowl in a microwave, just until the sugar dissolves. Do not boil. Meanwhile, in a mixing bowl, whisk together the eggs, yolks, and cinnamon by hand. When the milk is hot, pour it gradually over the egg mixture, whisking all the while. Add the vanilla. Slowly pour the hot liquid over the bread, letting it soak in. Push the bread down into the liquid to encourage its absorption, then let the pudding rest for 10 minutes.

5] Sprinkle the 2 tablespoons sugar over the pudding. Place the pudding pan inside the larger pan. Fill the pan with warm water to come ¾ of the way up the sides of the baking dish and bake for 30 to 35 minutes, until a knife inserted near the center of the pudding comes out clean and the top is puffed and golden. If you prefer a crispier top, sprinkle some confectioners'

Confectioners' sugar

sugar over the pudding and run it under the broiler just until the sugar browns. Place the pudding on a cooling rack.

SERVING. Rich Bread Pudding is good at any temperature. If you want to serve it warm, when it is creamiest, let it cool on the rack for 15 minutes before cutting. (It's best to cut and serve the pudding from its baking pan.) Once cool, you can leave the pudding on the rack, lightly covered with waxed paper, for a few hours, and serve it at room temperature, or you can refrigerate it and serve it chilled. At any temperature, give the pudding a sprinkling of confectioners' sugar before serving. (For extra comfort, and there are those days when too much comfort is still not enough, whip up a pot of Custard Sauce [page 193], replacing the Grand Marnier with Calvados or applejack. Put your portion of pudding in a bowl and drench it with sauce.)

STORING. Covered with plastic, the pudding will keep in the refrigerator for 2 days.

BEST MATCH. Milky tea with a drizzle of honey is the drink for this sweet.

❀ **PLAYING AROUND.** (Apple Butter or Sugary Rum-Banana Bread Pudding) To make a pudding that cuts the preparation time but keeps the spirit, omit the caramelized apples and the raisins. Substitute a loaf of cinnamon raisin bread for the egg bread and spread each slice with some apple butter. Prepare the custard, minus the cinnamon, as directed and proceed. You can twist the original pudding another way by replacing the caramelized apples and raisins with Sugary Rum Bananas. Use 2 firm, ripe bananas, cut into thin, crosswise slices; follow the directions and ingredients list for caramelizing apples, but substitute rum for the Calvados and skip the raisins.

Prune Bread Pudding Cups

These individual cups of creamy bread pudding are studded with small pieces of sweet prunes and bound by a rich allspice-infused custard made with brown sugar. They are easy to make, foolproof actually, and good warm or cold, so they're an ideal do-ahead when you feel a comfort crisis coming on. § Makes 8 Servings

1½ c. milk
1 c. heavy cream
¾ c. packed light brown sugar
1½ tbsp. whole allspice berries
8 thin slices firm-textured white bread, crusts removed
¾ c. pitted prunes, finely diced or coarsely chopped
3 large eggs
2 egg yolks
¾ tsp. pure vanilla extract
2 tbsp. granulated sugar

1] Pour the milk, cream, and brown sugar into a medium-size saucepan. Tap the allspice berries with the back of a heavy knife or cleaver to bruise them slightly and add the berries to the pot. Bring the mixture to the boil, stirring to dissolve the sugar. Remove from heat, cover, and let steep for 10 minutes. Don't worry if the mixture looks curdled.

2] Center a rack in the oven and preheat the oven to 375°. Butter eight 6-ounce custard cups or ramekins; set aside. Cut the bread into ½-inch dice, and put the pieces in a mixing bowl. Add the prunes to the bowl, tossing to combine. Divide the bread and prune mixture evenly among the ramekins.

3] Put the eggs, yolks, and vanilla in the mixing bowl. Whisk to combine. Strain the steeped milk, discarding the allspice berries, and add to the eggs, whisking to mix. For easy pouring, you can transfer the custard to a pitcher.

4] Pour about ⅓ cup of custard into each ramekin. Push the bread down into the custard with your fingers or a spoon. Add more custard slowly until the cups are filled. Let stand for 10 minutes so the bread can absorb the custard.

5] Sprinkle the granulated sugar over the tops of the puddings. Place the ramekins in a large roasting pan. Fill the pan with enough warm water to come halfway up the sides of the ramekins. Bake for 20 to 25 minutes, or until a knife inserted near the center of a pudding comes out clean and the tops are puffed and golden. Remove the puddings to a rack to cool.

SERVING. These can be served warm, after cooling for about 20 minutes, at room temperature, or chilled; each has its admirers, although for comfort, nothing beats warm. These need no adornment; just put the little cups on a saucer and serve with a spoon.

STORING. Puddings will keep in the refrigerator overnight covered with plastic wrap.

BEST MATCH. Infusing the milk in this pudding with allspice guarantees that tea is the right beverage.

❀┃ **PLAYING AROUND.** (Apricot-Ginger Bread Pudding Cups) Other fruit and spice combinations can be used successfully with this method of making bread pudding. A favorite of mine is apricots and ginger. Replace the allspice with 8 slices of peeled, fresh ginger, each the size of a quarter, and substitute an equal amount of plump dried apricots for the pitted prunes.

Summer Pandowdy

A pandowdy is a truly American dessert, a sweet from the time of Johnny Appleseed. Traditionally made with apples, a pandowdy consists of sliced fruit topped with a rolled-out biscuit crust. (A cobbler is similar but its crust is usually dropped by spoonfuls on top of the fruit.) It is baked until brown and bubbly and served, while still warm, by breaking the crust with a spoon, placing it upside-down in bowls and topping it with the cooked fruit and syrup. The origin of the name is obscured but many believe it has to do with the dessert's homey, if not downright dowdy, look and the habit of making it in a cast iron frying pan. This is a warm weather version and one that, in addition to its luscious, lightly spiced fruit and soft, cream-biscuit top, has a lot going for it in the looks department.
§ *Makes 6 to 8 Servings*

THE FRUIT

1½ lb. (about 12 small) fresh, ripe apricots, stoned and quartered (or an equal weight of nectarines, stoned and cut into eighths)
1 pt. fresh blueberries
½ c. packed light brown sugar
½ tsp. ground cinnamon
Grated zest from half a lemon
1½ tsp. fresh lemon juice
1 tbsp. cold unsalted butter, cut into slivers

THE CRUST

2 c. all-purpose flour
3 tbsp. sugar
1 tbsp. baking powder
5 tbsp. cold unsalted butter, cut into bits
¾ c. heavy cream
1 tbsp. heavy cream
1 tsp. sugar

1] THE FRUIT. Butter a deep-dish pie pan or an 8-inch square baking dish (a glass, ceramic, or enamel pan has just the right look for this sweet); set aside. In a large bowl, gently stir together the fruit, sugar, cinnamon, lemon zest, and juice. Turn this into the prepared pan. Scatter the butter over the fruit. Position a rack in the center of the oven and preheat the oven to 425°.

2] THE CRUST. Place the flour, 3 tablespoons sugar, and the baking powder in a large mixing bowl. Whisk to combine. Work the bits of butter into the flour with your fingertips or a pastry blender until the mixture resembles coarse meal. Add the ¾ cup cream and stir with a fork. The mixture will be stringy. Knead gently for about 45 seconds and it will become smooth.

3] Roll the dough out on a lightly floured surface until it is about ¼ inch thick. Trim it to about ½ inch larger all around than the top of your baking dish. Cut a small circle out of the center of the crust to serve as a steam vent, and carefully place the crust over the fruit. (It's easy to put the crust on the fruit if you lift it with 2 wide metal spatulas.) Do not press the crust against the edges of the pan. Gather the scraps, re-roll them to a thickness of ⅛ inch, and cut out decorations. (This is optional, but nice. Geometric shapes are easy, attractive decorations. If you have broader artistic talents, you may want to create trees, fruits, or a still life. The dough is very malleable and fun to work with. Just keep the decorations thin, because the baking powder will give them a good rise in the oven.) Brush the decorations with water and "glue" them onto the top of the pandowdy. Brush the crust and decorations with the remaining tablespoon of cream and sprinkle with the teaspoon of sugar.

4] Place the pandowdy on a baking sheet with raised sides and bake for 10 minutes. *Lower the oven temperature to 350°* and cover the crust with a foil tent, shiny side out. (Just lay the tent over the crust, leaving space between the center of the crust and the peak of the tent. It should be loose, so don't tuck it in anywhere.) Continue baking, 35 to 45 minutes longer, until the crust is golden and the fruit bubbly. Remove from the oven and cool on a rack.

SERVING. The pandowdy is at its best after it has cooled on the rack for 15 minutes, but it's still awfully good at room temperature. I like my pandowdy plain and dowdy, served crust down and eaten with a spoon, but it's swell with a scoop of vanilla or cinnamon (page 143) ice cream melting over the fruit.

STORING. This should be eaten the day it's made; the closer to the time you take it from the oven, the better.

BEST MATCH. Serve Summer Pandowdy with tall glasses of minted iced tea.

❀| **PLAYING AROUND.** (Apple Pandowdy) Return to tradition and make an Apple Pandowdy: Use 3 pounds of tart, crisp apples instead of apricots and berries.

Vanilla or cinnamon ice cream, optional

Raspberry Peach en Papillote

Few things are as soothing as warm baked fruit and perhaps nothing is easier than this recipe in which the fruit is baked in its own little pouch. I've written this recipe for baking in a "papillote," or folded package, made of aluminum foil. Traditionally, a papillote is made from a roughly heart-shaped piece of parchment paper. If you're accustomed to using parchment, use it for this dessert. I've suggested foil because it's easier to handle and much more likely to be stocked in the cupboard, a plus for this dessert because I think you'll want to make it often and frequently on the spur of the moment. The recipe multiplies by any number and can be prepared hours ahead of time, stored in the refrigerator, and put in the oven just 12 minutes before you're ready to serve. § Makes 1 Serving

½ **ripe, firm peach, peeled and stoned**

½ **tsp. cold unsalted butter**

½ **tsp. best-quality raspberry jam, with or without seeds**

1½ **tsp. cold unsalted butter, cut in slivers**

1½ **tsp. best-quality raspberry jam, with or without seeds**

3 **fresh raspberries, optional**

1 **tsp. Grand Marnier or Framboise (raspberry *eau-de-vie*)**

Vanilla ice cream, optional

1] Position a rack in the center of the oven and preheat the oven to 350°. Cut a 10-inch circle of aluminum foil. Fold the circle in half, shiny side in, then open it flat. This is to mark the center line.

2] Cut the peach crosswise into ¼-inch-thick slices, keeping the shape of the fruit intact. Hold the foil circle so the fold line is perpendicular to you. Place the ½ teaspoon of butter and the ½ teaspoon of jam close to the center of the fold on the right side. Lift the peach on a knife to keep its shape and place it lengthwise on top of the jam. Press gently against the fruit with your palm to fan it slightly. Top with the slivers of butter, the rest of the jam, and the berries, if you are using them.

3] Fold the left half of the foil circle over the right. Roll the edges of the bottom half of the foil over the top edge. Seal all of the packet but a 1-inch opening. Pour in the liqueur and seal the opening. Roll up the edges one more time to get a tight seal, crimping about ¼ inch of the edge. *(The packet can be made and refrigerated several hours ahead.)* Bake on a baking sheet for 8 to 10 minutes, or until the packet is well-puffed. Bake an additional 2 minutes if the packet has been chilled.

SERVING. Serve the papillote immediately, either placing the packet on a plate and cutting it open at the table or opening the packet in the kitchen, lifting out the fruit and pouring over the aromatic baking syrup. It almost goes without saying that the fruit and syrup are fabulous over vanilla ice cream.

STORING. Once baked, the dessert must be served immediately. However, the little packages can be prepared and refrigerated up to 6 hours ahead of time.

BEST MATCH. I think a double espresso is just right with this fragrant sweet, but you can offer a not-too-spicy citrus tea or a berry tea, such as raspberry or black currant.

☀| PLAYING AROUND. (Pear, Nectarine, or Pineapple en Papillote) Following the same procedure, substitute a peeled and cored pear half or half of an unpeeled nectarine for the peach. Both taste good with raspberry jam and Grand Marnier or Framboise. For a very different taste, substitute 5 thin pieces of fresh, ripe pineapple for the peach, brown sugar for the raspberry jam, and kirsch or dark rum for the liqueur; omit the fresh raspberries.

Sweet Plums with Tart Cream

This is a very simple dessert, nothing more than fruit with a sprinkling of sugar and a spoonful of cream, but it is deeply satisfying, offering the additional appeal of an aromatic kitchen—as the fruit juices start to bubble they release a *welcoming sweet, spicy scent. Serve this dessert when the last of the Italian prune plums are at the market and the weather has just turned chilly. § Makes 4 to 6 Servings*

THE FRUIT
2 lb. purple Italian prune plums, cut in half lengthwise and stoned
¼ c. packed light brown sugar
¼ c. granulated sugar
½ tsp. ground cinnamon
⅛ tsp. ground cloves

THE CREAM
½ c. sour cream
1 tbsp. sugar
½ c. heavy cream, chilled

1] THE FRUIT. Place a rack in the center of the oven and preheat the oven to 350°. Butter a 9-inch pie pan, preferably glass because it's nice to be able see the fruit juices. Starting at the outer edge of the pie plate, make a circle of plum halves, skin side facing the edge of the pan. Continue to make concentric circles with the fruit, pushing the fruit in one circle against the fruit in the preceding circle so the rings are compact and the fruit is standing almost upright. Fill the small center space with one or two halves. Mix the sugars and spices together in a small bowl and sprinkle evenly over the fruit. Place the pie pan on a baking sheet and bake for 40 to 50 minutes, or until the fruit can be pierced easily with a knife and the juices are bubbling. Remove the pan from the oven and place on a rack.

2] THE CREAM. By hand, whisk the sour cream and sugar together in a medium bowl. Whip the heavy cream with a mixer just until it holds soft peaks. Stir a spoonful of whipped cream into the sour cream, then fold the rest in gently with a spatula. (*The cream can be made earlier in the day and kept refrigerated until serving time.*)

SERVING. The perfect time for serving this sweet is 15 minutes after the fruit has come from the oven. The plums will still be warm enough to melt the cream slightly and I think this is most appealing. But this is a dessert that can be served at room temperature or even chilled. Bring the plums to the table in the pie pan and spoon generous servings into dessert bowls or plates.

STORING. Wrapped with plastic, the fruit will keep in the refrigerator for 2 days. The cream will keep, in an airtight container, for 1 day.

BEST MATCH. These warm plums need nothing more than a cup of strong coffee, served sweet and black.

❀| **PLAYING AROUND.** (Fruit Variations) The technique of packing fruit in concentric circles and sprinkling them with lightly spiced sugar before baking works well for other soft fruits, such as apricots and nectarines. You can use peaches; just blanch and peel them before baking.

Pear-Cranberry Crisp

The key to a great crisp is a crunchy topping. Mine gets its toothsome texture from whole wheat flour, shredded coconut, brown sugar, and chopped walnuts. This combination works with almost any fruit you put under it. Once you've added it to your repertoire you can mix, match, and play favorites. § Makes 6 to 8 Servings

THE TOPPING

½ c. all-purpose flour
¼ c. whole wheat flour
½ c. packed light brown sugar
½ c. shredded unsweetened
    coconut
¾ c. walnuts
1¼ tsp. ground cinnamon
Grated zest of 1 orange
½ c. (1 stick) cold unsalted
    butter, cut into 3 pieces

THE FRUIT

3 lb. (about 6 large) ripe Bartlett
    or Anjou pears, peeled and
    cored
2 tbsp. fresh orange juice
1 c. cranberries, fresh or frozen
    (not thawed)
⅓ c. sugar

Ice cream or sweetened whipped
    cream, optional

1] **THE TOPPING.** Place all the ingredients in a food processor and pulse until the mixture forms large curds, about 1 to 2 minutes. Leave the topping in the work bowl until you're ready for it. (*The topping can be made up to 3 days ahead and refrigerated in an airtight plastic bag.*)

2] **THE FRUIT.** Place a rack in the center of the oven and preheat the oven to 375°. Have ready a deep-dish pie pan or a 2-quart porcelain souffle mold. Quarter the pears and cut each pear quarter lengthwise into 3 slices and place in a large bowl with the orange juice. As you add more slices, toss to coat the fruit with juice. (The juice will keep the fruit from darkening.) Add the cranberries and sugar and stir to mix well.

3] Turn the fruit into the pie pan. Sprinkle the topping evenly over the fruit, pressing down gently if needed so the crumbs don't fall off the fruit at the edge of the pan. Place the crisp on a baking sheet with raised sides and bake 40 to 45 minutes, until the top is brown and the fruit juices are bubbling. Remove the crisp from the oven and place on a cooling rack.

SERVING. Let the crisp cool on the rack for at least 20 minutes before serving. Crisps are also good at room temperature or chilled. Serve the crisp directly from the pan, spooning portions into dessert bowls. You can serve this with ice cream or lightly sweetened whipped cream, but both the flavor and texture can stand on their own.

STORING. The crisp will keep, covered, in the refrigerator for 2 days.

BEST MATCH. If the crisp is warm, serve hot coffee; if it's chilled, very cold milk. Cider, hot or cold, is another good choice.

❀| **PLAYING AROUND.** (Pineapple-Banana Crisp) While you're bound to come up with fruit combinations that will become personal classics, this is an exotic duo I adore: Omit the orange zest in the topping. Cut 6 bananas into ¼-inch rounds and cut 1 small pineapple (about 1¾ pounds) into very thin pieces (approximately 2 cups). Omit the orange juice and substitute ¼ cup maple syrup for the sugar.

Honey-Yogurt Mousse

This mousse has a mellow flavor and a very creamy texture. The recipe retains the warmth of honey and cuts its often overpowering sweetness with a hefty dose of plain yogurt. You can make *this with excellent results using supermarket-brand honey rounded with vanilla extract or you can experiment with more exotic honeys, such as chestnut or lavender. § Makes 6 to 8 Servings*

¼ c. cold water
1 pkg. unflavored gelatin
2½ c. plain yogurt, at room temperature
1 c. honey
1½ tsp. pure vanilla extract (needed if supermarket-type honey is used)
1 c. heavy cream, chilled
6 to 8 tsp. Brickle (candied almond pieces available in supermarkets) or toasted chopped almonds, optional

1] Pour the water into a small saucepan and sprinkle in the gelatin. Allow the gelatin to soften for 5 minutes. Place the pan over gentle heat and warm, stirring constantly, just until the gelatin melts, about 1 to 2 minutes. Remove from heat and reserve.

2] By hand, whisk the yogurt, honey, and vanilla together in a large bowl. Gradually whisk in the gelatin, stirring constantly so you don't get strings of gelatin. Whip the heavy cream until it holds soft peaks. Gently whisk it into the honey mixture. Spoon half of the mousse into 6 to 8 wine glasses or ramekins and dust with a teaspoon of Brickle or nuts if desired; cover with the remaining mousse. Chill until set, about 3 hours.

SERVING. The mousse can be served as soon as it chills and sets. Its comfort comes from its texture and simplicity, so serve it plain.

STORING. The mousse will keep covered in the refrigerator for 2 days.

BEST MATCH. First choice would be hot tea, but black coffee would offset the flavors of this mousse nicely.

❀| **PLAYING AROUND.** (Almond-Crusted Honey-Yogurt Mousse Tart) This mousse makes a good tart piled into a toasted almond crust (page 150) and an even better tart coupled with a layer of chocolate truffle cream (page 186).

Slippery Slidey Lemon-Clove Cup Custard

Cup custard is one of the all-time great nursery sweets, soft and slippery, sliding with a slither down your throat, soothing, warm, and comforting yet cool and sleek. The custard I've created maintains all the slip and slide we fell in love with in childhood but comes in a sharp, citrusy flavor made for adults.
§ Makes 4 Servings

2 lemons
3 whole cloves
1¾ c. milk
3 large eggs
½ c. sugar
¼ tsp. pure lemon extract

1] Cut the zest from the lemon in long strips, avoiding the white pith. Reserve the lemons for another use. Place the zest, cloves, and milk in a medium saucepan and bring the milk just to the boil. Remove from the heat, cover the pot, and allow the mixture to steep for 15 minutes.

2] While the milk is steeping, place a rack in the center of the oven and preheat the oven to 325°. Butter four 6-ounce custard cups; set aside. Set aside a roasting pan that is large enough to hold the custard cups.

3] In a medium-size mixing bowl, working by hand or with a mixer, whisk together the eggs and sugar until the sugar dissolves and the mixture turns pale. Strain the steeped milk, discarding the zest and cloves, and gradually stir it into the bowl; stir with a wooden spoon and try not to create too much foam. Stir in the lemon extract.

4] Strain the custard into a pitcher for easy pouring. Divide the custard evenly among the cups and skim off any large bubbles that appear on the surface. Place the cups in the roasting pan and fill the pan with warm water to come halfway up the sides of the cups. Bake the custards 40 to 45 minutes; they'll still jiggle when shaken lightly. Remove the custards to a rack to cool to room temperature. Chill, covered with plastic wrap, for at least 2 hours before serving.

SERVING. Serve the custards in the cups or unmold onto small plates by running a knife around the edge of the cup to break the seal.

STORING. Covered, cup custard will keep in the refrigerator for 2 days, but it's best served fresh, when the lemon flavor, which diminishes quickly, is sharpest.

BEST MATCH. Tea is the beverage that should keep company with custard, and Constant Comment, a spice tea, is the nicest with Lemon-Clove Cup Custard.

✿| **PLAYING AROUND.** (Vanilla-Ginger and Espresso-Cinnamon Cup Custard) The technique of infusing milk with flavoring lends itself to many variations. For a vanilla custard with the zing of ginger, omit the lemon and cloves and add to the milk the pod and pulp of a split and scraped vanilla bean and 3 slices of peeled fresh ginger, each the size of a quarter. Boil and steep as in the Lemon-Clove recipe. For an Espresso-Cinnamon Custard (a love-at-first-slippery-spoonful flavor), omit the lemon and cloves and boil and steep the milk with a 3-inch piece of stick cinnamon. Add 2 teaspoons of instant espresso powder to the egg-sugar mixture. As you'd expect, this custard cries out for an accompanying cup of brewed espresso.

Outrageous Rice Pudding

Soft, creamy, and soothing, rice pudding is a baby food you never outgrow. This version, easily made on the top of the stove, has all the comforts *of a childhood pudding, and all the flavor, depth, and richness of a grown-up indulgence.*
§ Makes 4 to 6 Servings

⅓ c. long-grain white rice (not converted)

3 c. milk

¼ c. sugar

1 vanilla bean or 1½ tsp. pure vanilla extract

1 tbsp. Grand Marnier or other orange liqueur

⅓ c. heavy cream, chilled

Cinnamon and freshly grated nutmeg, optional

1] Place the rice in a medium saucepan and cover with cold water. Bring to the boil and boil 1 minute. Drain the rice and rinse with cold water. Put the milk and sugar in the saucepan. Split the vanilla bean lengthwise and scrape the seeds into the pot. (If you're using vanilla extract, wait—you'll add it later.) Add the vanilla bean and rice and bring to the boil over medium-high heat, stirring occasionally to dissolve the sugar. Lower the heat so the mixture simmers very gently. Cook at the simmer, stirring frequently, until the mixture thickens and just a thin film of milk floats over the rice kernels, about 35 to 40 minutes. Remove from heat and discard the vanilla bean.

2] Add the vanilla extract, if you're using it, and the orange liqueur. Scrape the pudding into a bowl. Place a piece of plastic wrap directly against the top of the pudding and cool to room temperature. Chill in the refrigerator for at least 2 hours. When the pudding is very cold, whip the heavy cream until it holds firm peaks. Fold the cream into the pudding.

SERVING. The pudding is ready to serve as soon as the whipped cream is added, or it can be covered and refrigerated until needed. For tradition's sake, individual servings of pudding can be sprinkled with cinnamon and a scraping of fresh nutmeg.

STORING. The pudding will keep covered in the refrigerator for 2 days.

BEST MATCH. Hot tea with milk and honey, light coffee with cream, or even steamed, sweetened milk make cozy companions to rice pudding.

❀| PLAYING AROUND. (Rice Pudding Ring with Berry Sauce) Give the rice pudding a dressy look by making it in a ring mold. When the pudding has cooled to room temperature, soften 1½ teaspoons (½ package) of unflavored gelatin in a small saucepan with 2 tablespoons of cold water. Place the saucepan over low heat and allow the gelatin to dissolve. Thoroughly mix the gelatin into the pudding. Whip ½ cup of heavy cream until it holds firm peaks and fold it into the pudding. Spray a 3-cup ring mold with PAM. Pack the rice into the mold and tap the mold sharply once against the counter to settle the pudding. Chill the pudding, covered with

Comfort on a Spoon

plastic, for at least 2 hours. *(The pudding can rest overnight if necessary.)* Unmold onto a serving platter by running a blunt knife around the mold and then dipping the mold briefly into hot water; about 15 to 20 seconds should do it. The pudding can be served as is, or you can fill the center of the mold with fresh, assorted berries and pass a berry sauce (page 201).

Thoroughly Modern Betty

This is a lively version of an old American dessert, the apple brown betty. Betties, usually made with stale bread crumbs and little or no flavoring, were economical sweets for farmers and pioneers. This rendition uses rich bread, brioche or challah, juicy pears, and sharp ginger, both fresh and ground. It's packed into a charlotte mold, chilled overnight, and turned out after it's baked. It's a crusty pudding with a punchy flavor. § Makes 6 Servings

10 tbsp. (1¼ sticks) unsalted butter

5 slices peeled fresh ginger, each the size of a dime

1 lb. (1 loaf) unsliced brioche or challah, crust removed, cut coarsely into cubes to make about 5 cups

⅓ c. sugar

2 tsp. ground ginger

4 ripe pears, such as Bartlett or Anjou, peeled and cored

1] Generously butter a 6-cup charlotte mold or soufflé dish. Line the bottom of the mold with a round of waxed or parchment paper, butter the paper, and set aside. Place the butter and fresh ginger in a saucepan and heat until the butter is melted; or you can do this in a microwave. Remove from the heat, cover, and steep for 10 minutes.

2] Place the bread in a mixing bowl. Remove the ginger from the butter and discard. Drizzle the melted butter over the bread, tossing with a fork so the cubes are moistened evenly.

3] In another bowl, combine the sugar and ground ginger. Cut the pears in half lengthwise and then crosswise into thin slices. Add the pears to the sugar and toss to coat evenly.

4] Place one-quarter of the bread cubes in the bottom of the mold, covering the base with an even layer. Distribute one-third of the pear slices over the bread. Repeat this layering two more times, and end with a layer of bread. Cover the mold with aluminum foil, fit a plate, or a piece of cardboard cut to size, inside the mold, and weight with a 2-pound can. Refrigerate, weighted, overnight.

5] Center a rack in the oven and preheat the oven to 375°. Remove the weight and plate or cardboard from the mold and bake, still covered with foil, for 25 minutes. Remove the foil and bake until the top is browned, about 30 minutes longer. Transfer to a rack and let the mold rest for 5 minutes.

SERVING. Run a knife around the sides of the charlotte mold to loosen the betty. Invert onto a serving platter and peel off the paper. Cut the betty into servings at the table and accompany with crème fraîche, whipped cream, or ice cream.

STORING. This betty is at its best just minutes after it comes from the oven. Leftovers can be nibbled at room temperature or reheated, but they won't have the same soft warmth as the freshly baked betty.

Crème fraîche, whipped cream, or vanilla ice cream

Comfort on a Spoon

BEST MATCH. The look and texture of this dessert are made for tea, but its flavor comes alive served with a full-bodied, black coffee.

❀| PLAYING AROUND. (Old-Fashioned Apple Brown Betty) Thoroughly Modern Betty is, of course, a twist itself, so you easily can go back to an Old-Fashioned Apple Brown Betty by substituting apples (preferably Staymans or Jonathans) for the pears. You'll find that apple and ginger are a great combination. But without the ginger, the dessert is also a marvelous vehicle for plump, steeped dried fruits. Try prunes steeped in tea or watered-down Armagnac (following the directions in the recipe for Quick Prune Pithiviers, page 166), or give Calimyrna figs the same treatment, using port instead of Armagnac. The technique for making this betty, and the results, are so wonderful they'll inspire variations.

ICE CREAM FOR ADULTS

Tangy Pear Mascarpone Sherbet
(Chocolate-Flecked Pear Mascarpone Sherbet)

Eggnog-Pumpkin Ice Cream
(Frozen Eggnog-Pumpkin Pie)

Ginger-Lemonade Sorbet
(Sorbet and Lemonade)

Cinnamon Ice Cream with Old-Time Creamery Hot Fudge
(Ice Cream Parlor Banana Split)

Deepest Darkest Double Chocolate Sorbet
(Custard Sauce)

Cardamom-Orange Ice Cream
(Cardamom-Orange Ice Cream in Orange Shells)

Raspberry Chocolate Truffle Ice Cream Cake
(Flavor Variations)

Coffee—Almond Crunch Tart
(Coffee—Hazelnut Crunch Tart)

Peanut Butter Fudge Ice Cream Sandwiches
(Peanut Butter—Coffee Ice Cream Sandwiches)

Tropical Freeze
(Chocolate-Banana—Filled Freeze)

ere's a collection of ice creams, sorbets, sherbets, and stunning ice cream cakes and pies in flavors and shapes never dreamed of by the Good Humor man. They're frozen fantasies for grown-up celebrations. There are two kinds of desserts in this chapter: ice creams and such to make from scratch, and cakes, tarts, pies, and sandwiches that you make by transforming storebought ice cream. Both are sensational.

The made-from-scratch ice creams, sorbets, and sherbets are wild and wonderful flavors, combinations such as pear-mascarpone, eggnog-pumpkin, or ginger-lemonade that take ice cream to another level. A scoop, solo, with a small cookie or, depending on the flavor, a ribbon of Old-Time Creamery Hot Fudge is a pleaser in any season and guaranteed to be an adult's idea of heaven. (Kids might feel this way about the Cinnamon Ice Cream, especially if you turn it into an Ice Cream Parlor Banana Split, so be prepared to share.)

The gorgeous Raspberry Chocolate Truffle Ice Cream Cake, Coffee–Almond Crunch Tart, Peanut Butter Fudge Ice Cream Sandwiches, and Tropical Freeze, a banana, rum, and coconut ice cream pie that tastes like a vacation, are ready-made parties just waiting in your freezer. Serve any of these to sophisticated adults and watch them dig in like kids.

Ice Cream for Adults

Tangy Pear Mascarpone Sherbet

Mascarpone is an outrageously rich, extra-creamy, mild, unprocessed cheese. Its texture is luxurious, a bit like thickened crème fraîche or satiny, beaten cream cheese. You can find it in specialty shops and Italian groceries, where it is dipped from large containers like ice cream. Buy it fresh and use it the same day to make this soft white, subtly pear-flavored, one-of-a-kind sherbet that gets its tang from fresh buttermilk.
§ Makes About 1 Quart

1¾ c. water
¾ c. sugar
2 tbsp. fresh lemon juice
1½ lb. (2 to 3) very ripe, fragrant
    Bartlett or Comice pears
¾ c. mascarpone
1 c. buttermilk

1] Mix the water, sugar, and lemon juice together in a nonreactive saucepan. Peel, core, and coarsely dice the pears and add them to the pan. Place the saucepan over medium heat and bring to a boil, stirring until the sugar is dissolved. Lower the heat and simmer steadily for 10 minutes. Remove the pan from the heat and cool to room temperature.

2] Puree the pears with some of their cooking syrup in a blender (which does a good job here) or food processor. Add the rest of the syrup and the remaining ingredients. Blend until perfectly smooth.

3] Turn the mixture into an ice cream maker and freeze according to the manufacturer's instructions. The finished sherbet will be slightly slushy and too soft to serve immediately; it needs to ripen in the freezer about 2 hours before you can use it.

SERVING. Scoop the sherbet into ice cream coupes or even martini glasses. Because there's not much sugar in this sherbet, it tends to become quite hard. Allow it to rest in the refrigerator 10 to 15 minutes, or blend it in a food processor for about 30 seconds, before serving.

STORING. Mascarpone Sherbet can be kept for 4 days in a tightly sealed container in the freezer.

BEST MATCH. While the sherbet is fine alone, it goes very well with a small cookie, such as a Flaky Cinnamon Twist (page 101) or Cocoa Snap (page 80), or a few Chocolate Truffles (page 172).

❀| **PLAYING AROUND.** (Chocolate-Flecked Pear Marscapone Sherbet) To add another dimension to this sophisticated sweet, finely grate (or grind in a food processor) 4 ounces of high-quality bittersweet chocolate. Add to the ice cream maker during the last 2 to 3 minutes of churning.

Eggnog-Pumpkin Ice Cream

This ice cream is like a frozen, crustless pumpkin pie. In fact, it was inspired by cookbook author Mildred Knopf's Holiday Pie, a creamy concoction based on storebought eggnog. While I rarely use prepared products, this is a case in which a convenience becomes a sensation.
§ Makes 1½ Quarts

1 qt. prepared eggnog (I use Borden's)
5 egg yolks
1 c. sugar
2 tbsp. molasses
1½ tsp. ground cinnamon
1 tsp. ground ginger
½ tsp. freshly grated or ground nutmeg
1½ tsp. pure vanilla extract
3 tbsp. brandy
2 c. (15-oz. can) pumpkin puree

1] Pour the eggnog into a medium saucepan and bring to a boil. The eggnog bubbles up, so keep an eye on it. While the eggnog is heating, beat the egg yolks and sugar together until they thicken and turn pale. Very gradually, pour the eggnog into the yolk mixture, whisking without stopping. Pour the mixture back into the saucepan and cook, stirring constantly, over medium heat until it thickens slightly, about 2 minutes. Strain the custard into a clean bowl.

2] Add the remaining ingredients to the custard, whisking gently to combine. The custard should cool before you put it into the ice cream maker. You can either place the bowl in a larger bowl filled with ice cubes and stir until cool or, if you're not in a hurry, just stir the custard now and then until it reaches room temperature. *(This base can be made up to 2 days ahead and kept refrigerated before freezing.)* Freeze the custard in an ice cream maker following the manufacturer's instructions. Transfer the ice cream to a freezer-proof container and ripen in the freezer before serving.

SERVING. Serve this extra-creamy ice cream after it has ripened in the freezer for 2 to 3 hours. If it is hard to scoop, allow it to rest in the refrigerator for 10 minutes before serving.

STORING. Eggnog-Pumpkin Ice Cream will keep in the freezer for 2 weeks.

BEST MATCH. Just like pumpkin pie, this is good with espresso or tea. For a double dose of holiday spirit, top Chocolate Pecan Tart (page 214) with a scoop of this ice cream.

❁| PLAYING AROUND. (Frozen Eggnog-Pumpkin Pie) Make this if you're not absolutely bound to tradition. Pack some of this ice cream into a nutty crust (page 150), freeze, top with whipped cream right before serving, and gobble it up after the turkey on Thanksgiving or Christmas.

Ginger-Lemonade Sorbet

Not for anyone with timid taste buds, this is a zesty, sharply flavored sorbet. In fact, sorbet sounds too polite for the assertive tastes we're talking about here. The mix of ginger, lemon, and fresh mint is bright, spicy, and very refreshing. This is the right stuff for the end of a heavy meal or when the weather is hot and humid and you're desperate for something super-cool. Unlike many other sorbets, this one keeps its soft, creamy texture for days in the freezer, so it's easy to keep some around. § Makes 1 Pint

1½ c. sugar

1½ c. water

2 oz. fresh ginger, peeled and finely minced (you can do this easily in a food processor) to make ¼ cup

2 tbsp. loosely packed fresh mint leaves

2 lemons, halved

1] Pour the water and sugar into a medium saucepan. Stir over medium heat until the sugar dissolves, then bring the mixture to the boil. Remove the pot from the heat. Add the ginger and mint leaves. Squeeze the juice from the lemons into the mixture and add the lemon halves to the pot. Cover and steep for 1 hour.

2] Pour the mixture through a strainer lined with cheesecloth, pressing against the solids to release the liquids. Freeze in an ice cream maker according to the manufacturer's instructions. (I find this mixture takes longer than others to freeze.) Pack in a freezer-proof container and freeze to firm.

SERVING. This sorbet is ready to scoop after about 2 hours in the freezer. If it becomes too hard to scoop, whirl it in a food processor to soften. Serve this potent sorbet in very small portions.

STORING. This will keep for about 2 weeks in the freezer.

BEST MATCH. Because the flavors of Ginger-Lemonade Sorbet are so strong, it's best served solo.

❀| PLAYING AROUND. (Sorbet and Lemonade) On the hottest day of summer, drop a scoop of Ginger-Lemonade Sorbet into a tall, frosty glass of fresh lemonade. Top with a mint leaf and cool out.

Cinnamon Ice Cream with Old-Time Creamery Hot Fudge

Ice cream's my greatest weakness and cinnamon and chocolate is my favorite combination, so these recipes get a workout in my house. The quick-to-make Hot Fudge, which is not very sweet and doesn't harden and tug at your teeth the moment it hits ice cream, is rich, glossy, and loaded with childhood memories of sundaes eaten on swiveling ice cream parlor stools. It pours out in thick ribbons over the cinnamon-spotted ice cream. Together these are perfect, but the ice cream and fudge are such good mixers it's nice to have them on hand to accompany other desserts. § Makes 1 Quart of Ice Cream, ½ Pint of Sauce

THE ICE CREAM

3 c. milk
1 c. heavy cream
6 egg yolks
1 c. sugar
1 tbsp. ground cinnamon
1 tsp. pure vanilla extract

THE SAUCE

3 oz. unsweetened chocolate
3 tbsp. unsalted butter
¼ c. cocoa, preferably a Dutch-processed brand, such as Droste or Poulain
1 tsp. instant coffee powder
¾ c. heavy cream
⅔ c. sugar
2 tbsp. light corn syrup
Pinch of salt
1 tsp. pure vanilla extract

2 tsp. coffee liqueur, such as Kahlúa, optional

1] THE ICE CREAM. Bring the milk and cream to a boil in a heavy-bottomed saucepan. Meanwhile, beat the egg yolks, sugar, and cinnamon together in a medium bowl until pale and thick.

2] While beating the yolk mixture constantly, gradually add the hot milk. Return the mixture to the saucepan and cook, stirring without stopping over medium heat, until the custard thickens, about 2 minutes. Strain into a clean bowl. Stir in the vanilla extract.

3] The custard should cool before you put it into the ice cream maker. You can either place the bowl in a larger bowl filled with ice cubes and stir until cool or, if time's not a problem, just stir the custard now and then until it reaches room temperature. *(This base can be made up to 2 days ahead and kept refrigerated before freezing.)* Freeze the custard in an ice cream maker following the manufacturer's instructions. Pack into a freezer-proof container and freeze to firm and ripen.

4] THE SAUCE. Melt the chocolate and butter in the top of a double boiler over hot water or in a bowl in a microwave. Remove from heat and blend in the cocoa and coffee powder; set aside.

5] Bring the cream, sugar, corn syrup, and salt to a rolling boil in a medium saucepan. Watch out—this will bubble up. Remove the pot from the heat and stir in the reserved chocolate mixture, the vanilla, and Kahlúa. Scrape the sauce into a bowl or jar. Serve after allowing the hot fudge to cool for 20 minutes, or place a piece of plastic wrap against the top of the sauce, cool to room temperature, and refrigerate.

SERVING. The ice cream is ready to scoop after ripening in the freezer for about 2 hours. To serve sauce that's been chilled, heat as much as you

Ice Cream for Adults

Whipped cream, optional

need in the top of a double boiler until warm and glossy or liquify it in a microwave, checking every 5 seconds. Scoop ice cream into coupes, drizzle over sauce, and, if you want, top with clouds of whipped cream.

STORING. The ice cream will keep in the freezer for 2 weeks. The sauce will keep in a tightly covered jar in the refrigerator for 2 months.

BEST MATCH. For something beyond heavenly, try Lucky Devil's Cake (page 99) with a scoop of Cinnamon Ice Cream and a hefty drizzle of Old-Time Creamery Hot Fudge. Add whipped cream only if you dare. Serve with milk or a dark-roasted coffee.

✺| **PLAYING AROUND.** (Ice Cream Parlor Banana Split) To whip up a split, cut a ripe banana in half lengthwise and lay it along the sides of a boat-shaped ice cream dish. Place 2 or 3 scoops of ice cream on top of the bananas. Now pour on some zigzags of Hot Fudge and a few spoonfuls of wet nuts (available in specialty stores). Pipe over broad ribbons of lightly sweetened whipped cream and decorate with good-quality chocolate sprinkles or jimmies (also available in specialty shops). Skip the cherry on top.

Deepest Darkest Double Chocolate Sorbet

This is sorbet that tastes as rich as ice cream. It's all that pure cocoa and best-quality bittersweet chocolate that does it. The color is the chocolate equivalent of black and the taste is truly chocolate—not sweet and very deep. I like this sorbet straight, but it's marvelous with a splash of liqueur. Try crème de menthe, anisette, or Grand Marnier. § Makes About 1 Quart

1 c. sugar

1 c. water

7 oz. high-quality bittersweet chocolate, such as Tobler or Lindt, coarsely chopped

¾ c. cocoa, preferably a Dutch-processed brand, such as Droste or Poulain

3½ c. water

3 to 4 tsp. liqueur, such as white crème de menthe, anisette, or Grand Marnier, optional

1] In a medium saucepan, stir together the sugar and water. Bring to a boil, stirring just to dissolve the sugar. When the syrup boils, remove the pot from the heat. Place the chopped chocolate in a large bowl and add some of the hot sugar syrup. Stir with a whisk. Gradually add the rest of the syrup, continuing to blend until smooth. Put the cocoa in the saucepan (there's no need to wash it) and mix in some of the water. Use the whisk to blend the water and cocoa to a smooth paste. Add the remainder of the water gradually and continue to whisk to blend. Combine the two mixtures and cool to room temperature.

2] Freeze the mixture in an ice cream maker, following the manufacturer's directions. If you want to add a bit of liqueur, pour it into the ice cream maker a minute or 2 before the sorbet is churned completely. Pack into a freezer-proof container and freeze to firm.

SERVING. Freeze for at least 2 hours before serving. Without the addition of liqueur, this sorbet has a tendency to freeze very hard. Allow it to soften at room temperature for a few minutes before serving or whirl it in a processor to restore its creaminess. Serve in scoops, with or without splashing liqueur over it.

STORING. This will keep in the freezer for 1 week.

BEST MATCH. I think this sorbet is best enjoyed on its own, followed by small cups of espresso with a spot of the flavoring liqueur mixed in.

❁| **PLAYING AROUND.** (Custard Sauce) Dress this elegant sorbet to the hilt by serving it with a Custard Sauce. Follow the recipe for Grand Marnier Custard Sauce (page 193), using the same liqueur in the sauce as you used in the sorbet. My choice here would be white crème de menthe—it's a flawless match with cocoa and bittersweet chocolate.

Cardamom-Orange Ice Cream

Cardamom is a flavor found frequently in Scandinavian foods, rarely in American. Too bad, because it's an appealing spice that manages to be both warm and cool. It has the warmth of cinnamon or nutmeg, and the light, refreshing edge of a more citrusy spice, such as ginger. This recipe gives free play to both sides of cardamom's personality. § Makes 1 Quart

1 orange
3 c. milk
1 c. heavy cream
16 cardamom pods
6 egg yolks
1 c. sugar
¾ tsp. pure vanilla extract

1] Using a small sharp knife, remove the zest from the orange in long strips. If necessary, cut away any white pith that remains on the zest. Reserve the oranges for another use. Place the zest in a heavy-bottomed saucepan and add the milk, cream, and cardamom pods. Bring to a boil over high heat. Remove the pan from the heat, cover, and let steep for 10 minutes.

2] Beat the egg yolks and sugar in a mixing bowl until pale and thick. Gradually add the hot milk (with the pods and zest) to the egg-sugar mixture, beating all the while. Return the custard to the saucepan and cook over moderate heat, stirring constantly, until the mixture thickens, about 2 minutes (or a bit longer if the milk has cooled). Remove from heat and stir in the vanilla. Strain the custard into a clean bowl, discarding the cardamom and zest.

3] The custard should cool before you put it into the ice cream maker. The fastest way to do this is to place the bowl in a larger bowl filled with ice cubes and stir until cool. You can also just stir the custard now and then until it reaches room temperature. *(This base can be made up to 2 days ahead and kept refrigerated before freezing.)* Freeze the custard in an ice cream maker following the manufacturer's instructions. Pack into a freezer-proof container and freeze to firm.

SERVING. The ice cream is ready to serve after it has firmed in the freezer for at least 2 hours. If the ice cream becomes too hard to scoop, soften in the refrigerator 10 minutes before serving or whirl in a food processor to restore its smooth texture. Scoop into coupes and serve plain.

STORING. The ice cream will keep in the freezer for 1 week.

BEST MATCH. This is lovely served with small cookies such as Pecan Flats (page 72), Orange Custard Bars (page 103), or Burnt Butter Baby Cakes (page 94). For a special occasion, serve with Chocolate Truffles (page 172).

❊⎜ **PLAYING AROUND.** (Cardamom-Orange Ice Cream in Orange Shells) For a somewhat old-fashioned presentation that's both elegant and easy, pack Cardamom-Orange Ice Cream into orange shells made by cutting off the top third of the oranges and scooping out the fruit, leaving a natural serving bowl; save the top slice. Fill with ice cream, freeze, and serve on small dessert plates with the reserved top slice of orange placed on the ice cream at an angle, like a jaunty beret.

Raspberry Chocolate Truffle Ice Cream Cake

This is a knockout. It is spectacularly beautiful, with stunning bands of raspberry pink and chocolate brown, and devastatingly delicious. While it looks like something bought at the fanciest shop, it's quite simple to make—it just takes some time. You've got to freeze each layer as you go along, so make it when you plan to be around the house. (Of course, once made, it can stay in the freezer for a month.) For this recipe, I turn vanilla ice cream into raspberry with the addition of fruit and eau-de-vie. If you've got a favorite ready-made raspberry ice cream, use it. § Makes 8 Servings

14 tbsp. (1¾ sticks) unsalted butter, cut into chunks
9 oz. high-quality bittersweet chocolate, such as Lindt or Tobler, broken into pieces
½ c. sugar
8 large eggs
1 pkg. (10 oz.) frozen red raspberries in syrup, thawed
2 tsp. Framboise (raspberry *eau-de-vie*), optional
2 pts. premium vanilla ice cream (I use Häagen-Dazs)

1] Lightly oil an 8- or 8½-inch springform pan. Place the bowl and beaters (or paddle attachment) of an electric mixer in the freezer to chill for at least 30 minutes.

2] Melt the butter and chocolate in the top of a double boiler over hot water, stirring frequently, or in a bowl in a microwave. Remove from heat and whisk in the sugar. Let the mixture stand, stirring occasionally, until the sugar is completely dissolved, about 5 minutes. Whisk in the eggs, one at a time. Pour one-third of this chocolate truffle mixture into the prepared pan and freeze for at least 30 minutes. Cover the remaining truffle cream with plastic wrap and set aside at room temperature.

3] Puree the raspberries in a food processor or blender. Add the Framboise, if desired, and pulse to mix. Place the vanilla ice cream in the chilled bowl and beat until softened, about 20 seconds. Add the raspberry puree and continue to beat until the mixture is just blended. Spread half of the ice cream over the frozen chocolate layer and freeze for at least 15 minutes. Return the bowl, beaters, and remaining ice cream to the freezer.

4] Pour half of the remaining chocolate mixture over the frozen ice cream layer and freeze for another 30 minutes. Beat the remaining ice cream to resoften, if necessary, and spread it over the frozen chocolate. Freeze for 15 minutes. Pour the last of the truffle cream over the top of the cake. Cover with plastic wrap, taking care not to touch the chocolate, and freeze for at least 6 hours.

SERVING. About 20 minutes before serving time, unmold the cake. Soak a kitchen towel in hot water and wrap it around the sides of the springform pan for a minute. Remove the sides of the pan and refrigerate the cake, still on the springform bottom, for 15 minutes before slicing.

STORING. Wrapped in a double thickness of plastic and foil, this cake will keep for 1 month in the freezer.

BEST MATCH. Serve this with espresso in your finest cups.

❁| PLAYING AROUND. (Flavor Variations) This technique and the suave chocolate truffle cream lend themselves to many variations. If raspberry's not your first-choice flavor, substitute coffee, vanilla, or butter pecan. Anything that goes well with chocolate (and looks good with chocolate's dark color) is fine.

Coffee–Almond Crunch Tart

The crunch in this tart comes from the crust, an almond-nutmeg mixture that's pressed into a fluted tart pan. It's just the right mate for an ice cream dessert because its flavor holds up in the freezer. It's also just the right mate to the smooth texture and flavor of the coffee-almond ice cream. Again, this is a made-up flavor, concocted from ground almonds and storebought coffee ice cream. § Makes 8 to 10 Servings

2 c. (8 oz.) blanched almonds (1 cup is used for the ice cream filling)

THE CRUST
¾ c. all-purpose flour

¼ c. sugar

½ tsp. freshly grated or ground nutmeg

¼ c. (½ stick) cold unsalted butter, cut into pieces

1 large egg

¼ tsp. almond extract

2 oz. semisweet chocolate, finely chopped (you can do this in a food processor)

THE FILLING
2 pts. premium coffee ice cream (I use Häagen-Dazs)

1 tbsp. Amaretto or other almond liqueur

2 oz. semisweet chocolate

1] Center a rack in the oven and preheat the oven to 350°. Lightly butter a 10- or 11-inch tart pan with removable bottom and set it aside. Spread the almonds on a jelly roll pan and toast them in the oven, shaking the pan once or twice, until they are pale brown, about 10 minutes. Set them aside to cool and turn off the oven.

2] THE CRUST. Place 1 cup of nuts in a food processor; reserve remaining almonds for the filling. Add the flour, sugar, and nutmeg and process about 10 to 20 seconds, until the ingredients are mixed and the nuts are finely chopped. Add the butter and pulse 4 or 5 times to distribute. Add the egg and extract and process until the mixture forms large curds, about 10 seconds. Remove the dough and wipe out the bowl.

3] Press the dough evenly over the bottom and sides of the buttered tart pan; freeze until firm, about 30 minutes. Preheat the oven to 400°. Cover the tart shell with aluminum foil, pressing against the dough to get a snug fit, and fill with pie weights or dried beans. Bake for 20 minutes, remove the weights and foil, and bake until the crust is golden, about 5 to 8 minutes longer. Remove the tart to a cooling rack.

4] Sprinkle the finely chopped chocolate over the bottom of the hot crust, and spread it evenly with a pastry brush or small offset spatula. Allow the crust to cool to room temperature. *(The crust can be wrapped well and frozen for up to 1 month before filling.)*

5] THE FILLING. Put the reserved toasted almonds in the food processor and grind to a paste, 1 to 2 minutes. Add the ice cream and liqueur and turn the machine on and off 8 to 10 times just to blend the ingredients. Stop to scrape the bowl as needed. Spoon the ice cream into the crust, smooth the top with a spatula, and freeze for at least 30 minutes.

6] Melt the chocolate in a double boiler over hot water or in a bowl in a microwave. Piping with a small plain decorating tip or drizzling with the tines of fork, create a design over the top of the tart with the melted chocolate. (A crosshatch is attractive, as is a series of zigzags.) Place the tart in the freezer to set the chocolate, about 5 minutes, then cover the tart with plastic wrap, and freeze for at least 4 hours before serving.

SERVING. Unmold the tart and slide it onto a serving platter. Cut the frozen tart with a sturdy finely serrated pie or cake knife. For an extra-special occasion, serve with Extra-Bittersweet Chocolate Sauce (page 192).

STORING. The finished tart can be wrapped in a double thickness of plastic and foil and frozen for 1 month.

BEST MATCH. Coffee would be the top pick with this Coffee–Almond Crunch Tart.

❀| PLAYING AROUND. (Coffee–Hazelnut Crunch Tart) This recipe is easily varied by substituting toasted and skinned hazelnuts for the almonds and Frangelico for the Amaretto. (Keep the almond extract.)

Peanut Butter Fudge Ice Cream Sandwiches

Peanuts and chocolate are a favorite all-American combination. Here they make a dessert sandwich. The "bread" is a terrific-on-its-own peanut butter brownie, the "butter," rich chocolate ice cream studded with nuts. It's a kids' sweet that grown-ups adore.
§ Makes 16 Sandwiches

THE BROWNIE

- ⅔ c. all-purpose flour
- ½ tsp. baking powder
- ½ tsp. ground cinnamon
- ½ c. chunky peanut butter
- ¼ c. (½ stick) unsalted butter, at room temperature
- ⅔ c. packed light brown sugar
- 1 tsp. pure vanilla extract
- 2 large eggs
- ½ c. mini chocolate chips

THE FILLING

- 1 pt. premium chocolate ice cream (I use Häagen-Dazs)
- ½ c. unsalted roasted peanuts, coarsely chopped

1] THE BROWNIE. Center a rack in the oven and preheat the oven to 350°. Butter a 9-inch square baking pan and set it aside. In a small bowl, whisk together the flour, baking powder, and cinnamon; set aside.

2] In an electric mixer, with a paddle attachment if available, beat the peanut butter and butter until creamy. Add the sugar and continue to beat until the mixture is light and fluffy, about 3 to 4 minutes, stopping to scrape the bowl as needed. Beat in the vanilla. Add the eggs, one at a time, and beat well after each addition. On lowest speed, add the dry ingredients and mix just until incorporated. Fold in the chocolate chips with a rubber spatula.

3] Scrape the batter into the pan. Bake the brownie for 20 to 23 minutes, or until a toothpick inserted in the center comes out clean. Run a blunt knife around the edge of the pan and turn the brownie out onto a rack; invert right-side up onto another rack and let cool completely. *(The brownie can be wrapped in plastic and refrigerated for up to 3 days or stored in the freezer for up to 2 weeks.)*

4] THE FILLING. Place the bowl and beaters (or paddle attachment) of an electric mixer in the freezer to chill for at least 30 minutes. Cut the brownie in half horizontally. You will have two very thin 9-inch layers. Place the bottom layer, cut-side up, on a cutting board that can go into the freezer.

5] Place the ice cream in the chilled bowl and beat until slightly softened, about 20 seconds. Add the chopped nuts and beat only until blended. Spread the ice cream evenly over the bottom brownie layer and cover with the top layer, cut-side down, pressing down gently. Cover with plastic wrap and freeze for at least 4 hours.

6] Using a long, sharp knife, trim the edges of the frozen brownie and cut it into sixteen 2-inch squares. Wrap each square in plastic and freeze for at least 30 minutes.

SERVING. Remove the squares from the freezer and let them rest at room temperature for about 5 minutes before serving.

STORING. Well wrapped, the squares can be kept frozen for 1 month.

BEST MATCH. Kids will reach for a glass of cold milk or hot cocoa with these, grown-ups may want to down a bar then pour a cup of coffee.

✿| **PLAYING AROUND.** (Peanut Butter–Coffee Ice Cream Sandwiches) Keep the peanuts in the filling but change the ice cream to coffee for a milder-flavored version of these treats.

Tropical Freeze

This dessert, a luscious ice cream pie, is like having a Caribbean vacation in your freezer. It has all the tastes of the hot tropics. The crisp crust, made from toasted coconut, is lined with slices of ripe banana and covered with swirls of banana-rum ice cream, a flavor created from a pint of rich storebought vanilla. It's a cinch to make and it's the perfect pick-me-up for the dead-of-winter blues. § Makes 8 to 10 Servings

THE CRUST

½ c. (1 stick) unsalted butter
2 c. (7 oz.) sweetened shredded coconut
5 butter cookies, such as Petit-Beurre, crushed
1 firm, ripe banana

THE FILLING

2 very ripe bananas
2 tsp. fresh lemon juice
1½ tbsp. dark rum
1 pt. premium vanilla ice cream (I use Häagen-Dazs)

1 firm, ripe banana, sliced and rubbed with lemon juice

1] THE CRUST. Butter a deep-dish pie pan or heatproof glass dish; set aside. Melt the butter in a heavy skillet over medium heat. Add the coconut and cook, stirring constantly, until it turns a golden color, about 8 minutes. Remove from heat and stir in the cookie crumbs.

2] Press the coconut-cookie mixture onto the bottom and sides of the pie pan. Cut the banana into thin rounds and arrange them over the bottom of the crust. Place the pie in the freezer and chill for at least 30 minutes.

3] THE FILLING. Cut the bananas into chunks and place them in a food processor. Process for 5 seconds. Add the lemon juice and rum and process until the puree is smooth, about 15 seconds longer. Add the vanilla ice cream and turn the machine on and off 8 to 10 times, just to blend the ingredients. Scrape the ice cream into the chilled crust, smooth the top, and cover the pie with plastic wrap. Freeze until very firm, at least 4 hours.

SERVING. Decorate the pie with banana slices (rubbed with lemon juice) right before serving. Bring the pie to the table in its pan and cut with a sturdy finely serrated pie or cake knife.

STORING. The pie can be kept, well wrapped, in the freezer for up to 1 month.

BEST MATCH. I like to enjoy this all by itself, followed by a cup of strong, black coffee, but for someone really ready for a vacation, the combination of Tropical Freeze and a frothy island drink, such as piña colada or banana daiquiri, is transporting.

❂| PLAYING AROUND. (Chocolate-Banana–Filled Freeze) Not as tropical, but really delicious. Just replace the vanilla ice cream with a pint of premium chocolate.

Café Society Sweets

Little Luxuries to Keep Coffee and Conversation Company

Fudge Buttons
(Ginger-Fudge Buttons)

Mixed Fruit with Bubbling Almond Cream
(Hazelnut Variation)

Espresso Cheesecake Brownies
(Orange or Lemon Cheesecake Brownies)

Orange Caramel Mousse
(Pineapple Caramel Mousse)

Jean-Marc's Honeycomb Tuiles
(Tiny Tuiles with Baby Balls of Ice Cream)

Quick Prune Pithiviers
(Apricot, Fig, Apple and Nut, or Pear Pithiviers)

Apple Paper Thins
(Pear Paper Thins)

Thick-Cut Candied Peels
(Chocolate-Dipped Peels)

Chocolate Truffles
(Endless Variations)

Linzer Doubles
(Out-of-This-World Ice Cream Sandwiches)

Glossy-Topped Black Cherry Chocolate Bars
(Sybarite's Special)

Raspberry Rugelach
(California Roll-ups and Other Variations)

Café Society Sweets are late-night luxuries, small sweets to serve with cups of steaming espresso or froth-topped cappuccino, snifters of brandy or cognac, or mugs of hot chocolate by the fire. These are, in many ways, the quintessential sweets: elegant, sophisticated, beautiful, and swell tasting.

Think of these baby brownies, paper-thin pastries, candied peels, sandwich cookies, and rich, creamy, spirit-spiked chocolate truffles as living-room sweets or after-dessert desserts. Serve them away from the dinner table after theater, the movies, a night on the town, or at the close of an evening at home with your dearest friends. But serve these only when you have time to linger: They're slow-eating sweets that make the evening last.

Fudge Buttons

Small, chocolaty, and slightly chewy, Fudge Buttons are gently flavored with orange zest and glazed with a white chocolate dip. They can be placed in pretty paper or foil cups for a dressier look or served just as they are, plain and perfect. § Makes 2 Dozen Cookies

THE BUTTONS

2 tsp. finely chopped orange zest

¾ tsp. granulated sugar

¼ c. plus 2 tbsp. all-purpose flour

Pinch of salt

¼ c. (½ stick) unsalted butter, cut into 4 pieces

2½ oz. high-quality bittersweet chocolate, such as Lindt or Tobler, coarsely chopped

⅓ c. packed light brown sugar

¼ tsp. pure vanilla extract

1 large egg

THE GLAZE

2 oz. white chocolate, such as Tobler Narcisse, broken into small pieces

1] THE BUTTONS. Place a rack in the center of the oven and preheat the oven to 350°. Lightly butter 2 miniature muffin pans, each with a dozen cups, and place them on a large baking sheet. (The muffin cups should be 1¾″ × ¾″ with a 1-tablespoon capacity.) Combine the zest and granulated sugar in a small bowl; set aside, stirring occasionally as the sugar becomes syrupy. In another bowl, whisk together the flour and salt.

2] In a heavy saucepan, melt the butter, chocolate, and brown sugar over very low heat, stirring constantly until smooth. Take the pan off the heat and allow the chocolate to cool for a minute. Keep working in the saucepan. One ingredient at a time, blend in the vanilla, egg, and zest, stirring until each is well blended. Add the flour mixture and stir until the flour is incorporated. The batter will be smooth and glossy.

3] Divide the batter evenly among the muffin cups, using about a teaspoon of batter to fill each one three quarters full. Bake for 9 to 10 minutes, until the tops spring back when touched. Place the tins on a rack and cool 3 minutes before removing the buttons. Finish cooling on the rack.

4] THE GLAZE. Melt the white chocolate in a small metal bowl over hot, not boiling, water, stirring constantly. The water should not touch the bowl. When the chocolate is smooth, remove it from the heat. Dip the tops of the buttons into the chocolate, allowing the excess to drip back into the bowl. Refrigerate buttons for 15 minutes to set the glaze.

SERVING. Serve the buttons as soon as the glaze has set. Ideally, they should be room temperature or only slightly chilled. Place the buttons in paper or foil cups or arrange them decoratively on a cake plate.

STORING. These buttons can be wrapped airtight and frozen for up to 1 month. Make certain to return them to room temperature before serving.

BEST MATCH. The fudge flavor seems to intensify when the buttons are teamed with a cup of steaming espresso. For a treat, serve these with a few Thick-Cut Candied Peels (page 170) on the side. They're a great pair.

❀| PLAYING AROUND. (Ginger-Fudge Buttons) Simply substitute an equal amount of very finely chopped fresh ginger for the orange zest.

Mixed Fruit with Bubbling Almond Cream

This dessert is simplicity itself—and splendid. Small bowls of mixed fruits, berries in summer, tropical fruits in winter, are covered with a rich, slightly crunchy almond pastry cream and a *sprinkling of brown sugar. They're set under the broiler briefly, so everything is cool except a thin layer of the bubbling cream and the crackly sugar top. § Makes 4 Servings*

THE ALMOND PASTRY CREAM

1 c. milk
1 large egg
3 tbsp. sugar
1 tbsp. all-purpose flour
1 tbsp. cornstarch
1 tsp. unsalted butter
½ tsp. pure vanilla extract
2 tsp. Amaretto or 1 tsp. almond extract
¼ c. slivered or julienned blanched almonds, pulverized

THE FRUIT

2 c. bite-size pieces of mixed soft fresh fruits, such as mango, papaya, strawberries, raspberries, blueberries, apricots, pears, bananas, oranges, cherries, figs
2 to 3 tbsp. sugar, depending on the sweetness of the fruits
¼ c. packed light brown sugar

1] **THE ALMOND PASTRY CREAM.** Scald the milk in a heavy-bottomed medium saucepan. While the milk is heating, whisk the egg, sugar, flour, and cornstarch together in a medium bowl. Gradually whisk the hot milk into the egg mixture. Pour the mixture back into the saucepan and cook over medium heat, stirring constantly and vigorously, until the cream thickens and one bubble breaks the surface, about 2 minutes. Remove the pan from the heat and strain the cream into a bowl. (You can wipe out and use the same bowl as before.) Stir in the remaining ingredients in the order in which they are listed. Press a sheet of plastic against the cream to prevent a skin from forming. When cool, chill several hours before using. (*The cream will keep tightly covered in the refrigerator for 3 days.*)

2] **THE FRUIT.** Taste the fruits and if they're not sweet enough to suit you, add sugar. Divide the fruit evenly among four 6-ounce custard cups, individual soufflé molds, or ramekins.

3] Place the cups on a baking sheet and top with the pastry cream. Sprinkle one-quarter of the brown sugar evenly over each serving. Place the cups under the broiler, about 3 inches from the flame, and broil until the cream bubbles gently and the sugar is crackly and caramelized. Check progress frequently and remove from heat as soon as the tops are caramelized.

SERVING. Place the ramekins on saucers and serve immediately.

STORING. Once assembled and caramelized, these won't keep.

BEST MATCH. These are heavenly with coffee, cappuccino, or espresso laced with Amaretto, and nice with a couple of Jean-Marc's Honeycomb Tuiles (page 164) or Raspberry Rugelach (page 178) on the side.

❀| **PLAYING AROUND.** (Hazelnut Variation) Of course you can change the fruits, but you can also substitute toasted and skinned hazelnuts for the almonds. If you use hazelnuts, you can still use almond extract as the accent flavor or substitute Frangelico, a hazelnut liqueur, for the Amaretto.

Espresso Cheesecake Brownies

One good thing on top of another: a layer of dense chocolate brownie topped with creamy espresso cheesecake and swirls of dark batter, *a lot of taste and texture for very little work.*
§ Makes 16 Brownies

THE BROWNIE

½ c. all-purpose flour
½ tsp. baking powder
⅛ tsp. salt
¼ tsp. ground cinnamon, optional
6 oz. high-quality bittersweet chocolate, such as Lindt or Tobler, broken into small pieces
½ c. (1 stick) unsalted butter, cut into 8 pieces
⅔ c. sugar
¾ tsp. pure vanilla extract
2 large eggs, at room temperature

THE CHEESECAKE

1½ tsp. instant espresso powder
1 tbsp. boiling water
8 oz. cream cheese, at room temperature
⅔ c. sugar
½ tsp. pure vanilla extract
2 large eggs, at room temperature
1 tbsp. all-purpose flour

1] **THE BROWNIE.** Position a rack one-third up from the bottom of the oven and preheat the oven to 350°. Butter a 9″ × 9″ baking pan and set aside. Place the flour, baking powder, salt, and, if desired, cinnamon in a bowl and stir with a whisk to combine; reserve.

2] Melt the chocolate and butter together in the top of a double boiler over hot water or in a bowl in a microwave. When melted, stir to blend. Add the sugar and mix well, using a small whisk (it's unnecessary to pour the chocolate mixture into a bowl). Add the vanilla and the eggs, one at a time, stirring after each addition until the mixture is smooth. After the eggs are added the chocolate may look grainy, but it will smooth as you stir it. Blend in the reserved dry ingredients. Set aside while you prepare the cheesecake.

3] **THE CHEESECAKE.** Dissolve the espresso powder in the boiling water; set aside to cool. Beat the cream cheese in a mixer, with a paddle if available, until it is very creamy. Add the sugar and vanilla and beat until the sugar dissolves, about 3 minutes. Blend in the espresso. Beat in the eggs one at a time. Beat at medium speed for a minute. On low speed, add the flour and beat just until blended.

4] The brownie batter will have thickened a bit while sitting, so give it a turn with a rubber spatula. Pour three-quarters of the batter into the prepared pan, spreading it evenly with the spatula. Pour over all of the cheesecake batter; it will spread by itself. Scatter teaspoonfuls of the remaining brownie batter over the cheesecake. Create a swirl pattern by dipping a table knife halfway into the batters and drawing it back and forth across the pan. Don't disturb the bottom layer and don't go across the pan more than once.

5] Bake for 30 to 35 minutes, until the top is lightly browned and the cake starts to pull away from the sides of the pan. Remove from the oven and cool on a rack for 10 minutes. Run a blunt knife around the sides before unmolding the cake onto a rack. Invert and cool right-side up on the rack. When the brownies reach room temperature, cover and place in the refrigerator to chill.

SERVING. These should be served cold (or even just minutes out of the freezer). Trim the edges and cut into 16 pieces, each about 2-inches square, or, if you're serving several small sweets, cut into 1-inch-square bits.

STORING. Wrapped airtight, these can be kept in the refrigerator for 3 days or frozen for up to 2 weeks.

BEST MATCH. Espresso is the obvious choice with these brownies, but they're equally good with cappuccino or a light, not-too-chocolaty hot chocolate.

❀| **PLAYING AROUND.** (Orange or Lemon Cheesecake Brownies) So many flavors go well with chocolate it's fun to change the flavor of the cheesecake topping in this recipe. Omit the espresso and substitute 1 teaspoon pure orange or lemon extract, or increase the vanilla extract to 1½ teaspoons for a traditional cheesecake flavor.

Orange Caramel Mousse

In dessertese, the term bittersweet *usually refers to chocolate, but it's an apt description of this mousse as well. The small amount of sugar in this recipe is caramelized to give it a pleasingly bitter flavor. The caramel, tart orange juice, and* tangy sour cream combine to produce a *refreshing, vibrant taste, a welcome contrast to mousse's traditional richness.*
§ *Makes 6 to 8 Servings*

¼ c. cold water
1½ tsp. (½ pkg.) **unflavored gelatin**
¾ c. **(6 oz. can) frozen orange concentrate, thawed, undiluted**
½ c. sugar
2 tbsp. cold water
½ c. sour cream
1 c. heavy cream, chilled

1] Pour the ¼ cup cold water into a small nonreactive saucepan and sprinkle over the gelatin. Allow it to soften 5 minutes. Stir the gelatin over low heat until it is dissolved. Add the orange concentrate and heat through. Remove from heat.

2] Put the sugar and the 2 tablespoons cold water into a medium-size nonreactive saucepan over medium heat. Stir occasionally until the sugar starts to melt. If some sugar spatters around the sides of the pot, wash it down with a small brush dipped in cold water. Bring the mixture to the boil. Continue to boil, without stirring, until the sugar turns a light golden caramel, about 12 minutes. When the sugar is caramelized, immediately remove it from the heat. While the sugar is boiling, return the orange-gelatin mixture to a very low flame.

3] Carefully whisk the warm orange-gelatin mixture into the caramel. Stand away from the pot, because the hot mixture may bubble up. If the caramel hardens a bit, particularly around the wires of the whisk, just place the mixture over low heat and whisk until the hardened caramel dissolves and the mixture is properly blended.

4] Pour the mixture into a metal bowl placed inside a larger bowl filled with ice cubes and water. Whisk the mixture until it cools and thickens a little, about 3 minutes. Whisk in the sour cream and continue to stir over ice until the mixture mounds lightly, about 6 to 8 minutes. Remove the bowl from the ice.

5] Whip the heavy cream until it forms soft peaks. Do not overbeat, or the mousse will be spongy (but still delicious). Whisk in one-half of the whipped cream, then fold in the remainder with a rubber spatula. Spoon the mousse into 6 or 8 individual ramekins or a 1-quart serving bowl and refrigerate.

SERVING. The mousse is ready to serve once it has set, after about 2 hours in the refrigerator. It is both pretty and delicious plain, but you can

Sliced strawberries or whole raspberries, optional

garnish it with a few sliced strawberries or whole raspberries if you want. Serve the mousse in the ramekins or, if you've made it in a bowl, scoop oval-shaped portions onto dessert plates using two large spoons.

STORING. The mousse will keep in the refrigerator, wrapped airtight, for 2 days.

BEST MATCH. Because of the tang provided by the caramel, oranges, and sour cream, this mousse can be served successfully with either strong tea or espresso. If you want orange to carry the night, serve with a garnish of Thick-Cut Candied Peels (page 170); to add a complementary flavor, place a few Chocolate Truffles (page 172) on the dessert plate.

❀I **PLAYING AROUND.** (Pineapple Caramel Mousse) For tang upon tang, replace the orange concentrate with an equal amount of pineapple juice concentrate. Whether you make an Orange or Pineapple Caramel Mousse, you'll find that using it to fill a chocolate tart shell (page 191) produces a late-night sweet worthy of your best china.

Jean-Marc's Honeycomb Tuiles

Honeycomb Tuiles have the look of a sweet you wouldn't think could possibly be made at home, yet they're easy and fun to bake. They are the creation of one of New York's most talented pastry chefs, Jean-Marc Burillier, who baked them as an after-dinner nibble for guests at Maxim's. A tuile is a traditional French cookie whose name means tile, *referring to the curved roof tiles prevalent in the French countryside. However, these are rather untraditional. Made with maple syrup and brown sugar, they develop an appealing honeycomb pattern over their shiny, translucent surfaces.*
§ Makes About 4 Dozen Cookies

4 tbsp. (½ stick) unsalted butter, very soft
¼ **c. packed light brown sugar**
¼ **c. maple syrup, at room temperature**
⅓ **c. plus 2 tbsp. cake flour**

1] In a small bowl, using a sturdy rubber spatula, or in an electric mixer, with a paddle if available, cream the butter, sugar, and maple syrup together until they are light in color and texture. Mix in the flour, stirring only until the dough is well blended. Cover the dough with plastic wrap and refrigerate for at least 3 hours before baking. (*The dough can be made to this point and refrigerated, well wrapped, for up to 1 week.*)

2] Adjust the racks to divide the oven into thirds and preheat the oven to 400°. Set aside 2 baking sheets and, if you want to curve the cookies, a metal ring mold, a rolling pin, or a slender bottle.

3] Roll scoops of dough between your palms to form balls the size of small cherries or hazelnuts. Place the balls 2 inches apart on the unbuttered baking sheets. Bake for about 7 minutes, until the cookies spread and are well browned and honeycombed. Immediately remove the sheets from the oven and allow the cookies to rest 30 seconds. Use a metal spatula to lift the cookies from the sheets. Work the spatula under an edge of the cookie, then push it beneath the cookie with a quick jerk. The cookie may crumple a bit, but it will unfold on the mold. Quickly place the cookie over the ring mold or rolling pin to curve it. Transfer the cookies to a flat surface when they are set. (They set in about a minute.) If the cookies harden and become difficult to remove from the sheets, put them back in the oven for 1 minute. If you want flat cookies, just cool them on a rack. Repeat until all of the dough is used.

SERVING. These are prettiest placed along a long, narrow platter so that one cookie's curve slightly overlaps the next (as though the cookies were a chorus line of small turtles).

STORING. If it's not humid, you can keep Tuiles for 3 days in an open tin. If the weather's against you, eat the cookies soon after they're baked. (Remember that unbaked dough can be kept chilled.)

BEST MATCH. At Maxim's, Jean-Marc served these with truffles and other petits fours. They are a natural with almost any crustless, fruity dessert and particularly good with Mixed Fruit with Bubbling Almond Cream (page 159). While coffee, espresso, or tea are just right with these, they are not so sweet that you can't serve them with champagne.

❀| PLAYING AROUND. (Tiny Tuiles with Baby Balls of Ice Cream) Once you get the hang of making these Honeycomb Tuiles, you can make them in almost any size, from mini to monster. For a change, make them tiny (about 1½ inches in diameter), leave them flat, and use them as a little saucer for whipped cream or a baby ball of ice cream.

Quick Prune Pithiviers

These are gorgeous. They have all the polish and style of professionally made pastries, yet they require no special skill to put together. Inspired by the traditional French Pithiviers, a puff pastry turnover that usually encases almond cream, these are filled with Armagnac-soaked prunes and nutty prune butter. Both the pastry and the prune butter are storebought. There's little to do but build the dessert, making layers of pastry, prune butter and fruit, bake, and bow to the praise. § Makes 8 Pastries

2 c. warm water
½ c. Armagnac
32 pitted prunes
2 sheets (1¼ pounds) storebought frozen puff pastry (I use Pepperidge Farm)
⅓ c. prune butter
2 tbsp. pecans, finely minced or pulverized
1 tbsp. Armagnac
1 large egg
1 tbsp. cold water
Sugar

1] Combine the warm water and the ½ cup Armagnac in a large bowl or a jar with a tight cover. Add the prunes and seal with plastic wrap or the cover. Allow the prunes to soak and plump at room temperature for 6 hours or in the refrigerator for up to 1 month. (You may want to make a few batches of these Armagnac-soaked prunes just to have on hand for dessert emergencies. They're spectacular over vanilla ice cream, pound cake, or rice pudding, or just spooned into a bowl with some softly whipped cream.)

2] Defrost the frozen puff pastry at room temperature for about 20 minutes, or until it is supple but still chilled. Roll one sheet of pastry to a thickness of ⅛ inch on a floured board and cut eight 3½-inch rounds; these are the bottoms of the packets. Brush off the excess flour and lift the rounds onto an unbuttered baking sheet. Chill until needed. Repeat with the second sheet, cutting eight 4-inch rounds for the tops. Chill until needed.

3] Center a rack in the oven and preheat the oven to 400°. In a small bowl, mix together the prune butter, pecans, and the 1 tablespoon Armagnac. In another small bowl, beat the egg with the 1 tablespoon cold water. Drain the prunes, reserving the liquid—it can be used to soak another batch of prunes. Remove the pastry bottoms from the refrigerator.

4] Place a heaping teaspoonful of the prune butter mixture in the center of each pastry bottom. Top with 4 prunes, packed together snugly. Brush the border of each round with a little of the egg wash. Top with the larger pastry rounds, pressing around the edges. Press the tines of a fork against the rim of each pastry to seal the packets well. Brush the pastries with egg wash, taking care not to let any drip down the edge and onto the baking sheet. (It will glue the pastry to the sheet and stop it from rising properly.) Cut a ¼-inch hole in the center of each pastry or slit it in 4 places with a sharp knife. Sprinkle lightly with sugar and bake 10 minutes. *Lower the oven temperature to 350°* and bake 10 to 12 more minutes, until golden.

Lightly whipped cream or softened vanilla ice cream, optional

Remove from the oven and use a metal spatula to lift the pastries onto a rack to cool.

SERVING. Serve these, warm or at room temperature, on individual dessert plates. They are lovely plain, but can be offered with a small spoonful of lightly whipped cream or vanilla ice cream that's been allowed to soften until it's almost a sauce.

STORING. These won't keep, so enjoy them the day they're made.

BEST MATCH. Tea and prunes are a natural pair, but this dessert is stunning followed by a snifter of Armagnac.

❀ PLAYING AROUND. (Apricot, Fig, Apple and Nut, or Pear Pithiviers) The possibilities for filling these little Pithiviers are limited only by your imagination. Apricots soaked in Grand Marnier and packed into the pastry with some storebought apricot butter or jam is an easy option. You can also try plump dried figs with cognac and a dab of apricot jam or orange marmalade; finely diced apples, nuts, and currants with a splash of brandy and some apple butter; or dried pears, port, and a film of red currant jelly.

Apple Paper Thins

Simple and satisfying, the ultimate midnight munch—a paper-thin, straight-edged pizza of buttery, sugary apples. This is apple pie that's not at all like mom's. The crust is a sheet of storebought puff pastry rolled to within a millimeter of its life and the apples are sweetened Granny Smiths. Everything can be put together in about 20 minutes, covered with plastic, refrigerated, and baked just before serving.
§ Makes About 10 Servings

1 sheet (slightly more than ½ pound) storebought frozen puff pastry (I use Pepperidge Farm)
3 Granny Smith or Golden Delicious apples
3 tbsp. unsalted butter, melted
3 tbsp. sugar
⅓ c. apple jelly

1] Defrost the frozen pastry for 20 minutes at room temperature, or until it is supple but still chilled. Working on a lightly floured surface, roll the puff pastry into a 15- to 16-inch square, ¹⁄₁₆ inch thick. Roll the pastry around your rolling pin (for easy transport), then unroll it onto a large unbuttered baking sheet. Brush off any excess flour and prick the pastry all over with a fork or the tip of a sharp knife. Lay a sheet of plastic wrap over the pastry and chill it while you prepare the apples.

2] Place a rack in the center of the oven and preheat the oven to 400°. Peel the apples and cut each in half lengthwise (from stem to blossom). Use a melon scoop to take out the core. Put each apple core-side down on a board and cut crosswise into very thin slices. (You should get about 16 slices from each half.) Remove the pastry from the refrigerator and arrange the apples on it in a single, slightly overlapping layer to make a rectangle of fruit about 11″ × 13″. Trim the pastry, leaving a 1-inch border all around the fruit. Brush the apples with the melted butter and sprinkle over the sugar. (*The recipe can be made to this point, covered with plastic, and kept refrigerated for several hours.*)

3] Bake for 20 minutes, turning the baking sheet around during this time if your oven heat is not even and one side is browning faster than the other. *Lower the temperature to 350°* and bake about 10 minutes longer, until the pastry is puffed at the edges and the apples are soft. Remove the pastry from the oven and slide it onto a board.

4] In a small saucepan, or a microwave, bring the apple jelly to a boil, stirring until smooth. Lightly brush the jelly over the apples.

SERVING. Cut the pastry into 30 rectangles approximately 2″ × 2¼″, and arrange the Paper Thins on a large serving platter with the bowl of whipped cream or crème fraîche in the center, if you are serving it. Allow guests to help themselves. If the pastries aren't too hot, don't be surprised to

Whipped cream or crème fraîche, optional

find friends using their fingers and dunking the pastries into the cream as though they were chips and dip.

STORING. This is best served immediately because the puff pastry tends to become soggy rather quickly.

BEST MATCH. These are wonderful served with a glass of Grand Marnier, room temperature or on the rocks. If you're serving just these Paper Thins, offer Eggnog-Pumpkin Ice Cream (page 141), even if it's not a holiday.

❀| PLAYING AROUND. (Pear Paper Thins) Substitute sweet Anjou pears for the apples and brush the pastry with a thin film of strained apricot preserves.

Thick-Cut Candied Peels

Candied citrus peels make perfect late-night nibbles. Although poached in a sweet syrup and coated with sugar, they remain tart and refreshing. Many restaurants offer candied peels after lavish meals and elaborate desserts not only because they go so well with coffee and cognac but also because their fresh, bright flavor wakes up the palate and seems to whisk away the weight of a grand meal. These are so much more distinctive than storebought you'll want to keep them on hand as a house special.
§ *Makes About 15 Servings*

3 thick-skinned oranges, such as navel oranges
1 large thick-skinned grapefruit
1 lemon
2 c. sugar
2½ tbsp. light corn syrup
1 c. cold water
2 c. sugar
2 tsp. ground ginger

1] Score the skin of the fruit into quarters, then peel off each quarter of rind, reserving the fruit for another use. For these confections you want to keep the pith (the fuzzy white inner part of the peel). Cut each quarter of orange peel into 3 slices, each grapefruit quarter into 4, and each lemon quarter into 2. (If you prefer, cut the peel into narrower strips; it won't affect cooking time.) Place the peels in a large saucepan and cover with cold water. Bring to the boil and boil 2 minutes. Drain the peels and rinse with cold water; then repeat the boiling and rinsing process once again. Drain the peels and set aside while you make the syrup.

2] In a 3-quart saucepan, bring 2 cups sugar, the corn syrup, and cold water to a boil. Boil the syrup for 20 minutes, washing down any crystals that may form on the sides of the pan with a brush dipped in cold water. Add the peels and bring the syrup back to the boil. Lower the heat to medium and simmer the peels for 25 minutes, stirring occasionally.

3] Line a jelly roll pan with waxed paper. Put the remaining 2 cups sugar and the ginger in the pan and mix with your hands. (This is a generous amount of sugar, but it makes the coating process easier.) When the peels are cooked, lift them out, one by one, with chopsticks or tongs; hold each peel over the pot for a few seconds to let the excess syrup drip back, then drop the peel into the sugar. Using a spoon or your hands, mix the peels and sugar until the pieces are coated. Shake or gently rub off the excess sugar from each peel. Transfer the peels to a rack, arranging them in a single layer. Allow the peels to dry overnight.

SERVING. The peels are ready to serve as soon as they are dry.

STORING. Once they are dry, store the peels in a covered container, using waxed paper to separate the layers. Peels will keep for 1 week at room temperature.

BEST MATCH. Of course these are divine with coffee or cognac, but they're also swell with mulled wine or cider or an old-fashioned buttered rum.

❂ | **PLAYING AROUND.** (Chocolate-Dipped Peels) When the peels are dry, dip the tips in warm melted chocolate. (Chocolate chips are great for this because you don't have to worry about maintaining a constant temperature for dipping as you would with couverture-type chocolate.) Allow the chocolate to set on a rack or waxed paper.

Chocolate Truffles

Truffles, rich chocolate candies dusted with cocoa, are the stuff of dreams. They're the bonbons you imagine satin-draped movie stars indulging in at midnight. In fact, while they're elegant—and very expensive at specialty shops —truffles are child's play to make. I've written the recipe for a basic truffle, just chocolate, cream, and a knob of butter, and then included eight variations. All are delicious and all freeze well. § Makes 2 Dozen Truffles

THE BASIC TRUFFLES

⅓ c. heavy cream

6 oz. high-quality bittersweet chocolate, such as Lindt or Tobler, coarsely chopped

2 tbsp. unsalted butter, at room temperature

About ¼ c. cocoa

1] **THE BASIC TRUFFLES.** Bring the cream to a boil in a small heavy-bottomed saucepan over moderate heat or in a bowl in a microwave. Remove the pan from the heat and add the chocolate and butter, whisking until smooth. Pour the warm chocolate mixture into a shallow bowl and press a piece of plastic wrap directly against the surface. Refrigerate for at least 3 hours.

2] Using a spoon, scoop 24 rounded teaspoonfuls of the cold chocolate mixture onto a sheet of waxed paper. Coat your palms with cocoa and roll each mound between your palms to form a ball. Dredge the truffles in the cocoa, tossing them gently from one hand to the other to remove the excess cocoa. Chill the truffles, covered, for at least 2 hours before serving.

VARIATIONS

Hazelnut-Frangelico. Reduce the butter to 1 tablespoon. Add 2 tablespoons Frangelico and 1 cup toasted and skinned chopped hazelnuts to the warm chocolate mixture before chilling.

Scotch-Raisin. Soak 1 cup raisins in ¼ cup Scotch in a covered container for at least 1 hour. Add this to the warm chocolate mixture before chilling.

Amaretto-Almond. Add 2 tablespoons Amaretto to the warm chocolate mixture before chilling. Toast 45 whole almonds, reserving 24 and finely chopping the remainder. Mold each truffle around a whole almond. After dredging the truffles in cocoa, roll them in the chopped nuts.

Cappuccino. Make a paste of 1 tablespoon boiling water, 1 teaspoon cinnamon, and 2 teaspoons instant espresso powder. Add the paste to the warm chocolate mixture.

Sweet Orange Rind–Grand Marnier. Use a zester to remove strips of rind from 3 oranges. Put the rind in a small saucepan, cover with cold water, bring to a boil and boil 1 minute. Drain and repeat the process. Bring 1 cup water and ⅓ cup sugar to a boil. Add the rind and boil 5 minutes. Drain.

When the rind is cool enough to handle, chop it fine and mix with 2 tablespoons Grand Marnier. Add the rind and liqueur to the warm chocolate mixture.

Macadamia-Rum. Add 2 tablespoons dark rum to the warm chocolate mixture before chilling. Reserve 24 whole macadamia nuts and finely chop 5 macadamia nuts. Mold each truffle around a whole macadamia nut. After dredging the truffles in cocoa, dip the tops in the chopped nuts.

Brandied Apricot. Soak 1 rounded cupful finely chopped or diced dried apricots in ¼ cup brandy in a covered container for at least 1 hour. Add this mixture to the warm chocolate mixture.

Kahlúa-Pecan. Reduce the butter to 1 tablespoon. Toast and chop 1 cup pecans. Add 2 tablespoons Kahlúa and the nuts to the warm chocolate mixture before chilling.

SERVING. The truffles should always be served chilled. Place them in paper or foil cups. If you've made several varieties, it's nice to serve them on a tiered cake plate, one type to a tier.

STORING. You can refrigerate the truffles, wrapped well, for up to 1 week or freeze them in an airtight container for 1 month. Remove from the freezer 5 minutes before serving.

BEST MATCH. Espresso, cognac, or even Armagnac are sumptuous accompaniments to truffles. (Some people enjoy truffles with champagne. I like the luxurious image of the combination more than the taste; I think chocolate is too sweet for champagne.) Several of the varieties would be nice paired with Thick-Cut Candied Peels (page 170). For an all-out splurge, prepare a chocolate plate including Truffles, Fudge Buttons (page 158), Glossy-Topped Black Cherry Chocolate Bars (page 176) and tiny squares of Espresso Cheesecake Brownies (page 160).

❀| **PLAYING AROUND.** (Endless Variations) After offering so many variations it may seem impossible that there are still more—but there are. Let yourself go and you'll find it easy to come up with many more combinations, such as Prune-Armagnac Truffles with Pecans or Brandied-Candied Fruit Truffles for Christmas.

Linzer Doubles

These offer all of the buttery richness and spice of a linzertorte in individual sandwich cookies. I make these with hazelnuts and add cocoa to the cookie dough for depth. I also cover each cookie with a thin layer of melted chocolate before spreading it with raspberry jam and topping it with its mate. There are many flavors and tastes in these cookies, and they all come together beautifully. § Makes 24 to 30 Cookies

2 c. hazelnuts, toasted, skinned, and finely chopped
1½ c. all-purpose flour
1 tbsp. cocoa
1¼ tsp. ground cinnamon
¼ tsp. ground cloves
⅛ tsp. salt
½ c. (1 stick) unsalted butter, at room temperature
½ c. sugar
½ tsp. grated orange zest
1 large egg
1½ tsp. Grand Marnier or other orange liqueur
3 oz. bitter- or semisweet chocolate
½ c. seedless raspberry jam
1 tsp. Grand Marnier or other orange liqueur

1] Whisk together the nuts, flour, cocoa, cinnamon, cloves, and salt in a medium bowl; set aside. In an electric mixer, using the paddle if you have one, beat the butter, sugar, and zest until light and creamy, about 3 minutes at medium speed, stopping to scrape the bowl as needed. Add the egg and the 1½ teaspoons liqueur and continue to beat. On low speed, gradually beat in the nut mixture, beating only until incorporated.

2] Divide the dough in half. Place one half on a sheet of waxed paper and cover with another sheet of waxed paper. Use your hands to flatten the dough into a disk, then use a rolling pin to roll the dough to a thickness of ¼ inch. (Turn the dough over and lift the paper frequently to avoid rolling deep crease marks into the dough.) Repeat with the other piece of dough. Keeping the rolled dough between the sheets of waxed paper, transfer the dough to 2 cookie sheets or cutting boards and freeze until very firm, about 45 minutes.

3] Place a rack in the center of the oven and preheat the oven to 375°. Lightly butter 2 cookie sheets or have 2 nonstick sheets ready.

4] Remove one piece of dough from the freezer, and peel off the top sheet of paper. Use a 2-inch round cookie cutter to cut the dough. Place the rounds on a buttered cookie sheet. (If the dough becomes soft or sticky while you're working, return it to the freezer to firm.) Chill or freeze the cookie rounds while you repeat this process with the second half of the dough. Gather up the scraps, roll them again between sheets of waxed paper, chill, and cut them.

5] Bake the cookies, one sheet at a time, for 11 to 13 minutes, until pale gold. Watch these carefully because they burn quickly. Transfer the cookies to a rack to cool.

6] Melt the chocolate in the top of a double boiler over hot water or in a bowl in a microwave. Using a small spatula or a butter knife, spread each cookie with a thin layer of chocolate. Set the cookies aside to allow the chocolate to set, or chill the cookies briefly.

7] Cook and stir the raspberry jam in a small saucepan over medium heat until it thickens slightly, or heat in a bowl in a microwave. Stir in the 1 teaspoon liqueur and set aside to cool. Place about ½ teaspoon of jam in the center of the chocolate side of half of the cookies. Gently press the remaining cookies, chocolate-side down, on top of the filling, rotating the cookies to spread the jam evenly.

Confectioners' sugar

SERVING. Just before serving, sift confectioners' sugar over the cookies.

STORING. The cookies will keep at room temperature in a covered container for a day or two. (Because of the jam they tend to get soggy.) They can be wrapped airtight and frozen for up to 1 month. It's best to freeze these without the dusting of confectioners' sugar.

BEST MATCH. Offer these with tea (a classic), coffee, or a hot toddy.

❀┃ **PLAYING AROUND.** (Out-of-This-World Ice Cream Sandwiches) Brush the cookies with chocolate but omit the raspberry jam. Soften some cinnamon ice cream (page 143) and sandwich a thick layer of ice cream between two cookies. Place the sandwiches in the freezer for about an hour to firm before serving. To store for up to 2 weeks, wrap the firmed-up sandwiches airtight and freeze.

Glossy-Topped Black Cherry Chocolate Bars

These bars have the finger-licking appeal of fudge brownies and the polish of the Black Forest Cake that inspired them. They are chock-full of cognac-soaked sweet cherries held in place by *the darkest, densest, moistest chocolate cake, and topped with rich, glossy, deep chocolate icing. § Makes 16 Bars*

THE CAKE

8 oz. dark, sweet, fresh Bing cherries, halved and pitted (you can also use frozen pitted cherries, thawed, drained, and patted dry)

1½ tbsp. cognac

½ c. all-purpose flour

½ c. cocoa, preferably a Dutch-processed brand, such as Droste or Poulain

Pinch of salt

½ c. (1 stick) unsalted butter, at room temperature

¾ c. sugar

1½ tbsp. light corn syrup

1 tsp. pure vanilla excract

2 large eggs

THE ICING

2 oz. unsweetened chocolate, coarsely chopped

2 oz. high-quality bittersweet chocolate, such as Lindt or Tobler, coarsely chopped

3 tbsp. unsalted butter, at room temperature

1 large egg

1 egg yolk

1½ tbsp. cognac

1] THE CAKE. Center a rack in the oven and preheat the oven to 350°. Butter an 8″ × 8″ pan and set it aside. Place the cherries in a nonreactive bowl and pour over the cognac. Allow the fruit to soak while you make the cake batter. Whisk the flour, cocoa, and salt together in a mixing bowl to combine; set aside.

2] In an electric mixer, fitted with a paddle if your machine has one, cream the butter, sugar, corn syrup, and vanilla until light and smooth, about 2 minutes at medium speed, stopping to scrape down the bowl as needed. Add the eggs, one at a time, and continue to beat at medium speed until well blended. Reduce speed to low and add the reserved dry ingredients, mixing only until incorporated. Remove the bowl from the mixer and stir the batter once or twice with a rubber spatula to mix in any dry ingredients that might have escaped blending. Fold in the cherries and cognac. Scrape the batter into the pan and spread it evenly with a spatula. (It will smooth as it bakes.) Bake for 30 to 35 minutes, or until a toothpick inserted in the center of the cake comes out clean. Cool 5 minutes in the pan before turning the cake out onto a rack. Invert the cake onto another rack so it's right-side up. Cool to room temperature.

3] THE ICING. Melt the unsweetened and bittersweet chocolates in the top of a double boiler over hot water or in a bowl in a microwave. Remove from heat and, working by hand, whisk in the butter, 1 tablespoon at a time. One by one, add the egg, yolk, and cognac. Beat until the icing is glossy and the whisk leaves thick tracks. Don't overbeat, or the color will lighten. Pour the icing onto the center of the cake and use a long metal spatula to ice just the top, not the sides, of the cake.

SERVING. The icing will set at room temperature and the cake can be served as soon as the top is dry, or it can be chilled or frozen before being cut into 2″ × 2″ bars and served. In fact, this cake never freezes rock solid and can be served straight from the freezer. Frozen, the Chocolate Bars taste the way high-quality ice cream would if it were cake.

    STORING. You can freeze this dessert for 1 month. Wrap it airtight after the icing has frozen.

    BEST MATCH. While these would be a good match to a tall glass of cold milk, they're really meant to be served with strong coffee to grown-up friends.

❁ PLAYING AROUND. (Sybarite's Special) For a Sybarite's Special, cut leftover bars into small chunks and mix into softened vanilla ice cream. You can mix the chunks into the ice cream with a spatula or use the paddle attachment of an electric mixer. Freeze the ice cream briefly to firm it if it becomes too soft in the process.

Raspberry Rugelach

Rugelach are small, intensely flavored roll-up cookies made with a tender cream cheese dough. It's a dough I love because it's a cinch to make and it's indestructible. It can't be overworked, *never gets tough, and always tastes good. It also has just the right tang to go with this filling of raspberry, cinnamon, currants, and chocolate chips. § Makes 3 Dozen Cookies*

THE DOUGH

4 oz. cold cream cheese, cut into 4 pieces
½ c. (1 stick) cold unsalted butter, cut into 8 pieces
1 c. all-purpose flour

THE FILLING

⅔ c. seedless raspberry jam
2 tbsp. sugar
½ tsp. ground cinnamon
¼ c. plump, moist currants
⅔ c. mini chocolate chips or chopped semisweet chocolate

1] **THE DOUGH.** Let the cold cream cheese and butter stand at room temperature for 10 minutes. Put the flour in a food processor. Scatter the cream cheese and butter pieces over the flour and pulse on and off 6 to 8 times. Now let the machine run, stopping to scrape the sides of the bowl frequently, until the dough forms large curds. Don't process so long that the dough forms a ball on the blade.

2] Turn the dough out onto a work surface and gather it into a ball. Divide the dough in half and shape each half into a square. Wrap the dough tightly in plastic wrap and chill for at least 2 hours before using. (*The dough can be refrigerated for up to 3 days.*)

3] **THE FILLING.** Remove one package of dough from the refrigerator and let rest at room temperature until malleable, about 10 minutes. Meanwhile, heat the raspberry jam in a saucepan over low heat or in a bowl in a microwave until it liquifies. Remove from heat and reserve. Butter 2 baking sheets, preferably nonstick, and set aside.

4] On a lightly floured surface, roll the dough out into a 10-inch square. Using a pastry brush, spread a thin coating of jam over the dough. Combine 2 tablespoons sugar and the cinnamon and sprinkle half of this mixture over the dough. Scatter half the currants and chocolate over the dough. Cover the dough with a sheet of waxed paper and, using your hands, gently press the ingredients into the dough. Remove the paper.

5] Mark the top and bottom edges of the dough at 2-inch intervals. Using these marks as guides, cut diagonally across the dough to make a harlequin, or diamond-shaped, pattern, then cut through the dough crosswise to make 18 equal triangles. (There will be 2 odd pieces of dough, at either end; these can be pieced together to make nibbles.)

6] Starting at the wide base of each triangle, roll up the dough so that each cookie looks like a miniature croissant. Place the cookies on the baking sheets with the points tucked underneath. Refrigerate the cookies for at least 30 minutes before baking, or freeze. (*Shaped cookies can be frozen for up to*

THE FINISH
1 large egg
1 tsp. cold water
2 tbsp. sugar

2 weeks, then baked without thawing.) Repeat with the remaining dough, jam, cinnamon-sugar, currants, and chocolate chips.

7] THE FINISH. Position 2 racks to divide the oven in thirds and preheat the oven to 350°. Beat the egg with the cold water to make a glaze. Brush a little glaze over each cookie. Sprinkle the cookies with the remaining 2 tablespoons sugar. Bake for 20 to 25 minutes, or until golden. (*Frozen cookies will take 5 to 7 minutes longer.*) Transfer the cookies to a rack and cool to room temperature.

SERVING. I think the many flavors in these cookies come together when they reach room temperature, but I'm never surprised when I find them being snatched from the cooling rack and eaten warm: minutes-from-the-oven rugelach have their fans.

STORING. Cookies can be stored at room temperature in an airtight container for 2 to 3 days or frozen for 1 month.

BEST MATCH. The raspberry in the rugelach cries out for tea, the chocolate for coffee, and in the end, either is good. Think of these when you want a tasty add-on with Mixed Fruit with Bubbling Almond Cream (page 159).

❀| PLAYING AROUND. (California Roll-ups and Other Variations) You can go traditional with these, brushing the rolled-out dough with melted butter (omitting the jam) and then sprinkling over chopped nuts (walnuts or hazelnuts) and a few chopped raisins or currants. You can also trade in the raspberry jam for apricot, the currants for small dices of dried apricots, and the chocolate for walnuts, and turn out a California Roll-up. For something very different, brush the rugelach with a thin film of red currant jelly and fill with plumped, dried cranberries and chopped pecans.

DINNER PARTY DAZZLERS

Desserts to Show Off

Apple Tatinettes
(Pear Tatinettes)

Frozen Chocolate—Peanut Butter Mousse Torte
(Frozen Parfait)

Minted White Chocolate Velvets
(Velvet Crème Brûlée)

Chilled Hazelnut-Chocolate Tartlets
(Chilled Almond-Chocolate Tartlets)

Frosty Double Chocolate Tart
(Extra-Bittersweet Chocolate Sauce)

Posh Pommes: Dinner Party Baked Apples
(Spicy Baked Apples)

Kir Coupes with Peaches
(Campari—Orange Juice Coupes)

Fifteen-Minute Magic: A Chocolate-Amaretti Torte
(Amaretto Custard Sauce)

Frozen Winter Sunshine
(Frozen Orange-Berry Terrine)

Mango-Berry Mousse with Raspberry Sauce
(Summer Fruit Mousse)

Chocolate Midnight
(Silky Smooth Chocolate Sauce)

Golden Cloud Cake
(Berry Cloud Cake)

Classic French Chocolate Gâteau
(Chocolate-Kirsch Cake)

When you're pulling out all the stops, pull out the desserts in this chapter: They'll make you a star. Here are big cakes with sumptuous fillings and billowy frostings, shimmering coupes, luscious mousses, elegantly understated tortes and tarts, and chocolate, chocolate, and more chocolate. The selection is wide enough for you to find the perfect match for any main course and stunning enough to allow you to depend on dessert to carry the night.

More than three quarters of these Dazzlers can be made in advance and kept in the freezer or refrigerator; some can even be frozen, frosting and all. And, as sensational as they look, many are a cinch to make.

If you make just one recipe from this chapter, I urge you to make Fifteen-Minute Magic: A Chocolate-Amaretti Torte. All you have to do is put the ingredients in the food processor, press the button, pour the batter into the pan, bake, cool, serve, and enjoy. It is truly magical.

Apple Tatinettes

Tarte Tatin is the ultimate French apple pie. It's baked upside down, producing caramelized apples and crispy pastry, then turned right-side up, usually producing burnt fingers. Everyone loves a good Tarte Tatin, yet few want to make it at home. But things are different with my mini-version. These Tatinettes are baked in a muffin tin and turned out easily onto a baking sheet. They are always beautiful, even if a few apples stick to the pan, and simple to make in stages so you can serve them hot from the oven, just the way they're presented in great French restaurants. § Makes 6 Tartlets

1 sheet (slightly more than ½ pound) storebought frozen puff pastry (I use Pepperidge Farm)

1 tbsp. unsalted butter

1 tbsp. sugar

2 pounds (about 5 or 6) Granny Smith or firm Golden Delicious apples

2 tsp. fresh lemon juice

4 tbsp. (½ stick) unsalted butter

½ c. sugar

3 tbsp. raisins, optional

2 tbsp. applejack or dark rum, optional

Crème fraîche or best-quality vanilla ice cream

1] Defrost the frozen pastry for 20 minutes or until it is supple but still chilled. On a floured surface, roll it to a thickness of ¹⁄₁₆ inch. Cut out six 3½-inch rounds from the dough. Place them on a baking sheet, prick them all over with a fork, and cover with plastic. Chill until ready to use.

2] Place a rack in the center of the oven and preheat the oven to 350°. You will need a muffin tin, preferably nonstick, that has at least 6 cups, each with a ½-cup capacity. Coat the cups with 1 tablespoon butter and sprinkle with the 1 tablespoon sugar. Peel, core, and halve the apples. Cut the apples crosswise into very thin slices, placing the slices in a large bowl and tossing them with the lemon juice as you work to prevent discoloring.

3] Melt the 4 tablespoons butter in a large heavy skillet over medium-high heat. Add the ½ cup sugar and stir until it is moist. Stir in the apples and sauté, stirring constantly, until the apples are well caramelized, about 8 to 10 minutes. (At first, the apples will give off juice and the fruit will be stewing in boiling liquid. As you continue to sauté, the juices will thicken, turn golden, and, finally, caramelize the fruit.) Add the raisins and applejack, if desired, and cook a minute to boil off the alcohol. Remove the pan from the heat. Spoon the mixture into the muffin cups, packing it down gently. (*The recipe can be prepared to this point a few hours ahead and left, covered, at room temperature.*)

4] Top the fruit with a pastry round, tucking the sides of the dough around the apples. The pastry will tuck in some places, crinkle and pop in others, but that's OK. Bake for 20 to 25 minutes, until the pastry is puffed and golden. Cover the tin with a cookie sheet and turn out the Tatinettes. Use a kitchen knife to return stray or stuck pieces of apple to each pastry.

SERVING. Place each Tatinette in the center of a dessert plate. Serve immediately with a scoop of ice cream or a dollop of crème fraîche.

STORING. While you can put the process on hold, as noted in the recipe, once the Tatinettes come out of the oven they must be served immediately.

BEST MATCH. This is a small, elegant dessert made to follow a big dinner. In the fall, it's a good match to such game dishes as venison with a sweet-pungent sauce or roasted pheasant with assorted wild mushrooms; in winter, think of this when you're serving a roast.

❂| PLAYING AROUND. (Pear Tatinettes) You can make Tatinettes with pears or a combination of apples and pears. Add coarsely chopped nuts to the mixture, if you like, or, if you can find them, wonderfully tart dried cranberries. (Make sure they're moist and not dried out when you add them to the recipe.) Tatinettes are also heavenly with Custard Sauce. Try the sauce on page 193, replacing the Grand Marnier with applejack or rum.

Frozen Chocolate–Peanut Butter Mousse Torte

I first tasted the combination of cognac and peanut butter at New York's 4-star Restaurant Lafayette and, yes, the French pastry chef used Skippy, the American childhood classic. The combo, odd at first hearing, is brilliant at first bite: the cognac intensifies and deepens the rich, distinctive taste of peanuts (and gives them enough class to show up for dinner). This dessert is termed a torte because of its layering: on the bottom, a crisp, sweet, roasted peanut crust; next, a layer of satiny chocolate truffle cream; and to finish, a cloud-light peanut mousse. Served straight from the freezer, this gorgeous torte is a very dressy, do-ahead dessert.
§ Makes 12 Servings

THE CRUST

¾ c. all-purpose flour
¾ c. roasted salted peanuts, without skins
¼ c. sugar
4 tbsp. (½ stick) cold unsalted butter, cut into 4 pieces
1 large egg, beaten

THE TRUFFLE CREAM

3 oz. high-quality bittersweet chocolate, such as Lindt or Tobler, coarsely chopped
4½ tbsp. unsalted butter, cut into 4 pieces
3 tbsp. sugar
3 large eggs, at room temperature

1] THE CRUST. Line the bottom of a 9½-inch springform pan with a round of waxed paper. Place the flour, peanuts, and sugar in a food processor. Process until the peanuts are coarsely chopped. Add the butter to the bowl all at once and pulse for 10 seconds to form a crumbly meal. Pour in the beaten egg and continue to process until large curds form. Press the dough onto the bottom of the prepared pan. Do not make a rim of dough; you need just a bottom layer for this recipe. Freeze the crust, uncovered, for 30 minutes before baking. *(If you want, you can make the crust ahead to this point and keep it in the freezer, well wrapped, for up to 2 weeks.)*

2] Center a rack in the oven and preheat the oven to 375°. Remove the crust from the freezer and cover it with a sheet of aluminum foil, pressing against the bottom to get a tight fit. Fill with pie weights or dried beans and place on a baking sheet with sides to catch any drips. Bake the crust for 15 minutes. Remove the foil and weights and bake about 5 minutes more, until the crust is golden. Cool on a rack. Remove the sides of the springform and turn the crust out onto the palm of your hand (your left palm if you're right-handed. This sounds harder than it is. The crust is so fragile you can't turn it out onto a rack—it would break when it hit the rack. If you spread your fingers, the peanut disk will fit nicely on your palm.) Carefully peel away the waxed paper with your free hand. Place the bottom of the springform on top of the crust and turn it over so the crust is resting in the pan. Replace the sides of the pan.

3] THE TRUFFLE CREAM. Melt the chocolate and butter in the top of a double boiler over hot water or in a bowl in a microwave. Remove from heat and whisk in the sugar. Let the mixture stand 5 minutes. One at a time, whisk in the eggs. Pour the chocolate cream over the crust and freeze for 30 minutes to set.

THE MOUSSE

½ c. chunky peanut butter (**Skippy is perfect for this**)

1 tbsp. cognac

3 eggs, separated

1 egg yolk

½ c. sugar

1 c. heavy cream, chilled

4] THE MOUSSE. In an electric mixer, using the paddle if you have one, cream the peanut butter and cognac on medium speed for about 1 minute. When well blended, add the egg yolks, one at a time, beating until smooth. This will be a stiff mixture. (If you have just one bowl for your mixer, transfer the peanut mixture to a large bowl and wash the mixer bowl thoroughly before proceeding.) In a clean, dry mixer bowl, with the whisk attachment in place, whip the egg whites until they form soft peaks. Gradually add the sugar and continue to beat until the meringue resembles marshmallow. Whisk one-third of the meringue into the peanut butter mixture to lighten it; fold in the remainder with a rubber spatula. In the same mixer bowl, whip the cream to the medium-peak stage, and fold it into the peanut mixture. Pour the mousse over the chilled chocolate, smooth the top, and freeze for at least 4 hours before serving. *(The torte can be made and frozen, wrapped airtight in the springform pan, for up to 3 days in advance.)*

SERVING. Do not thaw the torte before serving. To unmold, wrap a kitchen towel dampened in hot water around the sides of the pan for 10 seconds. Release the sides and lift the torte from its base onto a serving platter.

STORING. Once defrosted, the torte can be kept in the refrigerator, well wrapped, for 1 day. Served from the refrigerator, the mousse layer of the torte will have a lighter, creamier, somewhat spongier texture.

BEST MATCH. Save this sleek, sophisticated torte for your most special dinners when you pull out all the stops and serve lobster or tender baby lamb. Follow with sweetened espresso and snifters of fine cognac.

❀| **PLAYING AROUND.** (Frozen Parfait) For a simpler, still-delicious-but-not-as-dazzling dessert, omit the crust and spoon alternating layers of the truffled chocolate and peanut butter mousse into tall, slim parfait glasses, ending with mousse. Freeze. Serve topped with a rosette of whipped cream and a sprinkling of crushed peanut brittle for crunch.

Minted White Chocolate Velvets

Velvets are a delightful bundle of contradictions: They are baked like cup custard but have the texture of mousse; they have a soft ivory color, the effect of lots of white chocolate, but chocolate is the underflavor; and they are unquestionably rich, but pleasingly cool and refreshing because of the mint. § Makes 6 Servings

5 egg yolks, at room temperature
3 tbsp. sugar
¾ tsp. pure mint extract
1¾ c. heavy cream
¾ c. milk
5 oz. white chocolate, such as Tobler Narcisse, finely chopped
6 sprigs fresh mint

1] Position a rack one-third up from the bottom of the oven and preheat the oven to 325°. Set aside six ½-cup ramekins and a roasting pan. In a medium-size bowl, whisk the yolks, sugar, and mint extract until they thicken and pale. (It's a quick job by hand, or you can use an electric mixer with a whisk attachment.)

2] Scald the cream and milk in a heavy saucepan over direct heat or in a microwave. Remove from heat and stir in the chopped white chocolate. The chocolate may not dissolve completely and it may look like egg drop soup on the bottom of the pan—it's O.K. Pour the chocolate mixture into the egg mixture a little at a time, stirring constantly. Skim the foam from the top of the mixture and strain the mixture into the ramekins.

3] Place the ramekins in the roasting pan; fill the roasting pan with hot water to come halfway up the sides of the ramekins. Bake the Velvets for 30 to 35 minutes, or until a knife inserted in the center comes out clean. Remove the ramekins from the pan and cool on a rack. When the Velvets are at room temperature, cover with plastic wrap (do not let the plastic touch the tops) and chill at least 4 hours before serving.

SERVING. Garnish the well-chilled Velvets with sprigs of mint and serve each in its ramekin on a doily-lined dessert plate.

STORING. The custards can be kept refrigerated, wrapped airtight, for up to 5 days.

BEST MATCH. These are splendid after such dishes as pasta with pesto, garlic chicken, or highly seasoned seafood preparations, particularly stews or bouillabaisse-type soups.

❋| PLAYING AROUND. (Velvet Crème Brûlée) Turn your Velvets into crackle-topped Crème Brûlée. When the Velvets are very cold (you can't do this with warm custard), sift 1 teaspoon of brown sugar evenly over each ramekin. Place the ramekins 4 or 5 inches from the broiler flame and broil for 30 to 60 seconds, or until the sugar is caramelized. Chill, uncovered, for 1 hour before serving.

Chilled Hazelnut-Chocolate Tartlets

These tartlets are among my favorite desserts, and not just because they are chocolate. They have the right blend of textures, crunchy and creamy; a lovely balance of flavors, intense and soft; a polished, professional look; and the convenient quality of freezability. All this and they turn out picture perfect and rave-review delicious every time, no matter the baker's expertise. § Makes 12 Tartlets

THE CRUST

¾ c. all-purpose flour
¾ c. hazelnuts, toasted, skinned, and coarsely ground
¼ c. sugar
⅛ tsp. salt
6 tbsp. cold unsalted butter, cut into 6 pieces
1 large egg, lightly beaten

THE FILLING

⅔ c. heavy cream
8 oz. high-quality bittersweet chocolate, such as Lindt or Tobler, finely chopped
2 tbsp. Frangelico or other hazelnut liqueur

THE TOPPING

¼ c. heavy cream
1 tsp. confectioners' sugar

1] THE CRUST. Put the flour, nuts, sugar, and salt in a food processor and pulse a few times to combine. Add the butter all at once and pulse 10 to 15 times, until the dough resembles coarse meal. With the machine on, add the beaten egg and continue to process until large curds form. Divide the dough among twelve 3-inch tartlet pans. Use your fingertips to press the dough evenly along the bottom and up the sides of the pans. Place the pans, uncovered, in the freezer to firm the crusts for 30 minutes before baking. *(You can make the crusts to this point and freeze them, wrapped well, for up to 2 weeks before baking.)*

2] Place a rack one-third up from the bottom of the oven and preheat the oven to 375°. Remove the crusts from the freezer and cover each with a square of aluminum foil, pressing the foil against the bottom and sides of the crusts to get a tight fit. Fill with pie weights or dried beans and place the pans on a baking sheet. Bake for 20 minutes. Remove the foil and weights and continue to bake for 7 to 10 minutes, or until golden brown. Place the crusts, still in their pans, on a rack to cool to room temperature.

3] THE FILLING. Bring the cream to a boil in a small saucepan; or you can do this in a microwave. Remove from heat and stir in the chocolate, mixing until smooth and glossy. Add the liqueur and blend well. Set the pan aside, uncovered, to cool for 5 minutes, stirring once or twice. Pour the mixture into the crusts and place in the freezer for at least 2 hours.

4] THE TOPPING. Beat the cream until soft peaks form. Add the confectioners' sugar and continue to beat until fairly firm. *(You can do this up to 1 hour ahead. Cover the cream tightly and refrigerate until needed.)*

SERVING. Place the frozen tartlets in the refrigerator for 1 hour to mellow and defrost slightly before serving. (For a change, or convenience, you can serve these tartlets almost frozen. The texture will remind you of fudge.) Remove the tartlets from their pans. Spoon a bit of the cream in the center of each tartlet or use a pastry bag with a star tip to pipe on rosettes. Bring the tartlets to the table on individual dessert plates.

STORING. Without whipped cream, the tartlets will keep in the freezer, wrapped airtight, for 2 weeks. Once removed from the freezer, they can be kept covered in the refrigerator for 2 days.

BEST MATCH. Choose this dessert for a luxurious finish to a dinner that starred pepper-crusted beef or an excellent, meaty, seared tuna. Follow with coffee while the taste of chocolate is still strong.

❀| PLAYING AROUND. (Chilled Almond-Chocolate Tartlets) Try this with almonds and Amaretto standing in for the hazelnuts and Frangelico.

Frosty Double Chocolate Tart

This tart has the understated elegance of pearls and a little black dress. The press-in cocoa crust (a snap to make) is filled with a satiny, snow-white blend of white chocolate, cream cheese, and whipped cream, a mix that can be served almost frozen. The finish is an intriguing web of dark chocolate. Plan ahead because each component needs a cooling period, but remember that you can put the process on hold anytime and that the dessert, stored in the freezer, will keep for 2 weeks. § Makes 6 to 8 Servings

THE CRUST

1 c. all-purpose flour

¼ c. sugar

¼ c. cocoa, preferably a Dutch-processed brand, such as Droste or Poulain

Pinch of salt

½ c. (1 stick) unsalted butter, very cold or frozen, cut into 8 pieces

2½ to 3 tbsp. ice water

THE FILLING

6 oz. white chocolate, such as Tobler Narcisse, coarsely chopped

3 oz. cream cheese, at room temperature and very soft

1 c. heavy cream, chilled

1] THE CRUST. Place the dry ingredients in a food processor and pulse just to combine. Add the butter all at once and pulse 10 to 15 times, or until the mixture is coarse and mealy. Gradually pour in 2½ tablespoons of the ice water, pulsing once after each addition, then processing until the dough is blended enough to hold together when pressed; you may need to add up to ½ tablespoon more of the ice water. Turn the dough out into the center of a 9-inch tart pan with removable bottom. Use your fingertips to press the dough evenly into the bottom of the pan and up the sides. There is a generous amount of dough, so you may have a little left over. Prick the crust well all over. Freeze the crust, uncovered, for 30 minutes before baking. *(You can make the crust to this point, wrap it airtight, and freeze it for up to 2 weeks before baking.)*

2] Position a rack one-third up from the bottom of the oven and preheat the oven to 350°. Remove the crust from the freezer and cover with aluminum foil, pressing against the bottom and sides of the crust to get a tight fit. Fill with pie weights or dried beans and bake for 20 minutes. Remove the foil and weights and bake 3 to 5 minutes longer, to firm the crust. Don't be concerned if your crust develops small cracks; the filling will not seep out. Cool the crust to room temperature in the pan on a rack.

3] THE FILLING. Place the chocolate in the top of a double boiler over hot, not boiling, water. Make sure the water is not touching the bottom of the chocolate pot. White chocolate is tricky, so melt it over the lowest heat and don't stop stirring for a second. As soon as the chocolate is smooth, remove it from the heat.

4] Use a rubber spatula to mash the soft cream cheese against the sides of a bowl until it is very smooth. With the spatula, beat the cheese into the hot chocolate. The mixture will look curdled and some oil may seep out around the edges, but don't worry. Scrape the mixture into the bowl of an electric mixer and beat on high speed, using the whisk attachment, until it comes together. The mixture will be smooth, glossy, and satiny. (If it's not, just keep beating.) Remove the chocolate-cheese from the mixer and put it into a bowl (you can use the same bowl you used to beat the cream cheese originally); set aside. Pour the heavy cream into the bowl of the electric mixer (there's no need to wash it) and whip until it forms soft, billowy mounds. Stir one-quarter of the whipped cream into the chocolate mixture, then gently fold in the rest. Fill the crust and smooth the top. Freeze, uncovered, for 20 minutes before decorating.

THE DECORATION
1 oz. dark chocolate, semi- or bittersweet

5] **THE DECORATION.** Melt the dark chocolate in the top of a double boiler over hot water or in a bowl in a microwave. Dip the tines of a fork into the chocolate and wave it across the top of the tart to make an attractive drip pattern—like a Jackson Pollock action painting. Freeze the tart at least 4 hours.

SERVING. Two hours before you're ready to serve, transfer the tart from the freezer to the refrigerator. To serve, unmold the tart and slide it onto a doily-lined cake plate.

STORING. After the tart is frozen, it can be wrapped airtight and kept in the freezer for up to 2 weeks.

BEST MATCH. The soothing taste and texture of this tart hit the spot after intensely flavored foods such as musky porcini risotto or the bistro favorite, calves' liver finished with vinegar. It's marvelous after a seafood mixed grill or almost anything à la Southwest—chilies and chocolate are a good match.

❀ **PLAYING AROUND.** (Extra-Bittersweet Chocolate Sauce) Melt 1 ounce unsweetened chocolate and 2 ounces semisweet chocolate; set aside. Scald ½ cup heavy cream, ½ cup milk, 2 teaspoons sugar, ½ teaspoon espresso powder, and a pinch of salt in a medium saucepan over medium heat or in a bowl in a microwave. Remove from heat. Gradually whisk the cream mixture into the chocolate. When smooth, whisk in 1 tablespoon butter. Chill. This sauce will not thicken or become sticky when it touches the cold tart.

Posh Pommes: Dinner Party Baked Apples

Leave behind all memories of huge, wrinkled, awkward-to-eat baked apples found in neighborhood delicatessens. These exquisite creations, inspired by a recipe from the famed French chef Georges Blanc, are a far cry from any baked apple you've ever had. They are worthy of your grandest dinners. The apples are scooped out, stuffed with a blend of cardamom-
and orange-spiced grated apple, sweet currants, and powdered almonds, and served with a silky, Grand Marnier–scented custard sauce. Although the apples need attention at intervals, they're easy to make and, following the do-ahead notes, can be baked while you and your guests are having dinner; just remember that the sauce needs time to chill. § Makes 6 Servings

THE GRAND MARNIER CUSTARD SAUCE

1 c. milk
½ vanilla bean or 1 tsp. pure
    vanilla extract
3 egg yolks
¼ c. sugar
2 tsp. Grand Marnier or other
    orange liqueur

THE APPLE SHELLS

3 large baking apples, such as
    Rome or Cortland (each
    about 10 oz.)
2 tbsp. fresh orange juice

1] THE GRAND MARNIER CUSTARD SAUCE. Place the milk in a small heavy saucepan. Split the vanilla bean lengthwise and scrape the pulp into the milk. Add the pod to the milk. (If you are using vanilla extract, do *not* add it now.) Bring the milk to the boil. While the milk is heating, whisk the yolks and sugar until they thicken and become pale. Add about ¼ cup of the boiling milk to the yolks, whisking constantly. Whisk in the rest of the milk, then return the mixture to the saucepan. Cook over medium heat, whisking vigorously and without stopping, for about 2 minutes, just to cook the eggs and thicken the mixture slightly. One bubble may pop at the surface, but the mixture must not boil. Strain the sauce into a clean bowl. Add the vanilla extract, if you are using it, and the liqueur. Cool the sauce at room temperature, whisking occasionally, and then chill. *(The sauce will keep covered in the refrigerator for 2 days.)*

2] THE APPLE SHELLS. Place a rack in the center of the oven and preheat the oven to 350°. Butter a large glass or enamel baking pan, and pour in ½ cup of water; set aside. Cut the baking apples in half crosswise. With a sharp knife and a small spoon, scoop out and discard the core and most of the flesh, making shells about ½ inch thick all around. Peel away a ½-inch strip of skin around the top edge of each shell. Brush the cut surfaces with the orange juice. Place the apples in the pan and bake for 10 minutes. Remove the apples from the oven but leave them in the pan. *(The apple shells can be prepared a few hours ahead and left covered at room temperature. Make certain to preheat the oven again before continuing with the recipe.)*

THE FILLING

**2 medium-size tart apples, such
as Granny Smith or Golden
Delicious (each about 5 oz.)
peeled, cored, and quartered**

¼ c. sliced or julienned almonds

2 tbsp. sugar

2 egg yolks

2 tbsp. sugar

⅛ tsp. salt

1 tsp. chopped orange zest

¼ tsp. ground cardamom

2½ tbsp. currants

**2½ tbsp. unsalted butter, melted
and kept warm**

**1½ tsp. Grand Marnier or other
orange liqueur**

**Toasted sliced almonds and
orange slices, optional**

3] THE FILLING. While the apples are baking (*or several hours ahead*), fit a food processor with a shredding disk and grate the tart apples. Press the grated apples between your palms to remove excess moisture and place them in a medium-size mixing bowl. Wipe out the processor and insert the metal blade. Pulverize the almonds and 2 tablespoons sugar by pulsing several times. Add the nuts to the grated apples. Process the yolks, the remaining 2 tablespoons sugar, the salt, zest, and cardamom until creamy, stopping to scrape the work bowl as needed; add to the apple-nut mixture. Add the currants and stir to mix. (*If you make this ahead, keep it covered at room temperature and stir to blend before using.*) Fill each shell with this mixture, mounding it in the center. Add more water to the baking pan if necessary, and bake for 20 minutes. Remove the pan from the oven and *raise the oven temperature to 375°.*

4] Stir together the melted butter and liqueur. Prick the apple stuffing all over with a fork. Slowly pour the butter mixture evenly over the apples, allowing it to seep into the filling; brush the last of the butter mixture over the cut surfaces of the apple. Add more water to the pan if it has boiled away, and bake the apples for 15 minutes longer.

SERVING. Pour a small amount of custard sauce onto each of 6 dessert plates so that it forms a thin layer. Center a right-from-the-oven stuffed apple on the plate and serve immediately, passing the remaining sauce in a small pitcher. For an extra-special presentation, decorate the rim of each plate with toasted sliced almonds and a few sections from a small orange, such as a clementine or mandarine.

STORING. These are at their best served warm but can be served at room temperature. They should not be refrigerated.

BEST MATCH. These are a perfect fall-to-winter foil for a pork roast, perhaps one larded with dried fruit and sauced with port, or a lavishly stuffed goose. Although subtle, these can stand up to strongly flavored main courses, so think of them when you're serving something smoky, like smoked turkey or ham, or something earthy, like mushrooms.

❀| **PLAYING AROUND.** (Spicy Baked Apples) Omit the cardamom and substitute an equal amount of ground ginger or cinnamon. If you choose ginger, garnish the plates with translucent slivers of stem ginger.

Kir Coupes with Peaches

Kir is the aperitif of choice in Dijon. Made with crème de cassis, a heavy, sweet, black currant liqueur, and a local white wine, Aligoté, it is often sipped in the late afternoon at outdoor cafés or served before dinner. My version uses the aperitif to end a meal with a light, cool touch. I've sweetened the traditional drink slightly, added peaches, and turned it into an elegant gelled coupe.
§ Makes 4 Servings

⅓ c. white wine
2 packages unflavored gelatin
¾ c. crème de cassis
2⅔ c. white wine
2½ tbsp. sugar
1 tbsp. fresh lemon juice
2 ripe peaches or 12 slices frozen peaches (unthawed)

Lightly sweetened whipped cream or additional crème de cassis, optional

1] Pour the ⅓ cup wine into a medium-size nonreactive mixing bowl. Sprinkle over the gelatin and allow it to soften.

2] In a nonreactive saucepan, bring the crème de cassis, 2⅔ cups white wine, the sugar, and lemon juice to a boil, stirring to melt the sugar. Pour a little of the hot wine mixture over the gelatin and stir until it dissolves completely. Pour in the rest of the wine. Chill the mixture, stirring occasionally, until it is the consistency of unbeaten egg whites. You can speed up this process by placing the bowl in a larger bowl filled with ice cubes and water; stir frequently. (If you don't mind having the peaches float to the top of the coupes, you can skip this initial chilling step.)

3] While the gel is chilling, bring a pot of water to the boil and blanch the fresh peaches for 15 seconds. Remove the peaches and peel them. Return the peaches to the pot, lower the heat, and simmer 10 minutes. Lift the peaches from the liquid with a slotted spoon, drain, cut in half, and remove the pits. Place 1 peach half in each of 4 wine glasses. If you're using frozen peach slices, divide them evenly among the glasses. Pour the slightly thickened gel over the peaches and chill until set, about 3 hours.

SERVING. I usually serve these plain, but they are also good with a small amount of lightly sweetened whipped cream or with a very small amount of crème de cassis poured over the top.

STORING. The coupes can be made up to 2 days ahead and kept tightly covered in the refrigerator.

BEST MATCH. This is a fabulous dessert for summertime favorites such as sautéed soft-shelled crabs or, if you really want to go regional in an amusing way, serve it after shrimp with Dijon mustard sauce. Think about offering a few of Jean-Marc's Honeycomb Tuiles (page 164) on the side.

❀| **PLAYING AROUND.** (Campari–Orange Juice Coupes) Move over to Italy by omitting the peaches, replacing the white wine with orange juice, and substituting Campari for the crème de cassis.

Fifteen-Minute Magic:
A Chocolate-Amaretti Torte

It's just 15 minutes from the moment you unwrap the first crunchy amaretti to the time you place this elegant, deeply chocolate torte in the oven. But the real magic is the spectacular taste. The combination of dark chocolate and sweet almonds appeals to everyone. I've made it for some of New York's best chefs and served it at family reunions and the response has always been the same: delight. When Alain Sailhac was chef at New York's Plaza Hotel he pronounced the cake delicious and a good example of how a simple dessert can be great. Indeed, this is great and surprisingly simple. You need absolutely no baking experience to turn out a perfect cake.
§ Makes 10 to 14 Servings

1 oz. unsweetened chocolate

3 oz. high-quality bittersweet chocolate, such as Lindt or Tobler

6 large, double amaretti (Italian macaroons available in specialty stores and some supermarkets; look for the Saronno brand)

¾ c. sliced or julienned blanched almonds

½ c. (1 stick) unsalted butter, at room temperature

½ c. sugar

3 large eggs, at room temperature

Cocoa or confectioners' sugar, optional

Heavy cream, lightly whipped, or premium-quality vanilla or coffee ice cream

1] Place a rack in the center of the oven and preheat the oven to 350°. Butter an 8-inch round cake pan. Line the bottom with waxed paper and butter the paper. Dust the inside of the pan with flour and tap out the excess. Melt the chocolates in the top of a double boiler over hot water or in a bowl in a microwave; set aside.

2] Place the amaretti and almonds in a food processor and pulse several times, until the mixture is evenly ground. Turn out onto a sheet of waxed paper and reserve. Put the butter, sugar, and eggs into the work bowl and process until the mixture is satiny smooth and no longer grainy, about 3 minutes. Stop to scrape the bowl occasionally to ensure that the batter is properly blended. Pour in the reserved amaretti-almond powder and the melted chocolate. Pulse just until the mixture is well combined.

3] Turn the batter into the prepared pan and bake 25 to 30 minutes. The cake will dome slightly and the top will look dry and, perhaps, cracked. Cool the cake on a rack for 30 minutes. Run a blunt knife around the edges of the pan and turn out the cake. Peel off the paper, invert, and cool right-side up on the rack. The cake is only about 1 inch high, but it packs a lot of taste.

SERVING. This is at its best at room temperature. Dust the top with cocoa or confectioners' sugar, if desired, and cut into very thin slices. (It's richer than it looks.) Finish each plate with a small scoop of ice cream or spoonful of unsweetened, lightly whipped heavy cream.

STORING. Wrapped in plastic, the cake will keep for 3 days at room temperature; wrapped airtight it can be frozen for 1 month.

BEST MATCH. It's hard to think of a meal that wouldn't be enhanced by this torte, but it's an especially good finish to a creamy pasta primavera or a refined Dover sole. For a special celebration, serve Fifteen-Minute Magic with a glass of Malvasia di Lipari, Sicily's heady dessert wine.

❂| **PLAYING AROUND.** (Amaretto Custard Sauce) For a dressy presentation, and a knockout flavor combo, film each plate with Amaretto Custard Sauce, then top with a slice of torte (minus the ice cream or whipped cream, of course). To make the sauce, follow the recipe for Grand Marnier Custard Sauce (page 193), omitting the Grand Marnier and flavoring the sauce with a vanilla bean or 1 teaspoon pure vanilla extract, ½ teaspoon pure almond extract, and 2 teaspoons Amaretto.

Frozen Winter Sunshine

You'd be hard-pressed to find another dessert as bright and refreshing as this terrine of frozen citrus segments suspended in juice. The random arrangement of pink grapefruit, lemon, lime, and sweet orange gives each frosty slice the look of a modern painting. The terrine's very easy to make, although time-consuming until you hit the right rhythm for separating the fruit from the membrane. Once made, however, it can be stored in the freezer for a month.
§ Makes 8 to 10 Servings

THE TERRINE

4 pink grapefruits
5 juice oranges
2 lemons
2 limes
⅓ c. sugar
2 pkg. unflavored gelatin
⅓ c. cold water
3 tbsp. Grand Marnier or other orange liqueur

THE SAUCE

½ pt. fresh raspberries or 1 pkg. (10 oz.) frozen raspberries in syrup, partially thawed
3 tbsp. sugar, or to taste, if using fresh raspberries

1] **THE TERRINE.** Working over a strainer placed over a nonreactive bowl, pare the fruit down to the flesh. Using a sharp, small knife, separate the fruit in segments from the connective membranes. Drop the membranes into the strainer and place the citrus segments in another nonreactive bowl. When all the fruit has been cut up, squeeze the membranes to extract as much juice as possible from them; discard the membranes.

2] Place the juice from the bowl, and whatever juices may have accumulated around the reserved fruit, in a nonreactive saucepan. (You should have about 2 to 2½ cups of juice.) Add the sugar and bring to the boil.

3] Meanwhile, pour the cold water into the bowl that held the juice. Sprinkle over the gelatin and allow it to soften. When the juice has come to the boil, pour a little of it over the gelatin and stir until the gelatin dissolves; then pour in the rest of the hot juice. Chill the mixture, stirring occasionally, until it is the consistency of unbeaten egg whites. (You can speed up this process by placing the bowl in a larger bowl filled with ice cubes and water; stir frequently.) Gently stir in the reserved fruit.

4] Rinse a 9″ × 5″ loaf pan in cold water and shake out the excess water. Pour the fruit and thickened juice into the pan and freeze overnight.

5] **THE SAUCE.** Place the fresh berries and sugar in a blender or processor and whirl until pureed. Push the puree through a strainer to remove the seeds, and add more sugar, if you want. If you're using frozen berries, just process or blend them. Strain, if necessary.

SERVING. Unmold the terrine by dipping it in hot water for 15 seconds and then turning it out onto a cutting board. Cut it into slices and allow the slices to rest at room temperature while you spoon a layer of puree over the bottom of each dessert plate. Place a slice on top of the puree and serve immediately, while still very frosty.

STORING. Wrapped airtight, the terrine can be kept in the freezer for 1 month.

BEST MATCH. Save this as the finale to a multicourse meal when guests will most appreciate its chill and refreshing taste. It's particularly good after spicy meals. Try it after an elaborate couscous, a garlic-laced cassoulet, or anything curried.

❀ PLAYING AROUND. (Frozen Orange-Berry Terrine) This is lovely as an all-orange terrine with a few raspberries or strawberries mixed in for color and surprise. For this version, use about a dozen oranges and a half pint of berries.

Mango-Berry Mousse with Raspberry Sauce

These are strikingly beautiful, luxuriously smooth, and richly flavored. The bright, fresh, slightly citrusy taste of mango is enhanced here by yogurt and turned into a creamy, irresistible mousse. I mold the mousse in slim layers, using the small metal rings sold for making English muffins. They're an attractive shape and when you embed a few dark berries in the mousse, pushing them up against the edges of the rings, and unmold the little desserts, the berries stand in bold contrast to the sunny-colored mousse. You could serve these easily at a black-tie dinner, they're that chic. § Makes 8 Servings

THE MOUSSE

2 large, ripe mangos
⅓ c. cold water
2 pkg. unflavored gelatin
2 tbsp. La Grande Passion or Grand Marnier or 1 tbsp. lime juice
1 pt. plain yogurt, at room temperature
3 tbsp. sugar
1 c. heavy cream, chilled
½ pt. fresh blueberries
½ pt. fresh raspberries

1] THE MOUSSE. Place a 4-inch metal English muffin ring in the center of each of 8 dessert plates; set aside. (English muffin rings are metal rings about 4 inches across and almost 1 inch high. They are inexpensive, available in housewares and kitchen supply shops, and usually sold in packages of four. If you do not have these rings, you can use tuna fish cans, scrubbed and tops and bottoms removed, or large, round cookie cutters [if they're smaller you can put two portions on each plate], or you can pour the mousse into small, attractive ramekins or custard bowls. You won't be able to unmold the dessert from ramekins or bowls, but the terrific taste will still be there.) Peel the mangos and remove the flesh from the pit, taking care not to include the stringy fibers found around the pit. Puree the fruit in a blender or processor. (You should have about 2 to 2½ cups of puree.) Pour into a large bowl.

2] Pour the cold water into a small saucepan and sprinkle over the gelatin. Allow to soften for 3 minutes. Stir over very low heat until the gelatin dissolves completely. Remove from heat and stir in the liqueur or lime juice. Whisking all the while, add the gelatin to the mango puree. Whisk the yogurt and sugar into the mango mixture.

3] Whip the heavy cream until it holds soft peaks. Whisk half of the cream into the mango, then gently fold in the rest with a rubber spatula. Fill each ring to the halfway mark with mousse. Arrange a layer of blueberries on top of the mousse; use about 1 tablespoon of berries for each serving, placing the berries evenly over the mousse and making sure some of them are at the very edge, touching the inside of the metal ring. (These will look pretty when the mousse is unmolded.) Cover the berries with the remaining

THE SAUCE

**½ pt. fresh raspberries, or
1 pkg. (10 oz.) frozen
raspberries in syrup,
partially thawed**

**2 tbsp. sugar, or to taste, if using
fresh raspberries**

mousse and level the tops with a spatula. Position 6 raspberries in a circle on top of each mousse, placing the raspberries on the mousse sideways with the broader ends facing the center. Refrigerate the molds at least 2 hours to set.

4] THE SAUCE. Puree the fresh berries and sugar in a blender or processor until smooth. Taste for sugar, and add more if desired. If you are using frozen berries, just puree them. Strain the sauce, if desired.

SERVING. To unmold, fold a paper towel in half diagonally. Starting from the straight edge and working down to the point, fold the towel until it is the width of the dessert ring. Dampen the towel with hot water, then wrap it around the ring for 30 seconds. Remove the towel and lift off the ring. Repeat with the remaining desserts. Wipe away any moisture on the plates. Pour some sauce around each of the desserts and serve immediately.

STORING. The molds can remain in the refrigerator overnight covered with waxed paper.

BEST MATCH. The bright flavor of mango is a palate refresher that's welcome after blackened anything, an elegant, full-flavored dish, such as scallops with cilantro, or a savory, herb-roasted loin of veal.

❀| **PLAYING AROUND.** (Summer Fruit Mousse) You can make this with several different kinds of purees. It is especially good made with the fruits of summer, such as peaches or apricots. Before folding in the whipped cream, taste the mixture for sugar and add more as needed.

Chocolate Midnight

A friend suggested I call this the Mmmmmm Cake because invariably everyone's first taste finishes with a chorus of "Mmmmmm." This is a sleek, long loaf of moist, tightly grained chocolate cake, almost as dark as midnight, rich with sour cream and butter, laced with two layers of raspberry jam, and finished with a gloss of soft, shiny chocolate–sour cream frosting. It's not hard to make (it's really just a one-bowl cake), and swanky as it is, it can be frozen, frosting and all. § Makes 12 Servings

THE CAKE

1½ c. all-purpose flour

½ c. cocoa, preferably a Dutch-processed brand, such as Droste or Poulain

1 tsp. baking powder

¼ tsp. baking soda

1 cup (2 sticks) unsalted butter, at room temperature

1⅓ c. sugar

2 large eggs, preferably at room temperature

1 c. sour cream, preferably at room temperature

THE FILLING

⅓ c. high-quality red raspberry jam, with or without seeds

1] THE CAKE. Center a rack in the oven and preheat the oven to 350°. Butter a 10″ × 5″ loaf pan and dust the inside with flour, tapping out the excess. Sift together the flour, cocoa, baking powder, and baking soda onto a large sheet of waxed paper; reserve.

2] In an electric mixer, using the paddle attachment if you have one, cream the butter and sugar together on medium speed until very light and fluffy, about 5 minutes, stopping to scrape down the sides of the bowl as needed. Add the eggs, one at a time, and beat for a minute after each addition. Reduce the mixer speed to low and add the sour cream. Still mixing on the lowest setting, add the sifted dry ingredients gradually, mixing just until incorporated. Remove the bowl from the mixer and give the batter a last stir with a rubber spatula.

3] Scrape the batter into the pan. Smooth the top with the spatula and then push the batter outward so it is slightly higher around the edges than in the middle. Bake for 55 to 65 minutes, or until a toothpick inserted in the center of the cake comes out clean. Remove the pan to a cooling rack and let rest 5 minutes. Unmold the cake onto the rack and cool (upside-down) to room temperature. *(The cake can be made to this point, wrapped airtight in plastic, and frozen for 1 month.)*

4] THE FILLING. The top of the cake will become the bottom layer. If it is uneven, level it using a serrated knife. Cut the cake horizontally into three layers, using the serrated knife and a gentle sawing motion. Put the layer to be used as the bottom, cut-side up, on a long serving platter or tray. Place 4 narrow strips of waxed paper just under the sides of the cake with the greatest portion of paper extending onto the platter. (You'll pull these out once the cake is frosted; they keep the platter clean.) Bring the jam and 1 teaspoon of water to a boil, stirring, in a small saucepan over low heat or warm in a bowl in a microwave. Remove from heat and spread half the warm jam over the bottom layer. Lift the middle layer onto the bottom layer (this is easily done with two broad metal spatulas) and spread with the remaining jam. Lift the top layer into place. With a small pastry or paint brush, brush away any crumbs sticking to the top or sides of the cake.

THE FROSTING

5 oz. high-quality bittersweet chocolate, such as Lindt or Tobler

½ c. sour cream, at room temperature

Lightly sweetened whipped cream, optional

5] THE FROSTING. Melt the chocolate in a bowl over hot, not boiling, water, making sure the water doesn't touch the bowl. Still over hot water, stir in the sour cream. If the mixture tightens and does not look glossy, don't worry, just continue to stir over heat; it will smooth out in a few minutes. Remove the bowl from the heat and frost the sides and top of the cake while the mixture is still warm. *(The frosting can be stored in a tightly covered container in the refrigerator for 3 days. Before using, warm over hot water or in a microwave.)* If you like, swirl the frosting on the top of the cake with the tip of a spoon to make dips and peaks, or frost the top smoothly and use the dull edge of a long knife to score a crosshatch or diamond pattern, lifting the knife with each score to produce a thin line of points. Carefully remove the waxed paper strips.

SERVING. The cake is ready to serve as soon as it is frosted. Cut with a serrated knife and, if you like, serve with a spoonful of whipped cream.

STORING. The cake can be kept uncovered at room temperature for 2 to 3 hours, or wrapped airtight and refrigerated overnight or frozen for 2 weeks. (To refrigerate or freeze, chill the cake unwrapped, then wrap when the frosting is firm.) Bring to room temperature before serving. (Chilled or frozen cake will have a firmer frosting than freshly made cake.)

BEST MATCH. Finish an elegant meal with this. It would not be too much after a roast and would be glorious after any elaborate seafood preparation. Follow with espresso or cappuccino, then cognac or Armagnac.

❀| **PLAYING AROUND.** (Silky Smooth Chocolate Sauce) For a triple dose of chocolate, serve this sauce made from the frosting recipe. You can make a small amount of sauce with whatever frosting is left over, or you can double the frosting recipe and use the excess for sauce. Place the bowl of frosting over a saucepan of hot, not boiling water, and gradually stir in a small amount of hot milk. (How much hot milk you use will depend on how much frosting you have.) Just add the milk a little bit at a time until you get the consistency you want. The sauce is ready to use when it's smooth. *(Store the sauce in the refrigerator for up to 3 days and reheat before using.)*

Golden Cloud Cake

Nothing is as pretty, or as welcome after a grand meal, as a light, gorgeous whipped cream cake, and few cakes are as light and gorgeous as this one. The cake itself is an airy genoise, the slightly dry, featherweight building block of French gateaux, moistened with rum syrup, hollowed out to make room for a tart, golden sunshine-colored blend of whipped cream and pureed apricots, then swathed in pure white cream. It's shamelessly rich and positively irresistible. § Makes 8 to 10 Servings

THE CAKE

⅔ c. all-purpose flour
¾ tsp. baking powder
4 large eggs
⅔ c. sugar
1 tsp. pure vanilla extract
2 tbsp. unsalted butter, melted and cooled to room temperature

1] THE CAKE. Center a rack in the oven and preheat the oven to 350°. Butter an 8″ × 3″ springform pan. Line the bottom with a round of parchment or waxed paper, butter the paper, and dust the pan with flour, tapping out the excess. Sift together the flour and baking powder; set aside.

2] Place the eggs and sugar in a metal bowl, preferably the bowl of an electric mixer. Whisk the ingredients together by hand until blended, about 1 minute. Place the bowl over a saucepan of simmering water and continue to whisk until the sugar dissolves and the mixture is slightly warm to the touch, about 3 minutes.

3] Remove the bowl from the saucepan, add the vanilla, fit the bowl to the electric mixer, and, using the whisk attachment, beat the mixture at medium speed for 5 minutes or until it triples in volume and the batter forms a ribbon that holds its shape for 10 seconds when the beater is lifted.

4] Sift half the dry ingredients over the batter and fold in with a rubber spatula. Don't overmix. Fold in the melted butter and then the remaining dry ingredients.

5] Scrape the batter into the pan and rotate the pan briskly just once to settle the batter. Bake for 30 to 33 minutes, until the top is springy to the touch and a toothpick inserted in the center of the cake comes out clean. Transfer the cake to a rack to cool for 5 minutes. Run a blunt knife around the edge of the cake and remove the sides of the pan. Turn the cake over onto another rack, remove the bottom of the pan and the paper, then invert back onto the cooling rack to rest, right-side up, until it reaches room temperature. You'll find that cutting the cake is easier if you allow it to set for a few hours or keep it wrapped overnight at room temperature. *(The cake can be made ahead to this point, wrapped airtight in plastic, and stored for up to 3 days at room temperature or 1 month in the freezer.)*

THE SYRUP

⅓ c. water

3 tbsp. sugar

2 tsp. dark rum

THE FILLING

6 oz. (¾ cup packed) dried apricots, preferably sweet, plump Turkish apricots

¾ c. water

½ c. heavy cream, chilled

½ tsp. pure vanilla extract

2 tsp. confectioners' sugar, pressed through a sieve

2 tsp. dark rum

THE TOPPING

1 c. heavy cream, chilled

1 tsp. pure vanilla extract

1 tbsp. confectioners' sugar, pressed through a sieve

8 slivers of glacéed apricots, optional

6] THE SYRUP. While the cake is baking or cooling, place the water and sugar in a small saucepan. Heat, swirling to mix and dissolve the sugar, until the syrup boils. Boil 1 minute, remove from heat, add the rum, and set aside to cool to room temperature.

7] THE FILLING. While the cake is cooling, place the apricots and water in a small saucepan. Bring to the boil, cover, reduce the heat, and simmer for 30 minutes, until the apricots are soft enough to be mashed with a fork and just a tablespoon or two of water remains. Transfer the apricots and liquid to a food processor and process, stopping often to scrape down the sides of the bowl, until the mixture is smoothly pureed. (If necessary, add up to 1 tablespoon more of water to the mixture as you process.) Cool the puree to room temperature.

8] Whip the cream until it holds soft peaks. Whisk in the remaining ingredients and continue to whisk by hand until the cream holds medium peaks. Fold in the cooled apricot puree. *(The filling can be made 1 day ahead and kept tightly covered in the refrigerator.)*

9] THE TOPPING. Just before you are ready to assemble the cake, whip the heavy cream until it holds medium peaks. Whisk in the vanilla and sugar and continue to whisk until the cream holds firm peaks. Cover with plastic wrap and refrigerate until needed.

10] Place the cake on a serving platter and insert 4 strips of waxed paper under the cake so the greatest part of the paper covers the platter. Using a serrated knife, slice off the top ½-inch layer of cake. Lift this layer off the cake and set aside. With the knife, outline a circle on the top of the cake ½ inch from the edge of the cake. Cut down through the outline to within ½ inch to ¼ inch from the bottom of the cake. Working with the knife and your fingers, remove the cake within this section, leaving a wall about ½ inch thick. Brush the inside of the cake with some of the rum syrup and fill with the reserved apricot cream. Use just enough cream to come level with the top of the wall of the cake. Brush a bit of syrup on the cut side of the reserved cake layer, turn the layer over, and place it on top of the filling, pressing down gently to reconstruct the cake.

11] Using an offset or icing spatula, frost the sides and top of the cake with three-quarters of the topping. Fill a small pastry bag fitted with a star tip with the remaining whipped cream and pipe 8 rosettes evenly spaced around the rim of the cake. Leave plain or place a sliver of glacéed apricot in the center of each rosette. Gently remove the strips of waxed paper. It is best to refrigerate the cake for 1 to 2 hours before serving to give the flavors time to meld.

SERVING. Bring the cake to the table on its platter, cut with a serrated knife, and serve using a wedge-shaped cake or pie knife.

STORING. The cake can be kept for up to 6 hours in the refrigerator. Take care not to place it near foods with strong odors.

BEST MATCH. While Golden Cloud Cake would be luscious after a fish meal, I think its ethereal taste and texture are most appreciated after more substantial dishes, such as strongly flavored game or poultry or any spicy or tomato-based preparation. Follow the cake with double servings of espresso.

✸| PLAYING AROUND. (Berry Cloud Cake) The dried apricot filling makes this cake a winter specialty. You can make a Berry Cloud Cake, a summer fantasy, by using ¾ cup heavy cream in the filling and folding in ¾ cup sweet red raspberries, taking care not to crush the berries. For both the syrup and the filling, omit the dark rum and use kirsch or Framboise instead. Decorate the rosettes with 8 perfect berries.

Classic French Chocolate Gâteau

This is the cake you see in every French pastry shop window, the classic layer cake: a chocolate genoise (drier than most American cakes), soaked in a bit of syrup (this one flavored with coffee), and filled and frosted with a smooth, dark chocolate buttercream. In this version, I've chosen a buttercream that tastes a lot richer than it is. Instead of the traditional egg yolk foundation, I use an egg white meringue. The result is just as full-flavored as the original, but lighter and less temperamental. Once filled and frosted, the Classic can be frozen and thawed the day of your dinner party. It's more convenient than having to trek to the nearest patisserie, and so much better than what's found at most shops. § Makes 8 to 10 Servings

THE CAKE

½ c. plus 2 tbsp. all-purpose flour
½ c. cocoa, preferably a Dutch-processed brand, such as Droste or Poulain
¼ c. cornstarch
1 tsp. baking powder
¼ tsp. baking soda
6 large eggs
1 egg yolk
1 c. sugar
4 tbsp. unsalted butter, melted and cooled to room temperature

THE SYRUP

4 tsp. instant coffee
4 tsp. boiling water
½ c. water
⅓ c. sugar

1] **THE CAKE.** Center a rack in the oven and preheat the oven to 350°. Butter two 8″ × 2″ cake pans. Line the bottoms with waxed or parchment paper, butter the paper, and dust the pans with flour, tapping out the excess. Sift together the flour, cocoa, cornstarch, baking powder, and baking soda; set aside.

2] Place the eggs, egg yolk, and sugar in a metal bowl, preferably the bowl of an electric mixer. Whisk the ingredients together by hand until blended, about 1 minute. Place the bowl over a saucepan of simmering water and continue to whisk until the sugar dissolves and the mixture is slightly warm to the touch, about 3 minutes.

3] Remove the bowl from the saucepan, fit the bowl to the electric mixer, and, using the whisk attachment, beat the mixture at medium speed for 5 minutes or until it triples in volume and the batter forms a ribbon that holds its shape for 10 seconds when the beater is lifted.

4] Sift one-third of the dry ingredients over the batter and fold in with a rubber spatula. Don't overmix. Fold in half the melted butter. Repeat with half the remaining dry ingredients and the rest of the butter. Fold in the last of the dry ingredients.

5] Divide the batter evenly between the pans. Bake for 25 to 30 minutes, until the tops are springy to the touch and a toothpick inserted in the center of the cake comes out clean. Remove the cakes to a rack to cool in the pans for 10 minutes. Unmold the cakes and remove the paper liners. Turn the cakes right-side up and cool to room temperature on racks. *(The cakes can be made ahead to this point and stored, wrapped airtight in plastic, for up to 3 days at room temperature or 1 month in the freezer.)*

6] **THE SYRUP.** In a small bowl, dissolve the instant coffee in the boiling

THE BUTTERCREAM

6 egg whites

1½ c. confectioners' sugar

¾ lb. (3 sticks) unsalted butter, at room temperature (but not soft), each stick cut into 8 pieces

8 oz. high-quality bittersweet chocolate, such as Lindt or Tobler, melted and cooled to room temperature

water; set aside. In a small saucepan, bring the ½ cup water and the sugar to a boil. Remove from heat, add the coffee mixture, and stir to combine; reserve.

7] THE BUTTERCREAM. Place the egg whites and sugar in a metal bowl, preferably the bowl of an electric mixer. Whisk the ingredients together by hand until blended, about 1 minute. Place the bowl over a saucepan of simmering water and continue to whisk until the sugar dissolves and the mixture is quite warm to the touch, about 5 minutes.

8] Remove the bowl from the saucepan, fit the bowl to the electric mixer, and, using the whisk attachment, beat the mixture at low speed until it is cool to the touch. Because this can take as long as 10 to 15 minutes it's best done in a heavy-duty mixer. Add the butter, one piece at a time. When all the butter is added the mixture will look uneven, perhaps even curdled. Increase the mixer speed to medium and beat until the buttercream comes together and is satin-textured. (Be patient, it will come together.) Return to low speed and add the melted chocolate. Remove the bowl from the mixer and complete the blending with a rubber spatula. If the buttercream is very soft, chill it briefly until it reaches spreading consistency.

9] FILLING AND FROSTING. Cut each cake horizontally into two equal layers. Place a layer, cut-side up, on a serving plate. Insert waxed paper strips under the cake with the greatest part exposed to protect the plate. Brush the layer with some of the reserved syrup. Spread with buttercream. Top with a second layer and repeat the process. Brush the cut side of the third layer with syrup and place it cut-side down on top of the cake. Frost the sides and top of the cake with buttercream, reserving some buttercream for decorating the top of the cake, if you want. Crumble the remaining layer and put the pieces in a food processor. Pulse to pulverize. Press the cake crumbs into the sides of the cake. Leave the cake as is or put the reserved buttercream into a small pastry bag fitted with a star tip and pipe rosettes or a swirl border around the edge of the cake. Remove the waxed paper strips and place the cake in the refrigerator, uncovered, for 2 to 6 hours to allow the flavors to blend.

SERVING. Remove the cake from the refrigerator 30 minutes before serving. Bring the cake to the table on its serving platter and cut into wedges with a finely serrated knife.

STORING. The cake will keep in the refrigerator for 1 day. It can be frozen for up to 1 month. Place the cake in the freezer uncovered, then wrap airtight when the frosting is firm and freeze. Bring to room temperature before serving.

BEST MATCH. Maybe it's the contrast in colors, but I think the Classic is paired most strikingly with delicate white dishes, such as sautéed scallops or creamy oyster stew. Serve the cake with a full-bodied coffee to accent the chocolate.

❁| **PLAYING AROUND.** (Chocolate-Kirsch Cake) A dessert with a new taste and a slightly different look. Replace the coffee and boiling water in the syrup with 1½ tablespoons of kirsch or Framboise. Reduce the chocolate in the buttercream to 3 ounces. Before adding the chocolate to the buttercream, remove two-thirds of the mixture to a small bowl and fold in 3 tablespoons of liqueur. Use this white buttercream to fill the cake.

HOLIDAY WRAP-UPS

Finishes for the Feasts

Chocolate Pecan Tart
(Mochaccino Ice Cream)

Banana-Pumpkin Pie
(Sour Cream Pumpkin Pie)

Pomander Cake
(Ginger-Lemon–Soaked Chocolate Cake)

Holiday Gingerbread Cake with Chocolate and Fresh Ginger
(Ginger-Infused Whipped Cream)

Christmas Clementines
(Brandied Orange Sorbet)

Mulled Wine Tart
(Blush Wine Tart)

Giant Cranberry Turnover
(Cranberry Conserve)

Peppermill Squares
(Iced and Berried Peppermill Squares)

Date and Nut Toasting Loaf
(Sweet Orange Marmalade Sandwiches)

Fruit Fritters for Chanukah
(Spiked Fritter Batter)

Valentine's Day Sweet Hearts
(Pink Butter)

Honeyed Ricotta-Almond Easter Cake
(Strawberry Sauce and Glistening Berries)

Gene Ford's Fourth of July Sparkler
(Philadelphia-Style Snow White Ice Cream)

Here's a year's worth of festive finishes to holiday meals, recipes that can become a lifetime's worth of traditions. I haven't included the customary pumpkin or pecan pies for Thanksgiving, nor the usual Christmas fruitcake, because I knew that if they weren't in your family recipe book you could find them in dozens of other books. But I have given you recipes for pumpkin pie – made with banana; pecan pie – laced with chocolate syrup; and fruitcake – a not-so-sweet cream cheese loaf cake chock-full of dates and nuts; as well as fritters for Chanukah, cheesecake for Easter, a Sparkler for the Fourth of July, and lots more—each a new take on the traditional.

If your experience is anything like mine – and I hope it will be – you'll make one of these desserts for a holiday and, before anyone's taken a bite, have to explain why you've strayed from the usual. No explanations are needed once everyone has had a taste, and when the holiday rolls around again next year, you'll have folks putting in their requests for "That chocolaty gingerbread cake you made last Christmas," or "Those pretty biscuits with the berries you surprised us with on Valentine's Day." It's the way traditions are born.

Chocolate Pecan Tart

Pecan pies with chocolate turn up regularly on restaurant menus these days with good reason— the combination's great. And while there are many versions of this pie around, I'm partial to the taste and look of mine. The chocolate in my recipe comes from syrup and provides just the right complement to meaty pecans, and the change from pie to shallow tart reduces the amount of filling per mouthful, a pretty trick that cuts the perception of sweetness as well. It's good plain, fine with whipped cream, fabulous with ice cream, and perfect for capping the Thanksgiving feast. § Makes 8 Servings

THE CRUST

1½ c. all-purpose flour

1 tbsp. sugar

⅛ tsp. salt

½ c. (1 stick) unsalted butter, very cold or frozen, cut into 8 pieces

3 to 4 tbsp. ice water

THE FILLING

½ c. chocolate syrup (I use Hershey's)

¾ c. light corn syrup

3 large eggs

3 tbsp. unsalted butter, melted and cooled to room temperature

¼ tsp. salt

1 tsp. pure vanilla extract

1 tbsp. cocoa

1½ c. pecans

1] THE CRUST. Place the dry ingredients in a food processor and pulse just to combine. Add the butter all at once and pulse 10 to 15 times, or until the mixture is coarse and mealy. Add 3 tablespoons of the ice water, a tablespoon at a time, and pulse after each addition. Pulse until the dough forms large curds and holds together when pressed. (If necessary, add up to 1 more tablespoon of ice water to achieve the right consistency.) Turn the dough out onto a work surface and pat into a disk ¾-inch thick. Cover with plastic and chill at least 20 minutes before using. Roll the dough out on a floured surface until it is about ⅛ inch thick and fit it into a 9-inch tart pan with removable bottom. Do not prick the bottom of the crust. Freeze, uncovered, for 30 minutes. *(The crust can be prepared ahead to this point, well wrapped, and frozen for up to 1 month.)*

2] Position a rack one-third up from the bottom of the oven and preheat the oven to 425°. Cover the crust with aluminum foil, pressing against the bottom and sides of the pan to get a tight fit. Add pie weights or dried beans and bake for 20 minutes. Remove the foil and weights and bake uncovered for about 5 minutes more, until lightly browned. Remove the crust from the oven and cool on a rack before filling.

3] THE FILLING. Reheat the oven, if necessary, to 425°. Place all of the filling ingredients except the pecans in a food processor. Process for 10 seconds, stop and scrape down the sides of the bowl, and process for 10 seconds more. Place the crust on a baking pan with raised sides to catch any drips. Scatter the pecans evenly over the bottom of the tart shell and pour over the filling. With a spoon or your fingers, poke the pecans down as they rise to the top. They won't sink, but the poking will give them a good coating of filling. Bake the tart for 10 minutes. *Reduce the oven temperature*

Lightly sweetened whipped cream or ice cream

to 325° and bake 20 to 25 minutes longer, until the filling is puffed and crusty and the tart shell is evenly golden. Remove to a rack to cool.

SERVING. The most popular way to serve this tart is warm (about 20 minutes after it comes from the oven), but it is just as outstanding at room temperature. (To my mind, the tart tastes too much like candy when it's served chilled.) Unmold the tart onto a serving platter, cut in wedges, and serve topped with softly whipped cream or ice cream.

STORING. Like most tarts, this is best the day it is made. However, you can keep the tart tightly covered in the refrigerator overnight and rewarm it in a 350° oven for 10 to 15 minutes before serving. (Don't put it in the microwave—it will turn very soggy.)

BEST MATCH. I created this recipe as a treat to follow the Thanksgiving turkey and all its fixings but find it's a year-round favorite, particularly satisfying after a dinner of roasted chicken, grilled fish, or almost anything that comes off the backyard barbecue.

❋| **PLAYING AROUND.** (Mochaccino Ice Cream) On the theory that there can never be too much chocolate in a chocolate dessert, I suggest you serve this tart with easy-to-make Mochaccino Ice Cream. Dissolve ½ teaspoon ground cinnamon and ½ teaspoon instant espresso powder in 2 teaspoons boiling water; cool to room temperature. Stir this mixture into 1 pint softened best-quality chocolate ice cream. Return the ice cream to the freezer to refirm for about 30 minutes before serving.

Banana-Pumpkin Pie

Banana is a sensational addition to pumpkin pie. It melds with the creamy texture of the custard and lends its own sweet, slightly perfumed flavor. I'm not crazy about warm pumpkin pie. I find that cooling the pie gives the flavors time to ripen and results in a fuller, more intense taste. It also gives the cook a break on

Thanksgiving. You can bake and freeze the pie crust ahead, then whip up the filling early Thanksgiving morning—it takes just 5 minutes. Bake the pie before the bird and it will be properly chilled by dinner time.
§ Makes 6 to 8 Servings

THE CRUST

1½ c. all-purpose flour

1 tbsp. sugar

⅛ tsp. salt

½ c. (1 stick) unsalted butter, very cold or frozen, cut into 8 pieces

3 to 4 tbsp. ice water

1 egg white, lightly beaten with a fork

THE FILLING

2 c. pumpkin puree (15-ounce can)

1 ripe banana, cut into large chunks

3 large eggs

1 c. packed light brown sugar

2 tbsp. unsalted butter, melted and cooled to room temperature

1½ c. heavy cream

1½ tsp. ground cinnamon

1½ tsp. ground ginger

⅛ tsp. ground cloves

⅛ tsp. freshly grated or ground nutmeg

⅛ tsp. salt

3 tbsp. dark rum

1 tsp. pure vanilla extract

1] THE CRUST. Place the dry ingredients in a food processor and pulse just to combine. Add the butter all at once and pulse 10 to 15 times, or until the mixture is coarse and mealy. Add 3 tablespoons of the ice water a tablespoon at a time, and pulse after each addition. Pulse until the dough forms large curds and holds together when pressed. (If necessary, add up to 1 more tablespoon ice water to achieve the right consistency.) Turn the dough out onto a work surface and pat into a disk ¾ inch thick. Cover with plastic and chill at least 20 minutes before using. Roll the dough out on a floured surface until it is about ⅛ inch thick and fit it into a 9-inch pie pan. Build up the edges a little so they rise above the lip of the pan. Crimp the edges and prick the bottom of the crust all over with the tines of a fork. Freeze, uncovered, for 30 minutes. *(The crust can be prepared ahead to this point, covered, and frozen for up to 1 month.)*

2] Position a rack one-third up from the bottom of the oven and preheat the oven to 425°. Cover the crust with aluminum foil, pressing against the bottom and sides of the pan to get a tight fit. Add pie weights or dried beans and bake for 20 minutes. Remove the foil and weights and bake uncovered for 8 to 10 minutes more, until lightly browned. Remove the crust from the oven and immediately brush it with the lightly beaten egg white to seal it. Cool to room temperature on a rack.

3] THE FILLING. Preheat the oven to 450°. Place the pie pan on a baking sheet with raised sides to catch any drips. Put all of the filling ingredients in a food processor. Process for 2 minutes, stopping to scrape the bowl occasionally. Pour the filling into the crust. Depending on the height of your crust, you may have some filling left over. The pie should be filled generously, but the custard should not spill over the edge. Cover the edges of the crust with a shield. (To make a shield, cut a 7-inch circle out of the center of a 12-inch square of aluminum foil. Place the shield on the pie shiny side up.) Bake for 10 minutes. *Reduce the oven temperature to 300°* and bake 35 to 45 minutes longer, or until a knife inserted close to the center of the pie comes out almost clean. Remove the pie to a rack to cool. Chill, lightly covered with waxed paper, when the pie reaches room temperature.

THE TOPPING
1 c. heavy cream, chilled
2 tbsp. confectioners' sugar
½ tsp. pure vanilla extract

4] THE TOPPING. *Up to 1 hour before serving*, whip the heavy cream until it holds soft peaks. Add the sugar and vanilla and continue to whip until the beater leaves clear tracks. Cover and refrigerate until serving time.

SERVING. Spoon the cream into a pastry bag fitted with a star tip and pipe rosettes across the top of the chilled pie, or use a spatula to swirl a layer of cream over the filling. Cut the decorated pie at the table.

STORING. Pumpkin pie is best eaten the day it is made.

BEST MATCH. Serve this along with Chocolate Pecan Pie (page 214) to finish the Thanksgiving (or any other fall/winter) feast. Together, the two desserts provide comfort, crunch, and chocolate—sure-fire, all-American pleasers.

PLAYING AROUND. (Sour Cream Pumpkin Pie) For a different, ultra-creamy version of holiday pumpkin pie, omit the banana and substitute an equal amount of sour cream for the heavy cream.

Pomander Cake

This cake is named for those sweet-scented, clove-spiked oranges that are bound with ribbons and made to hang in closets. A must for winter holiday parties, the Pomander is a cocoa layer cake, moistened with a clove and orange syrup, filled with whipped cream and pieces of poached oranges, and finished with a crown of snow-white cream. It's a standout, rich but light enough to encourage indulgence.
§ Makes 8 to 10 Servings

THE CAKE

½ c. plus 2 tbsp. all-purpose flour

½ c. cocoa powder, preferably a Dutch-processed brand, such as Droste or Poulain

¼ c. cornstarch

1 tsp. baking powder

¼ tsp. baking soda

1½ tsp. ground cloves

6 large eggs

1 egg yolk

1 c. sugar

4 tbsp. unsalted butter, melted and cooled to room temperature

THE SYRUP AND ORANGES

2 c. sugar

2½ c. water

8 whole cloves

2 thin-skinned oranges, very thinly sliced

1½ tbsp. Grand Marnier or other orange liqueur

1] THE CAKE. Center a rack in the oven and preheat the oven to 350°. Butter two 8″ × 8″ cake pans. Line the bottoms with a round of waxed or parchment paper, butter the paper, and dust the pans with flour, tapping out the excess. Sift together the flour, cocoa, cornstarch, baking powder, baking soda, and ground cloves; set aside.

2] Place the eggs, egg yolk, and sugar in a metal bowl, preferably the bowl of an electric mixer. Whisk the ingredients together by hand until blended, about 1 minute. Place the bowl over a saucepan of simmering water and continue to whisk until the sugar dissolves and the mixture is slightly warm to the touch, about 3 minutes.

3] Remove the bowl from the saucepan, fit it to the electric mixer, and, using the whisk attachment, beat the mixture at medium speed for 5 minutes or until it triples in volume and the batter forms a ribbon that holds its shape for 10 seconds when the beater is lifted.

4] Sift one-third of the dry ingredients over the batter and fold in with a rubber spatula. Don't overmix. Fold in half the melted butter. Repeat with half the remaining dry ingredients and the rest of the butter. Fold in the last of the dry ingredients.

5] Divide the batter evenly between the pans. Bake for 25 to 30 minutes, until the tops are springy to the touch and a toothpick inserted in the center of the cake comes out clean. Transfer the cakes to a rack to cool in the pans for 10 minutes. Unmold the cakes and remove the paper liners. Turn the cakes right-side up and cool to room temperature on racks. *(The cakes can be made ahead to this point and stored, wrapped airtight in plastic, for up to 3 days at room temperature or 1 month in the freezer.)*

6] THE SYRUP AND ORANGES. Combine the sugar, water, and whole cloves in a medium saucepan and bring to a boil over high heat. Cook, stirring occasionally, until the sugar dissolves and the mixture is clear. Add the oranges and return the liquid to a boil. Lower the heat so the mixture

THE CREAM
1½ c. heavy cream, chilled
⅓ c. confectioners' sugar

Storebought candied oranges
and thin chocolate squares,
optional

simmers. Cook until the orange rinds are softened, about 20 minutes. Remove from heat and let the oranges cool in the syrup for 10 minutes.

7] Remove the oranges with a slotted spoon and place them on a cutting board. Finely chop them. Measure out 1 cup of the syrup and add the liqueur to it. (You can discard the remaining syrup or save it for another purpose.)

8] **THE CREAM.** Beat the cream until it holds firm peaks. Sift the confectioners' sugar over the whipped cream and fold it in with a rubber spatula. Transfer half the cream to another bowl and stir in the chopped orange.

9] Cut each cake horizontally into two equal layers. Break one of the top layers into pieces, place in a food processor, and process until you have fine crumbs; set aside. Place a bottom layer of cake, cut-side up, on a serving platter or cake stand. Insert waxed paper strips under the cake with the greatest portion exposed to protect the plate. Brush one-third of the syrup over the layer. Cover evenly with half of the whipped cream-chopped orange mixture. Place the other bottom layer, cut-side up, over the filling. Brush with half of the remaining syrup and spread with the rest of the whipped cream–orange mixture. Brush the cut side of the top layer with the remaining syrup and place on top, cut-side down. Cover the entire cake with the reserved whipped cream. Press the cake crumbs into the sides of the cake. Alternately, cover just the top of the cake with whipped cream, leaving the sides exposed, as I did in the jacket photograph. Leave the top plain or decorate with storebought candied oranges and thin chocolate squares or triangles. Remove the waxed paper strips and place the cake in the refrigerator, uncovered, for 2 to 6 hours to allow the flavors to blend.

SERVING. Remove the cake from the refrigerator 30 minutes before serving. Bring the cake to the table on its serving platter and cut into wedges with a finely serrated knife.

STORING. The decorated cake is best eaten the day it is made.

BEST MATCH. The Pomander Cake is a smash ending to an elegant Christmas dinner, perhaps one that features a crown roast or well-sauced game birds; or it can ring in the New Year following a luxe meal of lobster. It's meant for the dressiest holiday dinner party and should be served with espresso (tea would be lost with it).

❀| **PLAYING AROUND.** (Ginger-Lemon–Soaked Chocolate Cake) Because chocolate is a good foil for so many spices, you can change this cake-and-cream format to match your mood. For a sharp, bright taste, go ginger-lemon by replacing the cloves in the cake with an equal amount of ground ginger and adding 12 dime-size slices of peeled fresh ginger and the grated zest of 1 lemon to the syrup. Bring to the boil, then steep for 30 minutes before straining the syrup. If you like, you can add a very small amount of slivered stem ginger to the whipped cream you use for the filling.

Holiday Gingerbread Cake with Chocolate and Fresh Ginger

One bite and I think you'll agree with me that chocolate in gingerbread is not so much a novelty as an ingredient that was always meant to be included. It's perfect with traditional spices and sweet molasses and is super as an icing. You'll want to have this around for the twelve days of Christmas, but you'd be making a mistake to file it under "holidays only." § Makes 9 Squares

THE CAKE

- 2 oz. unsweetened chocolate
- 1½ tbsp. finely chopped peeled fresh ginger
- 2 tsp. granulated sugar
- 2 c. all-purpose flour
- 2 tsp. ground ginger
- ¾ tsp. ground cinnamon
- ¼ tsp. ground cloves
- 1 tsp. baking soda
- 11 tbsp. (1 stick plus 3 tbsp.) unsalted butter, at room temperature
- ¾ c. packed light brown sugar
- 3 large eggs, preferably at room temperature
- ½ c. molasses
- 1 c. buttermilk, preferably at room temperature

THE ICING

- 3 oz. high-quality bittersweet chocolate, such as Lindt or Tobler
- 1 tbsp. strong brewed coffee (you can make this with instant, if necessary)
- 3 tbsp. unsalted butter, at room temperature
- 3 tbsp. confectioners' sugar

1] THE CAKE. Position a rack in the center of the oven and preheat the oven to 350°. Butter a 9″ × 9″ baking pan. Melt the chocolate in the top of a double boiler over hot water or in a bowl in a microwave; reserve. Combine the ginger and granulated sugar in a small bowl and set aside. Whisk together the flour, spices, and baking soda; reserve.

2] In an electric mixer, with a paddle if available, cream the butter and brown sugar on medium speed until light and fluffy, about 3 minutes. Stop to scrape the bowl as necessary. Add the eggs, one at a time, and beat for 1 minute after each addition. The mixture will look curdled, but that's OK. Add the molasses and beat until smooth. Reduce the mixer speed to low and add the chocolate, then the ginger. Still on low speed, add the dry ingredients in 3 additions alternately with the buttermilk, beginning and ending with the flour mixture. Do not mix more than is necessary to blend the ingredients. Pour the batter into the prepared pan and bake for 35 to 40 minutes, until the cake starts to pull away from the sides of the pan and a toothpick inserted in the center of the cake comes out clean. The cake domes and cracks in baking but settles as it cools. Transfer the cake to a cooling rack for 10 minutes then unmold it. Invert the cake back onto the rack to cool to room temperature before icing. (The edges of the cake may look burnt. Don't worry—they can be trimmed.)

3] THE ICING. Melt the chocolate with the coffee in the top of a double boiler over hot water or in a bowl in a microwave. With a small whisk, beat in the butter 1 tablespoon at a time. Sift the confectioners' sugar into the icing and blend. Let the icing stand for 10 minutes at room temperature before pouring it over the gingerbread. Smooth the icing with a long metal spatula, icing just the top of the cake, and allow it to set for 30 minutes.

SERVING. If the edges are overbaked, trim them before cutting the cake into 9 even squares. Serve with whipped heavy cream, crème fraîche, ice

Sweetened whipped cream, lightly sweetened crème fraîche, or ice cream, optional

cream, or the unusual Ginger-Infused Whipped Cream described in Playing Around, below.

STORING. The gingerbread can be wrapped airtight and kept at room temperature for 3 days or frozen for 1 month.

BEST MATCH. While this could easily take its place on the Christmas groaning board, I think it makes the perfect trim-a-tree-party treat paired with a well-spiked eggnog. It's also lovely cut into very small squares and served with hot coffee at a holiday open house.

❀| PLAYING AROUND. (Ginger-Infused Whipped Cream) For a great topping, warm 1 cup of heavy cream and 8 dime-size slices of peeled fresh ginger over gentle heat; do not allow to boil. Remove from heat and cover immediately. Allow the cream to steep until it cools to room temperature. Refrigerate until the cream is very cold, at least 2 hours. Strain and discard the ginger. Whip the steeped cream to soft peaks. Fold in confectioners' sugar to taste and serve. This method of flavoring whipped cream is a marvelous trick I learned from Jean-Marc Burillier, an extraordinary New York pastry chef. Use it any time you want a subtly flavored cream. Try it with orange zest, cardamom pods, or vanilla beans.

Christmas Clementines

No matter how much everyone's eaten over the holidays, these are a welcome sight at the end of the meal. Cool, fresh, and bright-tasting, these lightly poached oranges are a not-too-sweet sweet. Look for clementines, the very small, seedless oranges that usually come to market in mid-December. But if clementines are not available, don't fret; this is a success with lovely, small, seedless navel oranges from California.
§ Makes 8 Servings

3 c. cold water
2⅓ c. sugar
3 cardamom pods, bruised
2-inch piece cinnamon stick
8 clementines or small navel oranges
3 tbsp. Grand Marnier or other orange liqueur
1½ tbsp. brandy

Shredded coconut, optional

1] Place the cold water, sugar, cardamom, and cinnamon in a 3-quart saucepan and bring to the boil over medium heat. While the syrup is heating, peel the clementines. The flesh should be fully exposed, so trim away a very thin layer of fruit with a small, sharp knife. Cut each orange in half crosswise. Reserve 2 pieces of peel, cut into 1-inch squares; discard the rest. Place the oranges and peel in the boiling syrup. Return the syrup to the boil, reduce the heat to low, cover, and poach very gently for 10 minutes.

2] Remove from heat and transfer the clementines to a serving bowl or a large, wide-mouthed canning jar. Measure out 1½ cups of syrup, discarding the spices. (Reserve the remaining syrup to sweeten or poach other fruits or make the sorbet in Playing Around, below.) Stir in the Grand Marnier and brandy and pour the syrup over the oranges. Cover with plastic wrap or the jar's lid and let cool to room temperature. Chill well.

SERVING. The oranges are so pretty in a bowl they can be brought to the table unadorned. (In canning jars wrapped with ribbons they make beautiful Christmas presents.) Spoon 2 halves for each person into dessert coupes or onto plates and ladle over syrup. For an ambrosial, old-fashioned combination, top each serving with a sprinkling of shredded coconut.

STORING. Packed in jars or refrigerator containers, these can be refrigerated for 2 weeks.

BEST MATCH. Serve solo (as the French would a *digestif*) and follow with strong coffee or hot tea.

❀| **PLAYING AROUND.** (Brandied Orange Sorbet) Use the leftover poaching syrup to make sorbet. Add enough fresh orange juice to the syrup to make 4 cups of liquid. Stir in 2 tablespoons Grand Marnier and 1 tablespoon brandy. Pour into an ice cream maker and freeze, following the manufacturer's directions.

Mulled Wine Tart

The first wine tart I ever had was prepared by Fredy Girardet at his world-renowned restaurant outside Lausanne, Switzerland. It was a rustic, comforting finish to a fancy meal and its flavor and texture—reminiscent of the filling in a lemon meringue pie—haunted me. Months later, mulling wine for a Christmas party, I realized I could build a perfect holiday dessert on his classic. (Girardet's wine tart is a classic not just because he makes it, but because it is based on a traditional regional sweet.) Several bottles of wine later I came up with this, a festive, rosy-colored dessert that's tart with the clean, sharp, high tastes of red wine, oranges, and spice— ideal after a holiday dinner at which too much is bound to be the norm. § Makes 8 Servings

THE CRUST

1½ c. all-purpose flour
1 tbsp. sugar
⅛ tsp. salt
½ c. (1 stick) unsalted butter, very cold or frozen, cut into 8 pieces
3 to 4 tbsp. ice water

THE FILLING

2 c. red wine (a hearty Burgundy is perfect)
½ small orange, unpeeled, thinly sliced
2-in. piece cinnamon stick
3 whole cloves
3 whole allspice berries
2-in. strip lemon zest
2 tbsp. unsalted butter
⅔ c. sugar
2½ tbsp. cornstarch

1] THE CRUST. Place the dry ingredients in a food processor and pulse just to combine. Add the butter all at once and pulse 10 to 15 times, or until the mixture is coarse and mealy. Add 3 tablespoons of the ice water, a tablespoon at a time, and pulse after each addition. Pulse until the dough forms large curds and holds together when pressed. (If necessary, add up to 1 more tablespoon of ice water to achieve the right consistency.) Turn the dough out onto a work surface and pat into a disk ¾ inch thick. Cover with plastic and chill at least 20 minutes before using. Roll the dough out on a floured surface until it is about ⅛ inch thick and fit it into a 9-inch tart pan with removable bottom. Prick the bottom of the crust. Freeze, uncovered, for 30 minutes. *(The crust can be prepared ahead to this point, well wrapped, and frozen for up to 1 month.)*

2] Position a rack one-third up from the bottom of the oven and preheat the oven to 425°. Cover the crust with aluminum foil, pressing against the bottom and sides of the pan to get a tight fit. Add pie weights or dried beans and bake for 20 minutes. Remove the foil and weights and bake uncovered for about 5 minutes more, until lightly browned. Remove the crust from the oven and cool on a rack before filling.

3] THE FILLING. Place the wine, orange slices, cinnamon stick, cloves, allspice, and lemon zest in a nonreactive saucepan. Heat until hot to the touch, but do not boil. Turn off heat, cover, and allow to steep for 1 hour.

4] Reheat the spiced wine. In a another nonreactive saucepan, melt the butter over medium-low heat, taking care not to let it brown. Add the sugar and stir with a small whisk to blend. Add the cornstarch and blend. Remove the saucepan from the heat and add a bit of the hot wine mixture, pouring it into the saucepan through a strainer to catch the solids. Stir to get a smooth,

THE TOPPING
1 c. heavy cream, chilled
2 tbsp. confectioners' sugar
½ tsp. pure vanilla extract

lump-free paste. Return the saucepan to the heat and pour in the rest of the mulled wine through the strainer. Heat for 6 to 8 minutes, stirring without stopping, until the mixture thickens. One bubble may pop on the surface, but do not allow the mixture to boil. Pour the filling into the cooled tart shell. Let rest at room temperature for 20 minutes, then refrigerate. *(The tart can be made to this point and kept uncovered in the refrigerator for 6 hours before serving.)*

5] THE TOPPING. *Up to 1 hour before serving*, whip the heavy cream until it holds soft peaks. Add the sugar and vanilla and blend in with a whisk. Cover and refrigerate until serving time.

SERVING. You can either smooth the cream over the tart using an offset spatula to get an even layer or slice the tart and serve spoonfuls of cream on the side.

STORING. The tart should be served the day it is made. Whatever you do, don't cover it, or the tart will turn an unappetizing shade of fuchsia.

BEST MATCH. Serve after Christmas dinner and follow with coffee or tea.

❂| **PLAYING AROUND.** (Blush Wine Tart) Months after Christmas, when you're looking for something very special, turn this into a Blush Wine Tart —it's just the treat for Valentine's Day. In one of my experiments, I discovered that using a blush Zinfandel from California produces a beautiful pastel pink tart with, oddly enough, an underflavor of grapefruit that's terrifically refreshing.

Giant Cranberry Turnover

Start with this if you've never baked and you'll instantly become addicted to the craft. The turnover is spectacular—stunning and scrumptious—and takes no special skills to put together. The filling is a fabulous mix of cranberries, dried apricots, and fresh pears. It's colorful, tart, tangy, refreshing after a big meal, and made in 10 minutes. Storebought frozen puff pastry is the dough—easy, professional looking, and good tasting. While cranberries are always associated with Thanksgiving, I think this Cranberry Turnover looks and tastes like a Christmas present. § Makes 4 to 8 Servings

THE FILLING

12 oz. (1 bag) cranberries, fresh or frozen (*not* thawed)

2 firm pears, such as Bartlett or Anjou, peeled, cored, and diced

½ c. dried apricots, diced

1 c. dark raisins

½ c. fresh orange juice

¾ c. sugar

1 tsp. ground cinnamon

¼ c. walnuts, coarsely chopped

1½ tbsp. Grand Marnier or other orange liqueur, optional

THE PASTRY

2 sheets (about 1¼ pounds) storebought frozen puff pastry (I use Pepperidge Farm)

1 egg

1 tbsp. cold water

2 tsp. sugar

1] THE FILLING. Place all of the ingredients except the nuts and liqueur in a large, heavy-bottomed saucepan. Bring to a boil over medium heat, stirring frequently with a wooden spoon. After about 5 minutes you'll notice the tracks left by the spoon don't fill in immediately. Cook another 2 to 3 minutes, until thickened. Remove the pot from the heat and stir in the nuts and liqueur. Spoon the filling into a large bowl and press a sheet of plastic wrap against the surface. Cool to room temperature. *(The filling can be made up to 1 month in advance and stored in an airtight container in the refrigerator.)*

2] THE PASTRY. Defrost the frozen pastry for 20 minutes or until it is supple but still chilled. Lay a sheet of pastry flat on a floured surface and lightly flour the top. Roll into a 12-inch square. Brush off the excess flour and roll up the pastry around your rolling pin. Unroll it onto a large, unbuttered baking sheet. Spoon the cooled filling into the center of the pastry, then spread it out into a 9-inch square. Roll the second sheet of pastry to a 12-inch square. Beat the egg and cold water together and brush this wash around the exposed edges of the bottom layer of pastry. Lift the second sheet of pastry onto your rolling pin and place it over the filling. Press down around the edges to seal. With a knife or pastry cutter, trim the dough to a 10-inch square. Brush the surface with the egg wash, being careful not to let it drip down the sides. Press the tines of a fork against the edges of the pastry to seal. Use a sharp knife to make 6 slits over the top of the pastry. (If you want, you can cut the scraps of pastry into thin strips, tie them into bows and "glue" them with egg wash on to the turnover as decoration.) Sprinkle the sugar over the turnover and chill, on the baking sheet, for at least 30 minutes.

3] Place a rack one-third up from the bottom of the oven and preheat the oven to 400°. Bake the turnover for 15 minutes, then *lower the temperature to 350°*; bake 20 to 25 minutes longer, just until the turnover is beautifully golden. Remove the turnover from the oven and slide it off the baking sheet onto a rack to cool.

SERVING. The turnover is delicious served after a 20-minute cooling period or at room temperature. The dessert is so pretty you'll want to cut it in front of your guests, so carefully transfer it to a large serving platter or attractive cutting board. Cut into quarters or eighths and serve plain or with a scoop of ice cream or whipped cream.

Vanilla ice cream or sweetened whipped cream, optional

STORING. This dessert, like most sweets made with puff pastry, can't be kept. Serve it the day it is made.

BEST MATCH. The fresh, bright, slightly tart taste of Giant Cranberry Turnover makes it the ideal ending to an extensive holiday meal. An easy match to the Christmas goose, it's just as right with roasted meats.

❀| **PLAYING AROUND.** (Cranberry Conserve) Double the filling recipe to make the best holiday conserve you've ever tasted. (Made in large batches it can be a lovely—and loving—Christmas present.) You can add other fruits, such as small pieces of dried pineapple, coarsely chopped orange zest, or plump dried cranberries. Pack the conserve into old-fashioned Mason jars and serve with grilled fish and poultry or use it as a topping for ice cream, lightly sweetened plain yogurt, or fromage blanc.

Peppermill Squares

Spiced cakes are a Christmas tradition. Think of gingerbread, lebkuchen, pfeffernüsse, and the French pain d'epice. While I wouldn't call these zingy squares traditional, their taste, and the thoughts they evoke, are very much in the Christmas spirit. I created these dense, fudgy sweets for a special issue of Food & Wine *magazine that celebrated spices. Finished with a smooth cream cheese frosting, these get their kick from a combination of white pepper, black pepper, and allspice, a mix made famous by the French food purveyor Hèdiard and popularized in a recipe by Madeleine Kamman. Shortly after the magazine came out, I got a letter from a woman in El Paso, Texas. She had made these little squares for her bridge group and the women were so excited by the recipe they decided to put together a cookbook to raise money for their chapter of Drive-a-Meal, a service that delivers meals to the elderly. When the book was published, it included this recipe and the story of how it inspired the group. It's easy to understand why this dessert holds a special place in my heart and why I think of it every Christmas.*
§ Makes 16 Squares

THE SQUARES

1 tbsp. black peppercorns
1 tbsp. white peppercorns
1½ tsp. whole allspice berries
½ c. all-purpose flour
Pinch of salt
½ c. (1 stick) unsalted butter, at room temperature
½ c. granulated sugar
⅓ c. packed light brown sugar
4 oz. semisweet chocolate, coarsely chopped
2 oz. unsweetened chocolate, coarsely chopped
1 tsp. pure vanilla extract
2 large eggs

1] THE SQUARES. Center a rack in the oven and preheat the oven to 350°. Lightly butter an 8-inch square pan and set it aside. Mix together the peppercorns and allspice berries. Put them in a pepper or spice mill and grind to a fine powder. Measure out 1 teaspoon of the pepper mix for this recipe and reserve the rest for another use. (It makes a terrific seasoning in place of your usual pepper.) In a bowl, whisk together the pepper mix, flour, and salt to combine.

2] Melt the butter in a heavy medium saucepan. Add the granulated and brown sugars and bring just to the boil over medium heat, stirring constantly. Stir in the semisweet and unsweetened chocolates and remove the pan from the heat. Stir until the chocolate is melted, then let cool for 5 minutes.

3] Still working in the pot, stir in the vanilla. Add the eggs, 1 at a time, mixing until blended. Gradually stir in the flour mixture. Pour the batter into the prepared pan. Bake for 30 to 35 minutes, or until a toothpick inserted in the center of the cake comes out clean. Remove the cake to a rack to cool for 10 minutes. Run a blunt knife around the edges of the pan to loosen the cake and turn it out onto the rack. Invert onto another rack and let the cake cool right-side up until it reaches room temperature.

THE FROSTING

4 oz. cream cheese, at room temperature

2 tbsp. unsalted butter, at room temperature

1 c. confectioners' sugar

½ tsp. pure vanilla extract

4] THE FROSTING. In a medium bowl, beat together the cream cheese and butter. Add the confectioners' sugar and vanilla and beat well. Spread the frosting over the top of the cake, leaving the sides bare.

SERVING. When you're ready to serve, trim the crusty edges of the cake and cut into 2-inch squares. I think these are particularly attractive arranged on a rustic, well-used bread board.

STORING. Peppermill Squares will keep for 3 days well wrapped in the refrigerator. Let the chilled squares stand for 10 minutes at room temperature before serving.

BEST MATCH. These are most appealing served late Christmas Eve when those waiting up for Santa need a boost. Give the kids milk or weak hot chocolate and serve the grown-ups strong coffee or equally strong cognac.

❀| PLAYING AROUND. (Iced and Berried Peppermill Squares) To turn this into a fancy holiday cake, replace the frosting with Deep Chocolate Glossy Icing (page 176). While the icing is still warm, cover the top of the cake with tightly spaced rows of halved strawberries. Dust the top of the cake sparingly with confectioners' sugar and cut at the table. Serve with lightly sweetened, softly whipped cream.

Date and Nut Toasting Loaf

Fruitcake is so much a part of the Christmas sweet scene that each year a rash of newly discovered heirloom recipes appears, many carrying headnotes to the effect that even if you don't like fruitcake you'll like this one. Not me. I don't like sticky green and red things in my cakes. But because I do like the oldtime connection between Christmas and fruitcakes, I created this very simple cream cheese loaf that's rich, buttery, and sweet with dates and nuts. It is good fresh, better after it has aged a day, and best lightly toasted or dipped in tea. This is the quintessential Christmas morning treat.
§ Makes 8 to 10 Servings

1 c. pitted dried dates, cut into 8 pieces
1 c. walnuts, coarsely chopped
2 c. all-purpose flour
2 tsp. baking powder
Pinch of salt
1 c. (2 sticks) unsalted butter, at room temperature
3 oz. cream cheese, at room temperature
¾ c. packed light brown sugar
4 large eggs, preferably at room temperature
1 tsp. pure vanilla extract

Butter, jam, honey, or cream cheese

1] Center a rack in the oven and preheat the oven to 325°. Butter a 9″ × 5″ loaf pan, dust with flour, and tap out the excess. Place the dates and nuts in a small mixing bowl. In another bowl, whisk together the flour, baking powder, and salt just to combine. Remove 1 tablespoon of the flour mixture and toss it with the dates and nuts, coating the small pieces with flour; set aside.

2] In an electric mixer fitted with the whisk attachment, cream the butter and cream cheese on medium-high speed until satiny and well blended, about 2 minutes. Add the sugar and continue to mix, stopping to scrape down the bowl occasionally, until the mixture is light and fluffy, about 3 minutes. Add the eggs, one at a time, beating 1 minute after each addition. Beat in the vanilla. Don't worry if the mixture looks curdled; it will come together when the dry ingredients are added. Set the mixer speed to low and add the dry ingredients, mixing only until the flour is incorporated. Avoid overmixing. Fold in the dates and nuts with a sturdy rubber spatula.

3] Scrape the batter into the prepared pan. Bake for 80 to 90 minutes. (If the cake starts to brown too quickly, cover with an aluminum foil tent, shiny side out.) Bake until the top is honey brown, bumpy, and cracked down the middle and a toothpick inserted in the center of the cake comes out clean. Cool the cake in the pan on a rack for 10 minutes before turning out onto another rack. Invert back onto the rack to cool to room temperature right-side up.

SERVING. The cake is ready to serve when it reaches room temperature. However, the taste and texture improve with a rest of at least 1 day. Wrap the cake in plastic and allow it to ripen at room temperature. Cut into ½-inch-thick slices and serve as is or lightly toasted. Offer butter, jam, honey, or cream cheese.

STORING. Wrapped in plastic, the cake will keep for 5 days at room temperature or frozen for 1 month.

BEST MATCH. This is a good starter for Christmas morning. Served with coffee or tea, it's enough to keep everyone happy until the feast begins; served with a creamy onion and ham omelet, it's a substantial breakfast add-on. I also like it late in the afternoon with a glass of sherry.

❀ | PLAYING AROUND. (Sweet Orange Marmalade Sandwiches) For a special Christmas nibble. Whip 6 ounces of softened cream cheese in an electric mixer. Mix in 4 tablespoons good-quality orange marmalade. Cut the cake into thin slices, toast lightly, spread half of the slices with Marmalade Cream Cheese, and top with the plain slices. Cut diagonally into halves or quarters.

Fruit Fritters for Chanukah

To commemorate Chanukah, the Festival of Lights, Jews around the world eat foods made with oil. In Israel, the traditional food is donuts; in Eastern Europe and most parts of the United States, the favorite Chanukah dish is potato latkes, or pancakes. These Fruit Fritters are fried in oil and so fit the bill for Chanukah. If they're not now part of a tradition, their sweet, rum-scented batter, warm, fruity interiors, and hot-from-the-pot snackability will start one. This recipe was inspired by a batch of fritters I made with Michel Attali, who for many years was the chef at Petrossian, the famed caviar restaurant in New York. As Michel fried his fritters he recalled apple beignets (fritters) from his French childhood; I fried mine and thought, "Wouldn't it be nice if these were what my son remembered one day?" § Makes 12 to 16 Servings

THE BATTER

1½ tsp. (½ pkg.) **powdered yeast**
½ c. **milk, at room temperature**
¼ c. **flat beer, at room temperature**
¼ c. **dark rum**
1 tbsp. **safflower (or other flavorless) oil**
Pinch of salt
1 tsp. **pure vanilla extract**
2 **eggs, separated**
1¼ c. **all-purpose flour**
½ c. **sugar**

THE FRUIT

1 tbsp. **fresh lemon juice**
1 tbsp. **sugar**
6 to 8 pieces **fruit, such as bananas, apples, pears, and pineapple, peeled and cored, the bananas cut crosswise into 1-inch chunks, the other fruit cut into ¼-inch-thick slices**

Oil for deep frying
Confectioners' sugar

1] **THE BATTER.** In a large mixing bowl, whisk together the yeast, milk, beer, rum, oil, salt, vanilla, and egg yolks. Switch to a sturdy rubber spatula and gradually blend in the flour. You'll have a thick, sticky batter. (The egg whites and sugar will be used later.) Cover the bowl with a kitchen towel and place in a warm, draft-free spot to rest for 1 to 1½ hours, or until the mixture rises slightly and the top is marked with small bubbles. *(The batter can be made ahead to this point and stored in the refrigerator, covered tightly, overnight.)*

2] **THE FRUIT.** Mix the lemon juice and sugar together in a bowl. Add the fruit and toss to coat. Allow the fruit to macerate for 15 to 30 minutes. Using a slotted spoon, transfer the fruit from the bowl to a surface covered with a double thickness of paper towels. Reserve the lemon-sugar liquid. Cover the fruit with more paper towels and pat dry. (Dry well, because the batter won't stick to wet fruit.)

3] Pour the lemon-sugar liquid into the yeast batter. Beat the egg whites in a clean, dry bowl with clean beaters until they hold soft peaks. Gradually add the sugar, beating until the mixture is glossy and resembles marshmallow. Fold the whites into the yeast batter.

4] Pour the oil into a deep fryer or deep saucepan and heat to 370°. Spear a piece of fruit with a long-tined fork, dip it into the batter to coat it evenly, and drop it into the hot oil, pushing it off the fork with a blunt knife. Fry a few fritters at a time, taking care not to crowd the pan. Cook, turning once, until uniformly golden, about 1 to 2 minutes on a side. Remove from the oil with a slotted spoon and drain on a double thickness of paper towels. Sprinkle with confectioners' sugar while still hot.

Jam or honey, optional

SERVING. If these don't disappear in the kitchen, pile them high on a platter. They are meant to be eaten out of hand, so have plenty of small napkins ready. You might also pass bowls of honey and jam for dipping.

STORING. Fritters must be eaten within minutes of being fried.

BEST MATCH. Cold cider or hot tea are nice with these.

❁| **PLAYING AROUND.** (Spiked Fritter Batter) You can change the batter's flavoring dramatically by substituting Frangelico, Amaretto, or Grand Marnier for the rum. No matter which liqueur you use, add the vanilla extract.

Valentine's Day Sweet Hearts

These are the epitome of straight-from-the-heart goodness and love: featherlight sweet cream biscuits, heart-shaped of course; a circle of brilliant red raspberry puree; a puff of soft whipped cream; and a few fresh berries. If you made nothing but the biscuits, you'd be the object of everyone's affection; make it all and you'll have cupid working overtime.
§ Makes 4 Servings

THE BISCUITS

2 c. all-purpose flour
3 tbsp. sugar
1 tbsp. baking powder
½ c. (1 stick) cold unsalted butter, cut into bits
¾ c. heavy cream
2 tsp. heavy cream

THE SAUCE

½ pt. fresh or frozen (partially thawed) red raspberries or strawberries
Sugar to taste

THE CREAM

½ c. heavy cream, chilled
2 tsp. confectioners' sugar
1 tsp. pure vanilla extract

1] THE BISCUITS. Position a rack in the lower third of the oven and preheat the oven to 425°. Place the flour, sugar, and baking powder in a large mixing bowl and whisk to combine. Add the butter to the bowl and, using your fingertips, a pastry blender, or two knives, work the butter into the dry ingredients until the mixture resembles fine meal. Make a well in the center and pour in the ¾ cup heavy cream. Using a fork, toss and stir until the mixture is moist and starts to come together. It may be shaggy; don't worry—it will smooth as you knead it. Still working in the bowl, gently knead the dough for about 45 seconds.

2] Place the dough on a lightly floured work surface and pat it into a disk. Dust the top of the dough with flour and roll out or pat it until it is ½ inch thick. Using a heart-shaped biscuit or cookie cutter, 2½ to 3 inches wide, cut out 8 hearts. (You can gather the scraps together, reroll, and cut out more hearts, if you want. You'll need only 8 for this recipe and the first 8 will be the best.) Brush the excess flour off the tops and bottoms of the hearts. Place them on an ungreased baking sheet and brush lightly with the 2 teaspoons cream. (Try not to dribble, because the cream will glue the biscuits to the pan.) Bake 13 to 15 minutes, or until deeply golden and almost tripled in height. Take the baking sheet from the oven and place on a rack until you need the biscuits.

3] THE SAUCE. While the biscuits are baking, puree the berries in a blender or food processor. Taste and add sugar until the sauce is as sweet as you like. If you use raspberries, strain the sauce if you find the little seeds unpleasant. Reserve.

4] THE CREAM. While the biscuits are baking, whip the cream until it holds soft peaks. Sift over the confectioners' sugar and add the vanilla. Mix in by hand with a small whisk. Refrigerate.

SERVING. These look nicest on large dinner plates with broad rims and standard 5- to 6-inch centers. Film each of 4 plates with puree. For each

THE BERRIES

½ pt. fresh red raspberries or hulled and sliced strawberries

serving, halve 2 biscuits. Spoon a little puree onto each cut side. Place the bottom halves of the biscuits side-by-side in the center of the plates and drop a spoonful of whipped cream on each. Lean the tops of the biscuits over the bottoms, leaving most of the cream exposed. Arrange berries in the cream, letting them peek out of the hearts. Spoon a puff of cream onto each plate, decorate with berries, and serve.

STORING. Love doesn't wait. Enjoy immediately.

BEST MATCH. This is not too sweet to be enjoyed with a flute of champagne or a glass of dessert wine. Espresso is a good match, too.

❀| **PLAYING AROUND.** (Pink Butter) Serve the heart-shaped biscuits for breakfast on Valentine's Day. Omit the puree, cream, and decorations and serve with Pink Butter: With a sturdy rubber spatula (or in a mini-processor), cream together 4 tablespoons very soft butter and 1 to 2 tablespoons strawberry jam. (Taste as you go.)

Honeyed Ricotta-Almond Easter Cake

I'm a loyal fan of America's favorite dense, rich, smooth cheesecake, the kind made with only cream cheese. So when I created this as an Easter cake for a friend, I expected to turn out something she would like but I wouldn't. Wrong.

I fell in love with the mellow honey warmth, ricotta creaminess, and appealing almond and Amaretti crunch of this dessert. I considered calling it Convert's Cheesecake.
§ Makes 10 to 12 Servings

THE CRUST

- 10 large, double Amaretti (Italian macaroons available in specialty stores and some supermarkets; look for Saronno brand)
- About ⅔ c. graham cracker crumbs, made from about 5 to 6 double crackers
- ¼ tsp. ground cinnamon
- 4 tbsp. (½ stick) unsalted butter, melted

THE CAKE

- 2½ c. ricotta cheese
- ½ c. heavy cream
- ¾ c. slivered or julienned blanched almonds
- ½ c. honey
- 1 large egg, separated
- 2 egg yolks
- 1½ tsp. pure vanilla extract
- 1 tsp. almond extract
- ½ tsp. ground cinnamon

THE GLAZE

- 2 tbsp. honey

1] THE CRUST. Butter an 8½- or 9-inch springform pan. Place the pan on a sheet of aluminum foil and draw up the edges of the foil to seal the pan. Pulverize the Amaretti in a food processor. Pour the Amaretti into a large measuring cup and add enough graham cracker crumbs to make a total of 1⅓ cups; pour into a mixing bowl. (Just wipe out the processor.) Add the cinnamon and melted butter and stir until the crumbs are moist. Press the crumbs evenly against the bottom and about two-thirds of the way up the sides of the pan. Place the pan in the freezer while you prepare the cake.

2] THE CAKE. Position a rack in the center of the oven and preheat the oven to 350°. Place all of the cake ingredients in the processor. Pulse several times to mix and to chop the almonds, and then process, stopping to scrape the bowl frequently, until the batter is smooth, about 3 minutes. Turn the batter into the pan and place the pan on a baking sheet. Bake for 70 to 80 minutes, until the cake is puffed and beautifully golden and shivers slightly when shaken gently. (If the cake is browning too quickly, make a tent of foil, shiny side out, and place it over the cake, taking care not to allow the foil to touch the cake.) Transfer the cake to a rack.

3] THE GLAZE. Warm the honey to liquify it and brush it over the top of the cake. (A feather brush is perfect for this job.) Cool for 20 minutes. Carefully run a knife around the sides of the cake to separate it from the pan. Remove the sides of the springform and cool the cake to room temperature. Chill for at least 6 hours before serving.

SERVING. It's easiest to serve this cake if you leave it on the bottom of the springform pan. The neatest slices are those made with a knife dipped in hot water and wiped dry.

STORING. Wrapped well, the cake can be refrigerated for up to 2 days.

BEST MATCH. This is a delightful ending to a leg of lamb or honeyed ham Easter dinner. It's good with tea or coffee laced with a splash of Amaretto.

❀| **PLAYING AROUND.** (Strawberry Sauce and Glistening Berries) For an even more festive presentation, serve wedges of cheesecake with Strawberry Sauce: Puree ½ pint (about 1¼ cups) fresh or frozen unsweetened strawberries. Strain. Sweeten with honey or sugar to taste. Pour a circle of sauce next to each serving. You can garnish each plate with a few honeyed berries: Choose large berries, with or without hulls. Pour some honey into a small deep bowl. Dip the berries into the honey and let the excess drip back into the bowl. Glistening berries can be used to garnish each plate or you can use the same technique to coat berry halves to decorate the top of the cake before cutting.

Gene Ford's Fourth of July Sparkler

Gene Ford, pastry chef at Claire, a popular New York fish restaurant, is known in town for his comfy, satisfying sweets, many recreated from childhood memories. This red, white, and blue pleaser is the dessert he serves to celebrate America's birthday. The base of the dessert is an old-fashioned angel food cake flavored and tinted with fresh strawberry puree. On top, gobs of whipped cream and a tumble of fresh, sweet blueberries and strawberries. Birthday candles are optional. § Makes 10 to 12 Servings

THE CAKE

1 pt. fresh, very ripe strawberries, hulled and halved

1½ tsp. sugar

12 large egg whites (or enough to measure 1 cup), at room temperature (egg whites should be from eggs at least 1 day old)

1¼ c. cake flour

6 tbsp. sugar

¼ tsp. salt

1 tsp. cream of tartar

¾ c. sugar

1] THE CAKE. Place the strawberries and the 1½ teaspoons sugar in a bowl and allow to macerate for 30 minutes. Drain the berries and puree in a blender or food processor. Measure out 1 cup and reserve. (Depending on the size of the berries, you may have a little puree left over. Save it for a mixed drink.) Center a rack in the oven and preheat the oven to 350°. Wash and dry a 10-inch tube pan with removable bottom and feet for cooling cakes upside-down; set it aside.

2] Place the egg whites in the bowl of an electric mixer, and put the bowl in a basin of hot water to heat the whites until they are very warm to the touch. This will help increase their volume when they are whipped. Meanwhile, sift the cake flour, the 6 tablespoons sugar, and the salt together 3 times.

3] Using an electric mixer with a whisk attachment, beat the egg whites until foamy. Add the cream of tartar and continue to beat on medium speed until the whites form soft peaks. With the mixer running, very gradually add the ¾ cup sugar. Keep beating until the whites are stiff but still glossy. (Gene says it's better to err on the side of underbeating.) Remove the bowl from the mixer and scrape down the sides with a rubber spatula. With the spatula, gently fold in the sifted dry ingredients in 3 additions. Fold in the puree in 2 additions and spoon the batter into the pan.

4] Rap the pan against the counter once to settle the batter—don't be too forceful—and place it in the oven. Bake exactly 35 minutes, without opening the oven door. At the end of this time, the cake will be puffed, springy, and slightly cracked, and a toothpick inserted in the center will come out clean. Remove the cake from the oven and turn the pan upside-down so it rests on its feet. Let the cake cool to room temperature. When the cake is cool, run a blunt knife around the sides of the pan and the center tube and unmold the cake onto a serving platter. Use the knife to loosen the

THE TOPPING

1 c. heavy cream, chilled

2 tbsp. confectioners' sugar, pressed through a sieve

½ tsp. pure vanilla extract

½ pt. fresh blueberries, washed and drained

½ pt. fresh strawberries, hulled and sliced

bottom of the pan and lift off. (You'll have the flat side on top. If you prefer the domed side up, first turn the cake out onto a rack and then invert onto a platter.) If the surface of the cake seems moist, blot it gently with paper towels.

5] THE TOPPING. *Up to 1 hour before serving,* whip the heavy cream until it holds soft peaks. Switch to a spatula and fold in the sugar and vanilla. Refrigerate, covered, until ready to use. Combine the blueberries and sliced strawberries in a bowl.

SERVING. To present the cake whole, fill the center with the whipped cream and spoon the berries over the cream and around the cake. Cut at the table using a serrated knife with a gentle sawing motion and give each person a portion of everything. You can also cut this in the kitchen and top each slice with cream and a cascade of berries.

STORING. The cake will keep in the refrigerator, lightly wrapped with plastic or waxed paper, for 4 days.

BEST MATCH. This is fine with hot espresso or cold tea, but it's sensational with strawberry malteds or ice cream floats.

✿| PLAYING AROUND. (Philadelphia-Style Snow White Ice Cream) For something very special, serve this sparkler with this easy-to-make ice cream instead of the whipped cream. (Unlike French ice cream, Philadelphia-style ice cream contains no eggs and is not made with a cooked custard base.) This is also Gene Ford's recipe, a recreation of his favorite ice cream from his hometown in Pennsylvania: In a medium saucepan, combine 2 cups heavy cream, 1 cup milk, ½ cup sugar, and 1½ vanilla beans, cut in half lengthwise. Stir over low heat until the sugar is dissolved and the mixture is very hot to the touch. Don't let it boil. Remove from heat. Lift out the vanilla beans and scrape the pulp into the cream mixture; discard the pods. Chill the mixture, then freeze in an ice cream maker following the manufacturer's directions. Makes 3 cups.

S • W • E • E • T

Index

Index

A Note About the Author

Food writer Dorie Greenspan has been baking professionally for over 10 years, and longer than that for family and friends. Her recipes have been published in Food & Wine *and* Elle *magazines, and her articles about food, wine, restaurants, and chefs have appeared in* Connoisseur, Elle, Travel Holiday, Food Arts, and Art & Antiques. *She is the editor and principal writer of* News from the Beard House, *the monthly newsletter of* The James Beard Foundation, *and editor of the* Travel Holiday Good Value Dining Guide. *She lives in New York and Westbrook, Connecticut, with her husband, Michael, and their son, Joshua.*

OPEN
COME IN